W9-DII-567

WITHDRAWN

MEDIEVAL CHURCH HISTORY

19.202

LECTURES

ON

MEDIEVAL CHURCH HISTORY

BEING THE SUBSTANCE OF LECTURES DELIVERED
AT QUEEN'S COLLEGE, LONDON

BY

RICHARD CHENEVIX TRENCH, D.D.
ARCHBISHOP OF DUBLIN

DENISON UNIVERSITY
LIBRARY
GRANVILLE OHIO

NEW YORK:
CHARLES SCRIBNER'S SONS,
743 and 745 BROADWAY.

All rights reserved.

BR
252
.T7
1877

DENISON UNIVERSITY
LIBRARY
GRANVILLE OHIO

19202

PREFACE.

I DELIVERED a good many years ago, and more times than one, courses of Lectures on Church History to a class of girls, at Queen's College, London. One course dealt with Early Church History, another with Modern, and between these was one on Medieval. This last course has constituted the groundwork of the present volume, published by request of hearers, but those hearers, as I must acknowledge, my own daughters. I had intended at the first to do no more than print the Lectures as delivered, with some slight occasional revision; and certainly had very imperfectly recognized how much more than this would be required. Little by little I became conscious that my present estimate of persons and of things was not always what it once had been, that later books demanded to be read, and later knowledge used; not to say that it was one thing to address a class of young ladies; who, however little one might know oneself upon a subject, were tolerably sure to know less; and another, to lay oneself open to the criticism of all comers. It has followed that much has been re-written, something withdrawn, not a little added. But with all this I have not sought to disconnect these Lectures from the place where they were first given and the hearers to whom they were first addressed. My general view of the manner in which a certain acquaintance with Church history

v

may be imparted to those who cannot make of it a special study, has not changed. What I then thought to be a better scheme for the distribution of the materials, than such schemes as are generally adopted, I think so still;—but on this and on other kindred subjects I have said something in an Introductory Lecture, which went before my entire subject, but which I have now prefixed to this present division of it, as being the only one that I shall publish. Not less have I kept the Lectures, in what they say and in what they do not say, as originally they were composed, namely as Lectures for girls of the upper and middle classes; and I have recognized here and there certain reticences and restraints of statement which this assumption of the age and sex of my hearers imposed upon me. More than this I have not considered that this circumstance required.

Bishop Blomfield, indeed, is reported to have excused a popular preacher, when some strong-thoughted lawyers complained that there was not sufficient body and resistance in his sermons; urging, that he had preached so long to bonnets as to have forgotten there were brains. I cannot think the antithesis of bonnets and brains to be a just one. How far the wearers of bonnets would bear the strain of competition with those thus assumed to be in exclusive possession of brains, supposing the matter in hand to be one which demanded originative power, on this I give no opinion; but having regard to receptive capacity, to the power of taking in, assimilating, and intelligently reproducing, what is set before them, my conviction after some experience in lecturing to the young of both sexes is, that there is no need to break the bread of knowledge smaller for young women than young men; and, save as already indicated, I did not in the original preparation of these Lectures, nor yet have I in the later revision of them, because my class was, or was assumed to be, a female one, kept anything back that I should have thought it desirable to set before young men of the same age and condition of life.

I had written so far in a somewhat anticipatory mood; for less than half my book was completed, although the scheme of it was fully made out, when I thus wrote. It has been finished under less favourable circumstances than those under which it was begun. Many hindrances, the results of a severe accident, have stood in my way. Every book not upon my own shelves which I have needed to consult, has had to be brought to me; I could not go to seek it; and this condition limits not a little the number which one has at command. As however I publish the Lectures notwithstanding, which I was under no sort of obligation to do, I have no right on the score of these hindrances to ask a more lenient judgment on the faults and shortcomings of my book than it otherwise might have found.

PALACE, DUBLIN: *Nov.* 26, 1877.

CONTENTS.

LECTURES

ON

MEDIEVAL CHURCH HISTORY.

LECTURE I.

ON THE STUDY OF CHURCH HISTORY.

In the study of any vast and complex subject, above all when it is one on which we can bestow only a very limited portion of our time and attention, which therefore it is quite impossible we can master in all its details, it is all-important for us that we should know beforehand what we should look for, on what concentrate our attention; what, as of real significance for us, we should keep in the foreground of our thoughts; what, as of secondary interest, we may allow to fall into the background; what, as indeed of no importance at all, we may dismiss and suffer to fall out of sight altogether. Our faculties are so limited, our memories can retain so little, the claims on our time are so infinite, art is so long and life so short, that all such economies of time and labour are precious, and can nowhere be superfluous or out of place. But hardly anywhere can they be so valuable, indeed I should say they are nowhere so indispensable, as in the study of Church history. The subject is so im-

mense, extending over so large a tract of time, over
such vast regions of space, having its points of contact
with so much of deepest interest in every other domain
of human activity, demanding to be looked at from so
many different points of view, while at the same time
it affects so closely our own position, and even our
own conduct, that we may well desire, if such can be
obtained, some preparatory helps to its study, some
touchstone which shall enable to discriminate and discern between that which is most worth our knowing,
and that which is of less worth, and that which is of no
worth at all.

I must complain of those who have written our
Church histories, that they are often very far from
helping us here as they ought. One is sometimes
tempted to make against them the same complaint
which the countryman made, who, having gone to see
for the first time some famous city, complained on his
return home that he could not see the city for the
houses. This has been sometimes cited as a very
foolish saying, but it expressed a very real fact; and,
looked at a little closely, there was nothing absurd
about it, but what indeed was very much the contrary.
What he felt that he wanted was a total impression,
with the great distinctive features of the city rising up
before him; and this, lost amid a labyrinth of streets
and lanes, and with no one to guide and place him on
some station of vantage, he felt that he had been unable to obtain. Now there are Church histories about
which one might make a similar complaint. The
writers of these have so crowded their pages with
smaller events, have so little aimed at giving due
prominence to the greater, have so filled their stage

with secondary and subordinate personages, that the really grand events and grand actors are in danger of being lost in the crowd; we fail to distinguish them from the multitude of far inferior importance, or of no importance whatever, who distract or obstruct our view. We cannot see the city for the houses.

Neither is the way of escape from this inconvenience so easy. If, hoping to avoid it, we betake ourselves to abridgments, saying to ourselves, "These at any rate, by the very necessity of the case, will deal only with what is primary, with what is worth remembering," we shall probably be quite disappointed in any expectation of the kind. Not to say that these abridgments are very often hungry, barren, dry skeletons from which all that constitutes the flesh and blood of history has been ruthlessly stript away; not to urge that they often justify too well the medieval proverb, *Compendia Dispendia*, we may very probably encounter in them the same mischief which we were labouring to avoid, and this in a more aggravated form. Shut up in closer limits, the writers have not the less sought to include a little of every thing and a notice of every body within these. Painting on a much narrower canvas, they have introduced into their picture almost as many figures as did those others into the ampler spaces at their command. And thus in these compendiums the same defects will often exist, and in a still more mischievous shape.

Let me say boldly that in my judgment the first question which one with such a task as mine, and shut in for the performance of it within such narrow limits, should ask himself is this,—not "How much can I put into my story?" but rather, "What can I omit, and

yet at the same time effectually tell that story? What
can I throw overboard, so lightening the sorely burdened ship, at the same time retaining, if not all of the
freight which is precious, yet at all events whatever of
that is *most* precious?" This is the question which in
these Lectures I shall constantly put to myself; and
shall seek to answer it on the principles which I have
already suggested. Instead of multiplying details,
which, if you wish to know them, you may obtain
almost anywhere, I shall endeavour to put you at
points of view for the taking in of those larger aspects
of the subject which more or less determine and dominate the whole. You must not wonder or complain
if, having such a story to tell, with so few hours in
which to tell it, I omit, foreshorten, trace outlines only,
leaving to you to fill in these frameworks at your
leisure. Then only you would have ground for complaint, if I wasted on trivialities, such as would inevitably be forgotten almost as soon as heard, the brief
time which we have at our disposal.

But there are other devices—technical and mechanical some of them will appear—which may yet materially assist you in obtaining a clearer oversight of
your subject, with mastery up to a certain point of it,
and of the relations of its several parts to one another.
For instance, there is the distribution of it into periods
of manageable length. None of the kingdoms of this
world have a history extending over a tract of time at
all approaching that over which this history of the
kingdom of God extends. And indeed how should
they have this? Those other kingdoms rise but to
fall; while this is a kingdom which endures throughout

all ages, having already endured for more than eighteen hundred years. It is needful then in the study of such a history to secure pauses for the mind, "landing-places," as Coleridge has called them. You may fairly claim to have this long story divided for you into shorter and, if I may say, handier portions. Now, if these divisions are to be of any real service, they must not be merely arbitrary and artificial. They should each of them represent a different act in that solemn drama of divine Providence which is being enacted on the world's stage. And here it is that I find fault with that which has hitherto been a very favourite device with Church historians. They have distributed, that is, the story which they had to relate into centuries; and, this done, have told all which belonged, or which seemed to belong, to one century before entering on the events of another. The Magdeburg Centuriators, the founders of modern Church history, proclaim by their very name that this is the scheme which they have adopted. To each of the thirteen centuries of which they treat they have attributed a volume of its own, and, down to Mosheim, such has been the popular arrangement. But this distribution by centuries, besides often cutting up the history into portions inconveniently small, lies under the fault which just now I noted, namely, that it is purely arbitrary; and, if it has some advantages, has inconveniences, which in my judgment very much outweigh these. The great movements of the Church adapt themselves to it very ill; often do not adapt themselves at all, altogether traverse and ignore it. These movements will not begin exactly at the beginning of a century, nor end exactly at its close, so to fall in with some artificial scheme of ours; and only when stretched on a bed of Procrustes, or on the same bed abridged and cut short, will they even seem to adapt themselves to it.

For myself I am persuaded that I shall do wisely in subordinating the chronological order and succession of events to the higher interests of my story. With this conviction I shall endeavour, so far as this may be, to have one central fact or idea in each of my Lectures, to group my materials round this, recapitulating what may be behind, anticipating what lies before, refusing altogether, so often as a higher interest seems to demand this, to play the part of annalist or centuriator, and seeking to marshal my materials according to quite other laws than those of time. Of course as events happen in time, and as the time when they happen often gives them their chief significance, time cannot be altogether ignored. I shall not, however, count myself bound to string the events which I care to record on the thread which it offers, but shall often prefer to arrange and combine them according to inner affinities of their own.

But this much being on this subject said, there are still errors on the one side and on the other which in the selection and distribution of our materials it behoves us to avoid. That kingdom of heaven which Christ founded in the world is not exclusively the Leaven working inwardly in the hearts of men. It is as little exclusively the Mustard seed, visibly growing up in the sight of all, and spreading forth its branches until it has covered with the shadow of them the whole earth. It is both of these; and our Lord, when He desired to set forth the future development of the Church which should unfold itself from Him as from its living seed, spake both these parables, one close upon the other (Matt. xiii. 31–33), that they might mutually complete one another, and that we might learn to give due prominence to both sides of the truth.

This is not always done. There are some Church historians, and those men of eminent piety—indeed no other would be likely to fall into this error—who have an eye only for the inward operations of grace in the hearts of individual believers. They trace with inexhaustible interest the working of the leaven, the transforming power of the truth, as it fashions into newness of life those who have hidden that truth in their hearts. Neander is the noblest representative of the historians with whom, despite of all their merits, we must find this fault. Not too spiritual, but too exclusively spiritual, what he gives us is often a succession of most interesting biographies, a history of the working of the leaven in the souls of men. But for that of the mustard seed, we may often search his great work in vain. As we read, we would fain hear more, we want *him* to care more and to tell *us* more, of the Kingdom, as it visibly shapes itself in the world, as it confronts the kingdoms of the world; and to trace for us with a more lively interest, and in bolder and firmer outline, the whole course of its outer fortunes no less than that of its inner life.

With other historians on the contrary this, which I have called the history of the mustard seed, is all in all. They bring before us the long array of Councils and of Popes; they detail at length the events adverse and prosperous which befell the Church, the outer conditions of its conflict with the powers of this world. They invite us to mark the visible growth of the tree, the spreading of its branches; how the birds of the air, the great ones of the earth, came and sought shelter in its branches, how this or that tribe or nation accepted baptism and was aggregated to the Church. But with all this the inward transforming power of the word of life, its secret energy, as it makes its presence felt in the hearts and thoughts and lives of men, of this they tell us little or nothing, for this they have no eye. If the others were at fault in making Church history merely a history of personal piety, these are still more in fault, not caring to tell us aught of that which after all is the distinctive mark of the children of the kingdom. In taking these two parables and giving to both of them their full rights, we shall find our best protection against onesidedness in this direction or in the other.

There is another point which you have a right to expect that we shall not permit you to miss, the relations, namely, of this history to contemporary profane history, and at the same time its difference and distinctness from that history. Two dangers are before us here; the one, to lose sight of its distinctness, that is, its supernatural character, to merge it in the world-history; the other, to lose sight of the fact that the Church exists for the world, quite as really as the world exists for the Church, so that there can happen no worse thing for it than to forget or to deny this. I know that there are some for whom the Church is at best nothing better than the organization of the moral life of a human community for the promotion of moral ends, and who therefore are quite consistent when they affirm that the lines which divide sacred history and profane exist nowhere except in our imaginations. All history, they urge, is sacred; and so in a manner it is, being the history of man; and certainly if a heathen moralist could say, *Homo sacra res*, much more, and with better right, should we. But these, emptying that history of a divine presence and a divine purpose, are indeed working toward quite another result, toward the making of all history profane. But that history, what is it for us? It is the record of the carrying out in time of a divine purpose for the knitting anew into one fellowship, under the headship of the Son of God, of all those who, receiving Him, do themselves become also sons of God. What other purposes beyond these the Church may exist to fulfil are only obscurely hinted in the Scriptures; and such, while we would not exclude, we as little dare to urge.

You have a right then to demand of us that we shall tell this story as a divine and a heavenly, not as an earthly and a mundane; that we shall justify the introduction of this man or of that event into our story by tracing their relation to the objects and ends which I have just mentioned; that we shall mark, and call upon you to mark, the great stream of tendency, which in the midst of confusions, eddies and perplexing back-waters is evermore setting heavenward. This is a divine history; what therefore we are to look for first and chiefly are the vestiges of God, the print of his footsteps, in it. But it is the history of the Church not as an institution which will know nothing of the world, which in fact has been separated off from the world to the end that the one might be saved, and the other perish; but as one rather whose separation from the

world is as much for the world's sake as for the
Church's own, that so there may be for the world a
City of Refuge, an abiding witness in the midst of it
for a higher life than its own ; which yet, higher as it
is, may be the portion, and on the simplest conditions,
of all. The history of the Church is the history of the
life of Christ in his members, not indeed without infinite faults, infirmities, shortcomings, sins, cleaving to
those in whom that life is working ; but, despite of all
these, a prolongation of the life which He began upon
earth, the history of a divine Society by Him founded,
and which, strange to say, like an inverted tree, has
its roots above and not below, in heaven and not on
earth. All that has been the true expression of this
divine life, all that has helped, and all too that has hindered, the unfolding of it, all the precious flowers and
fruits by which it has made its presence known, it is
of these which any true Church history should tell us.

Here then we have something of a clue to guide us
through that which else might prove an inextricable
labyrinth. Let us have grasped the events, let us
have recognized the persons, that have effectually
wrought to the unfolding of this higher life, and then
whatever else we may have missed, the leading threads,
the true *stamina* of the history, are in our hands. Let
us on the contrary have missed these, let us not have
attempted, or attempting let us have failed, to disengage these from the multitude of facts and people with
which they are mingled, and among which they are in
danger of being lost, and however well we may be up
in names and dates, in martyrdoms and persecutions
and heresies, in Fathers, in Councils, in Popes, in
events of this century and events of the other, still the

real meaning and purpose of Church history will have escaped us.

I would not willingly bring this my introductory Lecture to a close without naming to you one or two faults, not so much intellectual as moral, into which, as it seems to me, some who have undertaken to tell this wondrous story have fallen, and have led others to fall; and in which, if we did not watch against them, we might also be very easily entangled ourselves; faults from which I would fain keep myself clear, and help to keep you clear. Beware then, I would say to you, above all of those who in their outlook over the Lord's field have an eye only for the tares, and none for the wheat; who point out to us the mountains of chaff on the Lord's floor, but who neither themselves see, nor help to make others see, the golden grains which are abundantly hidden among this; who seem never so well pleased as when, at the expense of the Church, they can gratify a proud and self-satisfied world. Such there are, though to be found more often in other lands than in our own. To have been a standard-bearer of the truth is no title of honour in their eyes, but rather the contrary. If they have any heroes, these are to be found among such as the Church has been compelled to put from her and to disown, not among those whom she has delighted to honour. But indeed they have seldom any heroes at all. At their touch all which was high becomes low, all which was heroic dwarfs and dwindles into littleness and meanness. The men who spent themselves in contending to the death for truths which should be dearer to us than light or life were enthusiasts whose earnestness may just redeem them from our contempt.

But there is much very short of this, against which it is well you should be upon your guard. That Church of the living God, some stages of whose growth we would fain trace for your instruction—you are not without it, but within. It is your shelter, appointed of God to be this. Nothing of its past history should be a matter of a mere curiosity or entertainment to you. You are heirs of whatever it has gained, you are losers by whatever it has lost or let go. But the temptation is strong to contemplate all this as from some "coign of vantage" external to it, admiring this and criticising that; adjudging praise to this man and blame to that; resolving that this one went too far, and that not far enough; that Tertullian was too fierce, and Jerome too touchy; that Luther might sometimes have kept a better tongue in his head, and so on. Dwell not, except where this is necessary that so you may not miss the lessons which God would teach us, on the faults and mistakes of those who have been called to do his work in his Church, and have done it. There is something better for us to dwell on in this work of theirs; for He who is wonderful everywhere, is nowhere so wonderful as in the congregation of his saints, that is, of those who with all their mistakes, their sins, their shortcomings were the elect of humanity, the bravest, the purest, the noblest whom the world has seen.

Accept then, I would say in conclusion, with all reverence the fact that the Church militant, if in all ages a success, is also in all ages a failure. The success may be more evident in one age and in one land, the failure may be more marked in another; but tokens of this and of that will never be wanting. Some may dwell almost exclusively on one of these aspects; we shall do well not to hide our eyes from either. For us who believe the Church to be a divine foundation in the world, it must be a success, even as it shows itself to be such by many infallible proofs. For us who know that the treasure of God's grace is contained in earthen vessels, it must be a failure no less, an imperfect embodiment of a divine idea. Let us boldly face this side of the truth no less than the other.

LECTURE II.

THE MIDDLE AGES BEGINNING.

I ventured in my former Lecture to find fault with the distribution of Church history into centuries, as a distribution purely arbitrary and artificial, and one to which the actual events and movements with which that history has to do refuse to conform. But suppose we were to say, This history presents itself to us under three leading aspects, one succeeding the other; its several periods having each its own characteristic features, and to all appearance a purpose and task of its own; I will therefore mentally distribute it into three portions, corresponding to these several periods, and call them each by a name of its own, Ancient, Medieval, and Modern. Here, supposing that assumption to be a correct one, would be a scheme of distribution natural and not forced, one answering to facts in the world of realities, one therefore which would afford genuine assistance to the learner, and help to bring real clearness into his studies.

But this much being admitted, it would still be necessary to define precisely the limits of these several periods: at what date Ancient Church history should be assumed to have closed and Medieval to have begun; and again, when Medieval came to an end and Modern commenced. That these are questions

14

not perfectly easy to answer is evident from the very
different limits and landmarks of each period on which
different writers have fixed.   To take, then, Ancient
Church history first :—there can indeed be no question
about the time of its beginning.   The day of Pentecost
would on all sides be acknowledged as the birthday,
the *dies natalis*, of the Church.   But about the date of
the termination of Ancient Church history there would
not be at all the same consent.   Some would assign
to it a duration of eight hundred years, would make it
reach to the revival of the Empire under Charles the
Great (800).   I must needs think that this is a duration as much too long as that of Hallam is too short,
who counts the Middle Ages to have commenced with
the invasion of Gaul by Clovis (486).   My conviction
is that we should articulate the history more justly if
we affirmed that, as Ancient history it closed, and as
Medieval began, with the Pontificate of Gregory the
Great (590).   In him, the last of the Latin Fathers,
the first, in our modern sense of the word, of the
Popes, we bid adieu to the old Greek and Roman culture and literature and habits of thought as the predominant and ruling forces of the world.   The ancient
classical world still lives on in bequests innumerable,
visible and invisible, not a few among these of priceless worth, which it has made to all after times.   But
another order of things is shaping itself; and Gregory
the Great, standing at the meeting-place of the old
and the new, does more than any other to set the
Church forward upon the new lines on which henceforth it must travel, to constitute a Latin Christianity,
with distinctive features of its own, such as broadly
separate it from Greek.

Then, too, there are several grand events in the fifteenth century which suggest themselves as world-epochs; fitted as such to mark the conclusion of the Middle Ages, the commencement of another age. There is the Invention of Printing (1440). There is the Fall of Constantinople, and with it of the Eastern Empire (1453). Closely connected with both of these, but still capable of being distinguished from them, even as it commenced before them, there is the Revival of Learning, to which, however, it is hard to affix an exact date. There is, lastly, the Discovery of the New World (1492), with the widening of men's thoughts to meet this outward fact. They are all events of an immense importance; and each one of them well fitted to toll the knell of a departing age, and to announce the birth of a new. They might every one of them plead its own fitness to be the merestone to mark where one era terminated and another began. But they have all of them primarily more or less of a mundane significance; and seeing that we are treating of a history which is not of this world, however it may be in it, I should be disposed to look a little further, to the Reformation (1517), and to conclude the period of the Medieval Church history with it. No doubt, in some respects, it is too late a day. We are already well advanced in the modern world; but grave inconveniences attend every other date, graver than those which attend this.

Modern Church history remains, that which is actually unfolding itself before our eyes, and in which we ourselves play a part. What the limits in time of this may be, what will come after it, if indeed it shall not prove a winding up of the present dis-

pensation, these "times and seasons" it is not for us
to know.

But these three periods, each of them including
many hundred years, are still too big to be conveniently handled. The larger blocks of time must
again be broken up into smaller sizes, the divisions
must be in their turn themselves subdivided. All who
have undertaken to tell the Church's story have felt
this, and that resting-places at shorter intervals must
be found. Thus Ancient Church history might again
be profitably distributed into three lesser portions.
The first of these would be properly characterized as
the Apostolic, reaching down as it does to the death
of the last of the Apostles, St. John (98), and embrac-
ing therefore something less than one hundred years.
This period has a distinctive character of its own, being
in the Apostles and Apostolic men authoritative and
constitutive for the after Church. Upon this follows
the period of the Church's conflict with Pagan Rome,
the period of the *Ecclesia pressa*, as it is sometimes
called, reaching down to Constantine's Edict of Tolera-
tion (311). Then, completing the period of Ancient
Church history, follow some two centuries or more,
during a good part of which the Church rides on the
high places of the earth, having exchanged the trials
of adversity for the temptations, at least as dangerous,
of prosperity.

In the same way Medieval Church history will fitly
fall into three subdivisions. The first, extending from
the Pontificate of Gregory the Great to that of
Gregory VII. (1050), will embrace the Middle Ages
in their formation, as a new order of things is gra-

dually shaping itself out of the chaos and confusion in which those Ages began, the breaking up of an old world, and little by little the construction of a new. The second period will reach from the Pontificate of Gregory VII. to that of Boniface VIII. or the Middle Ages in their glory, and at their height. To this, their creative period, belong all those magnificent births which they have bequeathed, some to the admiration, and all to the wonder, of the after world—the Crusades, the rise of Gothic Architecture, the Schoolmen, the Mystics, the Mendicant Orders, the Universities. To this belongs the struggle, so grand and so terrible, between the world-king and the world-priest, the Emperor and the Pope, with the complete triumph for the time of the latter; and thus to this also belongs the Papacy in the most towering heights to which it ever ascended.

Then follows the period from Boniface VIII. to the Reformation, or the Middle Ages in their decline and decay. Their productive vigour is exhausted; they are unable to bring forth any new births, or to maintain at their height such as they have received from the times which went before. These Ages, once so confident in themselves, but now defeated in so many of their dearest hopes, are losing heart; they have ceased to believe in themselves any more, and so give clearest intimation that whatever good purposes they and the institutions which were proper and peculiar to them were capable of serving, these they had served already; that the one crowning favour which some of the most characteristic among them could now confer on the Church and the world would be to pass away, if so a new and a better might succeed in their room.

The period of Modern Church history, being as yet only partially unrolled, being one, moreover, which we do not contemplate from any external point of view, but in which we ourselves are involved, is less capable of being further subdivided than either which went before. At the same time the Peace of Westphalia (1648) offers a convenient resting-place for the mind. With that the political, though not the religious, conflict between the Reformed and the Roman Catholic communities in Western Christendom came virtually to an end. That remarkable reaction, which had so signally counter-checked the early triumphs of the Reformation, winning back to the Roman Obedience much which at one moment appeared lost to it for ever, in its turn had run its course; and, having discovered what it could effect, and what it could not, was then compelled to own that the attempt to crush the Reformation by mere force, as something which had no right to exist, must for ever be renounced.

Hitherto we have contemplated the Church as existing under conditions of *time*. But it subsists also under conditions of *space;* and at different epochs has, so to speak, shifted its ground, at all events shifted its centre, and occupied different portions of the area of the civilized world. We may profitably lay out a geographical as well as a chronological ground-plan for our study here. And first, is there any order which we can trace in the midst of all their confusion in these changes of its local dwelling-place? And if so, can we recognize the law which has in different ages determined the bounds of its habitation? I think there is, and that we can; and we shall be the more confident that this is so, when we find in the main the great changes of place coincident with those other changes in time of which we have just been speaking.

Thus I do not need to remind you at how early a day the Church chipped its Jewish shell, refused any more to be bound in Jewish swaddling clothes; how the Word of life, rejected by them who had the prior right to its blessings, was offered to the heathen, and eagerly embraced by them,—the Apostles, St. Paul in chief, planting Churches in all the principal cities of the Greek and Roman world. Thus during the first period, the Roman Empire, that zone of fertile land which surrounds the great inland sea, to which we now restrict the name of "the Mediterranean," was the chief, almost the exclusive, sphere of the Church's activity. Here and there might be some missionary effort beyond, or even an outlying Church, as in Persia, or beyond the Danube, but these were accidental and exceptional. I have called it the Græco-Roman world, for the Asiatic cities, such as Antioch and Ephesus, which play so important a part at this time, had been thoroughly hellenized—this was one of the fruits of Alexander's conquests—indeed the Greek spirit was immeasurably stronger and more living in them than in Greece itself. Such is the appointed sphere in which the Church lives and moves for the first five or six hundred years of its existence. At first overlooked, then repelled as an intruder, slandered, fought against, persecuted, trampled under foot, it yet makes good its position, overcomes by patience, by meekness, by the word of the testimony, by the blood of the Cross; until at length it appropriates the classical language and culture, fills them, so far as they are capable of being filled, with the spirit of a new life ; and within the limits of the Roman Empire there rises up, first a Greek and then a Latin Church literature of inestimable price for all after times.

But the Roman Empire is doomed. Christianity can delay its perishing, but cannot avert it. God has something better in store for his Church. It shall display its power, not in arresting for a while the decay of an old and dying civilization, not yet upon nations the best period of whose life had been long overlived before it was planted in their midst ; but upon those whose best is all in the future. The rude and unsophisticated children of the North break down the barriers which Roman arts and arms had so long, and for the last century or two so painfully, maintained against them. They settled in all the fairest provinces of the Western Empire. Ere long, however, they own the mighty power of the Gospel of Christ; of his Church which has stood erect when all other institutions have gone to the ground before them. These races, barbarous indeed, but full of native energy, with many noble possibilities which only waited the word of the Cross to call them out, accept the yoke of Christ; and after a little while the message of the Gospel is carried back by them among the tribes of their kindred which had remained in their primitive seats. The Church is travelling westward and northward, making conquests there which shall serve as a compensation for the immense losses which it is enduring in another quarter, where the great Arabian heresiarch and the Caliphs, his successors, are doing their work only too well, so that in lands which were once the very cradle of Christianity, it now barely exists through the sufferance and contempt of its foes. The Church is not so much Greek and Latin, with these two hemispheres balancing and completing one another, as Latin and Germanic. I use this word and not German, to indicate that I include therein all families of the Teutonic stock. What is Greek indeed still subsists, but has fallen so far behind that it can hardly be counted any more in the running.

In Modern Church history there is a still further shifting of the centre of the Church's life. Rome is not this centre any more, neither do the nations occupying the soil of the Latin Empire stand in the forefront of things. Repelling and repudiating, as all these did, the Reformation, in which was the Church's hope for the future, they too have fallen into the rear. As the Greek Church fell behind in the second period, so the Latin, as represented by Rome and the Churches in communion with her, is falling behind in the third. Not we ourselves, but those who come after, must declare of us whether we, into whose hands the lamp of faith has now passed, shall have run aright the race set before us; whether we shall have accomplished the glorious destiny which has been placed within our reach, but which only too easily we may miss. It is yet to be seen whether England, this Esther which has been so strangely exalted to one of the chief thrones in the world, will listen to the voice which is saying to her, "Who knoweth whether thou art come to the kingdom for such a time as this?" or whether this kingdom shall be taken away from her, and given to some other who shall know how to use its opportunities better.

It is the second of the three periods thus marked

out with which we, in this present course of Lectures, have to do.   We start with the Pontificate of Gregory the Great.   Let us seek to take a brief oversight of the aspect which Western Christendom presented, when he was called to the helm of the sorely tossed ship of the Church, and trace with this some chief features of his own work.   And first let me observe that, whether for good or for evil, he must be accepted as the true founder of the Medieval Papacy.   It is the source of infinite confusion, and throws back the historic exist- ence of the Papacy to a period at which, in its later developments, it did not exist at all, when we speak of a Pope before his time.   None, of course, would deny that the Bishop of Rome bore that title before; but he only bore it, as all other Bishops did.   It was not till about the sixth century that the title began to be re- stricted to one Bishop of the West; this restriction be- ing, no doubt, an indication that the difference between him and other Bishops was making itself so felt as to demand its utterance and expression in words.   Much, no doubt, in the conditions of the world around wrought together for the marking out of the difference between him and all those others whose office was not in itself inferior to his, and for giving a new emphasis to this difference; yet in the main it was the virtues of Gre- gory, these, it is true, seconded by his rare gifts of go- vernment, which gave to the office that he held so far higher a significance, and so much greater a weight than ever it had possessed before.

Those virtues were indeed eminent, and endured the proof, being tried to the uttermost in a very evil time. For in truth the outlook which the Church in his day presented was so dark and gloomy that it could scarcely have been darker or gloomier, to whatever side he turned. After long wars which had utterly wasted Italy, and left Rome itself little better than a desert, famine and pestilence consuming what the sword had spared; after troubles and confusions which had loosened or quite dissolved the bands of ecclesiastical discipline, the Byzantine Emperors, thanks to the genius of Belisarius and Narses, had recovered their Italian dominions (553), though soon to lose for ever the main part of them again. This meant that the Bishop of Rome was once more their subject; and if, out of prudential motives, treated sometimes with a certain deference, yet not secure from the worst outrages and indignities, if he failed to jump with all the varying doctrinal humours of the Byzantine Court. Nor was this a mere chimerical danger. One of Gregory's successors, Martin I., refusing to conform to the shifting changes of the Imperial theology, was sent in chains to the East, put there on his trial; and being condemned, tasted the worst which the malice of foes could inflict (655).

But there were dangers nearer and more urgent. It was but a few years before Gregory's elevation that the Lombards, pressed upon by other tribes in their previous seats to the North-East, had occupied those fertile plains of Upper Italy to which they have bequeathed a name which has long survived their comparatively short-lived dominion there (568–744). The Lombards were still Arians; but though their Arianism sat loosely upon them, it was excuse enough for every sort of fanatic outrage on the Catholic faith and the holders of it; while in other ways they were less accessible to the influences of Roman culture than any

other of the Teutonic tribes. Rome and the Roman
Bishop were in constant danger from them. Tardy
and insufficient was any help which could be looked
for from the Imperial Exarch at Ravenna. The Emperor and the Emperor's representative could oppress,
but could not protect; while the star of deliverance
which, rising in the land of the Franks, should bring
freedom to the Church at once from the Greek and
the Lombard, was not yet visible above the horizon.

Nor was the outlook beyond much more encou-
raging. In the conversion of the Arian Goths of Spain
and their king to the Catholic faith was almost the one
glimpse of light and comfort which Gregory, as he
looked around him, could anywhere have found.
Frightful calamities following hard upon one another
had reduced the once glorious North African Church
to a faint shadow of what once it had been, that shadow
itself in less than a century wholly to disappear (670).
The line of the Danube and the Rhine, lost to the
Church during the confusions of the preceding centuries, was only being slowly regained; while the serried
strength of Teutonic heathenism beyond remained unassailed as yet, and, until its strength had been effectually broken by the stronger hand of Charles the
Great, was an abiding menace to civilized and Christian Europe. Of England, for the most part heathen
still, I shall speak in another Lecture.

In the East the prospects of the Church were not
less cheerless. The long ignoble agony of Byzantine
Christianity had fairly begun. The Council of Chalcedon (451), while it renewed the Church's protest
against Nestorianism, so chilly and rationalistic, had
condemned no less the more spiritual errors of Euty-

ches and the Monophysites; but its wise moderation
had profited nothing.   The decisions which should
have been the end, proved unhappily rather a new beginning of strife, or at any rate a new departure for it.
In some parts of the Empire, as notably in Egypt, the
Monophysites far outnumbered the Catholics, these
and those furiously raging against one another; while
the Emperors, seeking to compose the quarrel, but
meddling as arbiters in a conflict which was not to be
settled by Imperial decrees, only inflamed the strife
which they thought to allay; and thus all was ripening
for that tremendous catastrophe, that judgment-doom
on the Eastern Church, which, unguessed as yet by
any mortal man, was even then at the door.   The
Arabian camel-driver who should change the whole
face of the East was some twenty years old when Gregory was called to the Pontificate (590); he had
reached his thirty-fourth or thirty-fifth year when Gregory died (604), though it was not till some seven
years later that he began openly to proclaim his
mission.

And yet we may say boldly that had the gift of
prophecy been added to the many gifts which Gregory possessed, had he known all which was even then
so near, it would not have shaken his confidence that
the kingdom of God is the one kingdom in the world
which cannot be moved; even as it was in this faith
that he did so much to bear up the pillars of a tottering Church and world.   Whether he was fully aware
that old things were passing away, and about to make
room for new, may very well be a question, as it is
always a question whether the primary actors in such
mighty transformations are themselves fully conscious

of them ; but certainly both in what he wrote and in
what he did, there are tokens of a sense upon his part
of an old world overlived, of a new world beginning.
Thus it may seem but a small matter, yet in fact is
very significant, that he should announce in the Pre-
face to his main theological work that he did not
intend to embarrass himself or his readers by any
painful adherence to the laws of the Latin language.
Much utters itself here. Plainly he has turned his back,
so far as this was possible, on the old Greek and Roman
world. Him, the foremost man of his age, the classical literature does not interest in the least. He has
only rebukes for a Bishop whom it does interest.
Then, too, the credulity which in the Middle Ages so
often took the place of faith, which failed to draw any
line of distinction between history and legend, is only
too strong in him, while in his own writings may be
detected germs of errors which appear full-blown at a
later age. All this must be freely admitted, while yet,
when all is said, he must be owned to complete, and
worthily, to complete, the grand quaternion of the
recognized Doctors of the Latin Church, and to close
the catalogue of these.

And this is not all. So many changes in the service-
book of the Church have found place during the twelve
hundred years which have since run their course, that
it is easier to acknowledge the greatness of our debt
to Pope Gregory as first and happiest of liturgic innova-
tors and reformers, organizer of the Church's worship
as it never had been organized before, than to define
exactly wherein that debt consists. Only I will mention that to him we owe that plain song or chant,
which still bears his name ; and which, if it wanted the

freshness, the movement, the popularity of the Ambrosian melodies which it displaced, very far surpassed them in dignity and solemnity; while it broke definitively away from all of Greek and Pagan which still lingered about and haunted those other.

But if the whole Latin Church owes him so much, there is a peculiar and special benefit for which English men and women are his debtors, and which we should prove most unthankful if we suffered to fall out of sight, this namely,—that, regarding as part of his high commission to take oversight of the heathen world, to reduce under spiritual culture the outfield of the nations, he saw and seized the opportunity for reannexing England to Western Christendom, from which it had now for nearly two centuries been violently torn away. The Conversion of England, by him auspicated and begun, will furnish the subject of my next Lecture.

LECTURE III.

THE CONVERSION OF ENGLAND.

THE conquest of Britain by the Saxons and Angles, and their own settlement in the land which they had conquered, differed in some most important features from corresponding events in other countries which had, like Britain, once formed part of the Roman Empire. In other lands it was a forcible taking possession of the soil by the intrusive race, who thrust out the old occupants from such parts of it as pleased them best; and this intrusion was no doubt carried through with no little violence and of suffering to the conquered people. At the same time, as Guizot shows long ago, it is easy to exaggerate the amount of this suffering; and one thing is beyond doubt, namely, that there was no extermination; that a *modus vivendi* was discovered, and the conquering and the conquered races contrived to subsist side by side; nay, more than this, that the conquering accepted before very long the language, the civilization, and in the end the religion of the conquered. It had been quite otherwise here. There had been no attempt at a transaction between the Saxon and the Briton. The invaders made a thorough clearance of the land as they advanced, winning their way now swiftly, now slowly, and at times coming to a stand. What remained of the British population, all which had not perished in an unavailing resistance, was pushed westward and northward ; to West Wales, that is to Cornwall, to North Wales, or Wales as we should call it now, and to other the northern parts of the Island.   Britain, or England as we must name it henceforth, was paganized anew.   A wedge of heathenism, thrust in between Christian Ireland and the Christian continent of Western Europe, it separated these, and was itself completely withdrawn from any share in their higher life.

It is to Gregory the Great we owe the foundation of the mission by which England was restored to its place in the commonwealth of Christian nations.   I pass by, though not as questioning its truth, the tender and graceful story of the Angles and the Angels, of Deira and De Irâ, of Ella and Hallelujah.   It is sufficient for me to remind you how this illustrious Bishop of the Western Church saw that the time had arrived for seeking to draw once more within the pale of Christendom this Island, which had been lost to it so long; recognized in the marriage of Ethelbert, King of Kent—King, that is, of the most civilized part of the land, and with an acknowledged superiority over the whole—to Bertha, a Frankish and thus a Christian Princess, an opening afforded which should not be neglected.   It was not a sudden thought.   The English mission, with its toils and dangers, he had once hoped to appropriate to himself.   But, raised to his present dignity, he must be content to select another, the Roman Abbot Augustine, to whom he added some forty companions more, who should make good that lack of service upon his own part which now was unavoidable. Need I tell you how the Roman Pontiff cheered, encouraged, and rebuked his missionaries, when these, having gotten as far as Gaul, would fain have turned back, terrified by the reports which they heard of the people to whom they were sent, "a people of a fierce countenance, whose language they could not understand?" Familiar also to us all is the story of the favourable reception which they found, such as must have made them abundantly ashamed of their unfaithful fears ; King Ethelbert himself before very long accepting the yoke of Christ (597), and drawing after him, as was the ever-recurring feature of these conversions, his chiefs, who in their turn drew after them the mass of the people.

Augustine, satisfied that a veritable work had begun, journeys as far as France ; is there consecrated by the Pope's Vicar, Vergilius, Metropolitan of Arles. Returning to England, he uses his liberty in selecting Canterbury as the future ecclesiastical centre of the land, and not London, which was heathen still ; but which Gregory, with his imperfect knowledge of the actual political conditions of England and the division of its kingdoms, had designed and named. And now some additional helpers joined him from Rome, with assistance in other shapes from the Pope, who watched with a tender solicitude over the Church which he had planted. Nor did he omit to send to Augustine the pall, at once a token of the archiepiscopal dignity which now was his, and of his holding this as the gift of the Pope. But more valuable than all the rest were the wise monitions with which the large-hearted Pontiff, who must have known his man, accompanied his gifts, urging as he did upon him that he should not push too far his demands of an exact conformity to Roman rules and usages in things indifferent on the part of his new converts. Whatever anywhere he found of good and edifying, let him adopt and make his own. It was not long before Augustine had ample room and opportunity for the exercise of that wisdom and moderation by Gregory enjoined on him here; but it must be owned that the opportunity was missed, and the admonition laid very imperfectly to heart. A good man, he was also a narrow and unconciliatory. The grand breadth and tolerance, at least in things secondary, of Gregory would in vain be looked for in him. On a review of his whole career, we have no choice but to say that, as will sometimes happen, the work was grander than the man who wrought the work, that he did not so much achieve greatness, as have greatness thrust upon him. And this showed itself so ere long.

Augustine, as I have said already, found England in the main a heathen land; and yet not so but that British Christians and a British Church existed still. The Teutonic invaders had destroyed all which they could destroy in the deserted Roman province, but had not been able to make a clean sweep of Christianity from the Island. Augustine felt it most desirable to come to some understanding with the heads of this Church, that they, acknowledging his authority, and with this, of course, that of his sender, might be underworkers with him for the evangelizing of the English people; a work not to be accomplished by the little band which he had brought with him, and the scanty reinforcement which had subsequently joined him. But the task of associating British and Roman Missionaries in a common work was one difficult and delicate, and, with all which we owe to Augustine, it must be freely allowed that he was not the man to effect it. On the other hand, it can as little be affirmed of the British Christians that they yearned to take that glorious revenge on their Anglo-Saxon enemies which was placed within their reach. These or the fathers of these had despoiled them of earth; they were little disposed in return to help their spoilers to heaven. The attempt, however, to arrange terms of co-operation was made. Augustine got together a Synod at which a certain number of the British Bishops were induced to attend; but these, offended at his assumption, refused to accept the Roman rule for the keeping of Easter, or otherwise to submit to the supremacy of the Bishop of Rome, of which they declared that they had not heard before, and which, hearing of now, they repudiated altogether. It was not very wonderful that this attempt at reconciliation, or, to describe it more accurately, this summons to submission, did not close the rent and rift between the Churches, but rather left it wider than before.

Let me note here that it is altogether a mistake, though a very common one, to assume that the difference about Easter, which did so much to keep them asunder, was a revival of the old dispute between the Churches of Asia Minor (Ephesus above all) and the rest of Christendom—the same which had been settled at the Council of Nicæ; and it is mistake reared upon mistake to adduce this as a proof that Britain had received her Christianity from the East; which it is just possible may have been the case, but for which there is no evidence here. In the Churches of Asia Minor, which professed to follow the tradition of St. John, the

E

method of calculation, fundamentally distinct from that of the West, was such that the Easter festival might fall upon any day in the week. Nothing of the kind could possibly happen in the British. Its Easter basis of calculation, if I may so call it, was identical with that of Rome. It was only that, in the application of a rule which was common to both, the other Churches of the West and Rome at their head, not being cut off from the superior astronomical knowledge of Alexandria, had learned from time to time to make allowance for certain disturbing facts, and had adjusted their calendar to these. The British Church meanwhile, separated for long years from the science of the Christian world, had failed to make the corrections in her calendar which were necessary, if Easter was to preserve its proper place.

The centre of interest shifts after Augustine's death, of which the exact year is not certainly known, from the little kingdom of Kent, in which alone his very moderate missionary successes were obtained, to the more important kingdom of Northumbria, where King Edwin, he too married to a Christian princess, after long hesitation, is won for the truth, to which he loyally cleaves, and for which in the end he lays down his life. For not inconsiderable as had been the triumphs thus far of the Gospel in the land, England was not converted or nearly converted yet. If the truth goes forth "conquering and to conquer," yet it has its defeats, its dark days, before the complete triumph arrive. The corn of wheat must die, or appear to die, before it bears much fruit. It seems indeed an almost universal law of mission work, that the definitive victory is not won without a temporary reaction of more or less severity. The powers of darkness, seen and unseen, the spiritual weaknesses which constitute the real background of every form of heathenism, these, with all whom they can enlist in their service, gather themselves up, as with the energy of despair, for a last and decisive struggle with the kingdom of light. A fierce tempest of wrath sweeps over the Church, and the patient work of years perishes, or seems to perish, in an hour. So fared it, though not to the full extent, in the Roman Empire. A Constantine might seem to have brought, but did not indeed bring, all to a happy end ; there must still be a Julian and an apostasy before a Theodosius came. And so fares it in cases innumerable. Ansgar must prove the truth of this in Sweden. Hungary twice relapses into heathenism, even after a St. Stephen had sat upon its throne. In our own days we have seen something of the same kind in New Zealand and Madagascar, It was not otherwise in the England of old. The fierce pagan King of Mercia, Penda by name, heads the heathen reaction ; and when Edwin falls in battle, it might seem as that with him had fallen the whole imposing but unstable edifice of Christianity in the north of the Island (633).

But Christ is mightier than Woden. The work, arrested for a while, goes forward again. Yet it is not the band of Italian monks, who are too few, nor yet missionaries from the British Church in Wales, who have too little heart for the task, by whom the conversion of northern England shall be accomplished. Other evangelists, and these from quite a different quarter, appear upon the scene, and take up the uncompleted work; and to them the chief glory of it must belong.

To the Celtic monks, who were also the travellers, the scholars, the missionaries of the sixth, the seventh, and the eighth century, England, and indeed all North-Western Europe, owes a debt of gratitude which is hardly as yet acknowledged to the full. Bede, though writing altogether from the Roman point of view, bears witness to the single-mindedness and devotion with which they addressed themselves to the missionary work. Two hundred years have elapsed since St. Patrick taught; but he had left multitudes behind him, his lineal spiritual descendants, in whose hearts was burning the same sacred fire which had once burned so brightly in his own. Not a few of these, passing over from Ireland, had chosen the little storm-beaten island of Iona among the Western Hebrides, with the hope that from it as from a centre might radiate the light of God's truth into all the darkness round; nor were they disappointed in their hope.

On all those points of discipline and ritual observance on which the British Church of Wales was at issue with Rome, they were at issue no less ; but there was nothing in their past history to estrange them from the English as the Britons were estranged ; and they threw themselves with a will, not one by one, but by troops and companies, into the work which was before them ; Aidan, called the Apostle of Northumbria, gentle, and winning souls by the gentleness of Christ, leading the way. The points of difference and divergence between these and the missionaries who had received their commission from Rome, came into no perplexing prominence so long as their several spheres of labour, north and south, lay apart from each other. But when, by the very successes which attended their labours, these came to touch one another, as before very long they did, the crisis, sooner or later inevitable arrived, and the question whether Celtic or Roman Christianity should be paramount in the land. It was a question which hung for a while in the balance. Rome triumphed in the end. We may regard the Council of Whitby (663) as the turning point. At this the advocates of the Roman celebration of Easter and of the British severally pleaded before Oswy, then the most powerful monarch in the Heptarchy. He, being assured by the advocates for the Roman use that this was according to the mind of St. Peter, and that St. Peter had the keys of the kingdom of heaven, to admit or exclude, did not think it prudent to put himself in opposition to one so powerful, and declared for this use.

The tide of popular favour set from this time forward more and more strongly in the direction of Rome; which little by little triumphed not in England only, but in Ireland and Scotland as well, until Iona, the latest stronghold of Celtic Christianity, was itself won (716). Many, it is true of the more ardent and independent spirits among the Scottish missionaries refused to accept the yoke and to bow to the obedience of Rome. Seeing no place for them here any more, they crossed the seas to found, or where this was already done, to strengthen and extend, the Mission Churches in Frisia and Northern Germany, which their brethren had already founded. A grand career was opened to them there, and they were not wanting to it (see p. 60) ; while yet in the end the same issues which the conflict had found in England, it found also abroad. The struggle with Rome being again renewed on the German soil found the same results. By the year 743, thanks mainly to Boniface,—of whom in another Lecture,—Roman Christianity was everywhere triumphant there.   The work of the Celtic missionaries was with their God.

Owning as we must that there were precious truths held with clearness by the Celtic Church—you will hear it often spoken of as the Church of the Culdees— truths which were already more or less obscure in the Roman, we are sometimes tempted to wish that the issue had been otherwise.   And yet it would be well to ask, Was there, in any Celtic Church which could then have been founded, that which would have enabled it, or the England which would have been formed and fashioned under its influence, to endure the tremendous strain of the next four hundred years? All was best as it was.   The centuries which followed showed only too clearly the weak points of Celtic Christianity.   Devoid of that unifying power, of that wonderful gift of order and organization which was the strength of the Roman, passionately throwing itself into tribal quarrels, and making them its own, it would have consumed itself in intestine strifes.   Instead of offering a basis of unity for the land, and refusing to recognize, as the Roman Church refused to recognize, the rivalries and enmities of Northumbrian and Mercian and South Saxon, it would have introduced new elements of discord and division ; and that unity of England, anyhow so hard to obtain, and so long struggled for in vain, would have become well-nigh or altogether impossible.   Neither could England, on the remote fringe as it then was of the civilized world, have afforded to be separated from the arts and culture of Western Europe, which all found their centre at Rome; and which, few and fragmentary as they were, were yet all which survived from the mighty wreck of old Greek and Latin civilization to carry the Church and the world through the dark and evil days which were before them both. At the same time, considerations such as these should not abate in the least our gratitude for all which we owe to these Celtic evangelists, who wrought so large a share in the conversion of England, and for whom that law of the kingdom of heaven was so signally true, "One soweth and another reapeth."

I cannot close this sketch of the first founding of our English Church without honourable mention of one who did more than any other to bring into harmonious working order and to knit into an organic whole that which hitherto had been little more than a mere assemblage of isolated missions. Theodore of Tarsus, a philosopher and divine, trained in the East, but having accepted a mission from the Pope (669), is deservedly an illustrious name in our ecclesiastical annals. To him we probably owe the rudiments of our parochial system. It was he who recast, according to later needs, the episcopal divisions of the land, which had been originally co-extensive with the kingdoms of the Heptarchy. If much has since perished of his arrangements—and the Danish Invasion swept much away—not a little still survives to the present hour. The victory of Roman over Celtic Christianity was already practically decided when he came; but he did much to reconcile the victors and the vanquished, a Wilfred, "of great parts and greater passions," as Fuller has it, and a Chad, clothed with that grace of humility which Wilfred sometimes lacked; nor shall we ascribe to Theodore too high an honour if we regard him as in some sort a second founder of the English Church, giving to it broader and safer foundations than an Augustine, or those who wrought merely in the spirit, at once narrow and timid, of Augustine, could have ever given.

Having brought this story thus far, to the events which determined the future character of the Church in this land, I must renounce any attempt to follow it further; and content myself with calling your attention to a few of the leading aspects which it presents, until such time as, with the Norman Conquest, our English Church may be said to have taken a new departure. Certainly it had accomplished much in the first hundred and fifty years of its existence. There are brilliant pages in its annals. A nation of heathens had been converted, not by violence, not by the sword, into a nation of Christians—most imperfectly converted, no doubt, but all save a few slight traces of heathendom had disappeared. There was much for which to thank God; and yet, with all this, it must be freely admitted that it did not in its later days altogether fulfil the promise of an earlier time. None, it is true, with good right, could call that tree a barren one which put forth such shoots as this did, which produced scholars such as Bede and Alcuin, a poet such as Cædmon, missionaries such as Willibrord and Boniface, a statesman such as Dunstan, a king such as Alfred. But for all this, there are grave shadows resting on the Anglo-Saxon Church; nor can these be adequately explained and their gravity diminished by a reference to the terrible calamities which after a while overtook this

Church, seeing that those calamities themselves can only be regarded as the just punishment of preceding sins.

There have been races, which under the transforming influences, primary and secondary, of the Gospel of Christ, have laid aside their inborn fierceness, but this without laying aside or losing the strength and energy of character of which that fierceness had been the perverted utterance ; races which have brought their energy with them into that new and higher sphere in which now they moved, and found room to exercise it there. Foremost among the races which thus kept all they before had which was worth the keeping, while they added much to this which only that higher civilization by Christianity rendered possible could give, were the Normans. These, as their name attests, were Northmen, once, Scandinavian pirates, with all the tameless strength of those wild sea-robbers ; who settling themselves down here and there, as in Neustria, in Calabria, in Sicily, in Greece, adopted the arts of peace, the creed, the language of those among whom they settled, with whatever of rarer and finer culture those might own ; but did this without bating one jot of their original vigour, manhood and love of adventure ; an aspiring race, subtle and crafty ; yet not relying on these serpentine gifts alone, for they were also strong to do and to dare ; the most brilliant chivalry of Europe, hewing out with the sword kingdoms and principalities for themselves, as was shown upon many a famous field and day ; and chiefly on that field of Senlac and day of St. Calixtus, field and day most memorable of all, when the Saxon battle-axes went down at length before the Norman spears, and the

F

fate of England for long centuries, we may be bold to say for all time, was determined.

But of Angles and Saxons it must be owned, that if they gained much when they bowed to the yoke of Christ, there was also something which, though they might have kept, they did at the same time let go. Among the grave shadows at which I hinted just now, I certainly will not reckon the devotion which the English Church felt and showed to the distant mother that bore her. And yet it must be freely owned that this devotion, romantic, childlike, and happily ignorant of much which would have put it to a severe test, was not always bestowed wisely or well. Its existence none can contest. Among all the Teutonic tribes, the English, being once converted, proved the most devoted children of the Church. More than thirty kings and queens descended from the throne to end their days in cloistral retreats. It would be difficult to number the other scions of noble houses, male and female, who thus sought to win heaven by the abandonment at once of the pomps and duties of earth. From no other western land were pilgrimages of rich and poor to the thresholds of the Apostles so frequent or so numerous. From no other land did there flow into the Papal exchequer such rich contributions. Peter's Pence, if afterwards adopted by others, was an English invention at the first.

It was the monks who had converted England. It was inevitable therefore that the monastic element should be strong throughout the whole of Anglo-Saxon life, from the throne to the cottage should pervade it all. This was natural and, in a land newly converted and only little by little to be weaned from innumerable

heathen superstitions and idolatries, was not in itself
to be regretted. Still this might easily be overdone,
and it was not long before it was overdone. It was
not long before all or nearly all of the public lands
were alienated for ever to churches and monasteries,
till little or nothing remained with which to recompense
those whose strong arms and courageous hearts had
shielded, or should hereafter shield, the throne and
uphold the State. Under whatever obligations to military service these lands may have been held, every
such alienation must have diminished the number of
those who should have borne arms in the country's
defence. The thane, whose place was in the forefront
of the battle, had assumed the tonsure, oftentimes his
sons with him. England was fast becoming a nation
of monks. Let a true piety, however ill-directed, have
had its share here; but love of ease, an ignoble shrinking from the task and toil of life, had also theirs in developing this cloistral religion in a manner so excessive. Already Bede, when as yet the danger was remote, asked with anxiety what would be the end of
these insane gifts, of this forgetfulness of arms and all
martial exercises on their parts who were the natural
defenders and guardians of their native land. It was
plain before very long what this end would be.

Keep all these things in mind, and also the fact, not
to be denied, that there was a coarse animalism from
which the Anglo-Saxon temperament was not free, a
sluggish self-indulgence, which such unworthy with-
drawals from toil and from danger must have done
much to foster and feed, and you have in good part an
explanation here of the frightful calamities which in
the eighth and ninth centuries overtook Christian

England, of the faint resistance which the spoilers and
destroyers who made it their prey encountered. A
people such as I have just described needed to be
emptied from vessel to vessel, if they were not hopelessly to settle down upon their lees. And the needful discipline was not wanting. The Dane first, and
the Norman after him, were stern but effectual reminders that men cannot with impunity leave unfulfilled
the duties to which God has called them, whatever else
in the way of will-worship they may substitute in their
room. These reminders were not altogether thrown
away, thanks above all other to Alfred the Great.
Many precious boons we owe to him, but this the most
precious, because it included or made possible all
other, namely, that the Danish invasion was a scourge
and no more, that the very life of Christian England
was not crushed out by it; as might very well have
been, if a monarch of less heroic mould, if one who
could only pray, a monk at heart, and not one who
could both pray and fight, had sat upon the throne at
this crisis of England's fate. Restorer and reviver of
Christian life and learning in the land, his spirit lived
in his son and grandson, scarcely the men of faith that
he was, but in many aspects splendid sovereigns, who
saw clearly the work which they had to do, and did it.

There were no grand characters among churchmen
in the later days of the Anglo-Saxon Church to correspond to these. Milman's judgment is severe but
true : "The Anglo-Saxon Clergy, since the days of
Dunstan, had produced no remarkable man. The
triumph of monasticism had enfeebled without sancti-
fying the secular clergy ; it had spread over the Island
all its superstition, its thraldom of the mind, its reck-

less prodigality of lands and riches to pious uses, without its vigour, its learning, its industrial civilization. Like its faithful disciple, its humble acolyte, its munificent patron, Edward the Confessor, it might conceal much gentle and amiable goodness; but its outward character was that of timid and unworldly ignorance, unfit to rule, and exercising but feeble and unbeneficial influence over a population become at once more rude and fierce, and more oppressed and servile, by the Danish Conquest."

Let me in conclusion ask you to observe how this work of the conversion of England exactly corresponded in time with the triumphant advance of the Mahomedan arms. Pertaining as these events severally do, the one to the extreme West the other to the further East, we may easily miss their connexion, might hardly believe that such connexion existed at all. And yet, in the providence of God, the one was set over against the other; and the West was knitting herself into the strength and unity which it would need for that collision with Mahomedan power, which sooner or later was certain to arrive. It is the rise of Islâm with which in my next Lecture I shall deal.

LECTURE IV.

ISLÂM.

WHILE the Church was making these spiritual conquests in the West, securely planting herself in regions
which should henceforth form her most flourishing
seats, organizing herself under a single head, dark
clouds were gathering and perils threatening in the
East, from a quarter where beforehand they might have
been looked for the least. Nor were these merely transient perils. The regions which had been her earliest
haunt and home, Palestine, Syria, Asia Minor, Egypt,
North Africa, these all were within little more than a
century torn from her; neither did these losses of
that first time at all exhaust the losses which she was
thus destined to endure. It was from Arabia that the
storm thus suddenly broke upon the Church, which
was to rend away so many of her fairest branches.
Up to this time Arabia had played little or no part in
the world's history. Satisfied with maintaining their
own independence—and with only some rare and recent exceptions they had defied or eluded the attempts
of the mightiest conquerors to place a yoke upon their
necks—the children of Ishmael had hitherto dwelt
apart in their solitary world. From this they were
now to come forth, and deeply to stamp themselves,
their manners, their customs, their faith, on a large
and important portion of the globe, and to win for the

faith which they professed the devoted adhesion of some sixth part of its inhabitants.

The Arabs had been, so far back as history knows anything about them, a free, warlike people, thinly scattered over their immense peninsula, their tribes oftentimes at war among themselves, oftentimes at war with their neighbours, if the freebooting excursions to which they were addicted deserved so honourable a name. Whatever original knowledge of the one God they may have possessed had been gradually overclouded and lost. In the times of their ignorance—for so the Musselmans fondly term the period before their prophet rose, and brought them back to the primitive patriarchal faith—the land had been full of idols and of idolaters, Sabæan star-worshippers and others. Nor did the presence of a considerable colony of Jews in Arabia, and of some Christians as well, do much to dispel the darkness of idolatry which brooded on the land. Themselves with scanty knowledge of their own faith, entangled in manifold superstitions and errors, they were little fitted to be witnesses against the superstitions and errors of others. Such very briefly was the political and religious condition of Arabia when Mahomet was born (569 or 571.)

Mecca was the place of his birth. Of his early life legend knows much, history very little. He belonged, though himself poor, to one of the noblest tribes in the land, to that, namely, of the Koreishites. To the members of this tribe appertained some not very clearly defined sacerdotal privileges; among others the guardianship of the Caaba, a heathen sanctuary or temple, which had been the Holy Place of the Arabs long before Mahomet, adopting and weaving it

into his scheme, gave to it its second consecration as
the middle point of Mahomedan worship. His youth
excited no special remark. Too poor to carry on
commercial affairs upon his own account, he transacted those of a rich widow, and this with such fidelity
and prosperous issues, that after a while she bestowed
upon him herself and her fortune. The affairs in
which he was thus engaged involved many journeys, and
brought him in contact with men of various countries
and diverse faiths; for Mecca was the centre of an
active commerce, and sent out its caravans eastward
and southward through the whole Arabian peninsula,
and to many regions beyond. Twice he visited Syria.
Probably in one of these journeys he fell in with that
mysterious Nestorian monk, who plays a part alike in
the Mahomedan and Christian tradition of his life, but
whose relations with him are wrapt in an obscurity so
deep. From him, as some will have it, Mahomet obtained whatever measure of acquaintance with things
Jewish and Christian he possessed. His knowledge,
indeed, of these, however gotten, was small, fragmentary, and inaccurate—ridiculously inaccurate one
might call it, were not the whole rise of Islâm too
terrible an event for the human race to allow the employment of such a word—a knowledge not derived
from the Scriptures themselves, but from sources the
most turbid, from Talmudic legends and apocryphal
gospels, and, as we may confidently affirm, not drawn
at first hand even from these.

Such a portentous birth as a new religion, and that
religion a false one, could scarcely come to pass without labour-pangs corresponding. Nor did it. Of much
we must remain ignorant; but this much we know,

that in or about his fortieth year he began to listen to
secret intimations that there was a divine mission for
him to fulfil, while there did not want other whis-
pers that these suggestive voices were not from above,
but below. The crisis of his life had arrived ; fleeing
from men, hiding in mountain caves, deeply sunken
in religious reverie—epileptic fits his enemies would
have it—seeing visions and dreaming dreams, now
lifted up as to heaven, and now cast down as to hell,
it was only after a long interior conflict that his life
wrought itself out for him into any distinctness of
purpose, and that he began to declare, as God's message by him to the world, There is no god but God,
and Mahomet is his prophet (611).

And yet something of the course by which he had
been led thus far I think we can trace. Doubtless in
the years which went before he had been deeply impressed with the moral and spiritual degradation of
his country. There are many clear tokens that amid
all the darkness of idolatry, all the falsehoods with
which the land was full, the sense of the unity of the
Godhead had not been quite obliterated from the
minds of his fellow-countrymen. It revived in strength
in his own. He saw truly what lay at the root of
all their miseries and dissensions, so that tribe was
evermore at war with tribe, and family with family ;
namely, that faith in a common Lord, the only true
bond which can bind men together, was wanting. He
saw that their very worship, being as it was the worship of things which were beneath them, and not of
One who was above, itself instead of drawing upward,
only dragged them down and debased them the more.
It was the custom until very lately never to name

Mahomet without some opprobrious addition to his
name—"the impostor Mahomet," "the Arabian false
prophet;" while, if I do not mistake, the pendulum is
now swaying in an opposite direction, and we may
soon have Mahomet placed on a level with Moses—
at the least, and the Korân, if a lower revelation than
the Bible, declared a divine revelation still. The truth,
as I am bold to affirm, is neither here nor there. If by
"impostor" we understand, and we can scarcely un-
stand less, one who devised a cunningly arranged
system of fraud and falsehood, which then, with the
full consciousness that it was such, he sought to im-
pose upon others, impostor Mahomet was not. De-
ceiver I believe that he often was, but only where, not
of course without his own sin, he was himself first deceived. On any scheme of simple and self-conscious
imposture it is altogether impossible to explain the results of his preaching, which has changed the face of
so large a part of the world, given birth to a religion
which for many centuries contended as on equal terms
with the Christian ; and which, if waning now like the
moon that is its symbol, yet still subsists a mighty
power and passion in the hearts, and moulding the
lives, of millions of our fellow men. "Lies," as our
proverb declares, "have no legs ; " at all events lies
which are nothing else but lies have not legs which
will carry them through some twelve hundred years
and more. Instead of dismissing without more ado
this religion as a lie, and its founder as an impostor,
we ought rather to ask ourselves what were the
sources of its strength to divide the light from the
darkness in the man and in the faith, and to do the
justice to both which they have a right to demand.

But first to follow to its close the outward history of the man. His claims to the prophetic office are met by contemptuous indifference, and then by bitter hostility, no where so bitter as at Mecca; for he too is a prophet who finds no honour in his own country. Driven from thence at length by the persistent enmity of his own tribe, and hardly escaping with his life, he and the few whom he has persuaded to believe in his mission take refuge at Medina, not so named before, but now acquiring this name of The City—the city, that is, of the prophet. This was in 622, some eleven years after he had begun to preach. The year is worth remembering, for the Hegira, or Flight to Medina, is the Mahomedan æra, the date from which they reckon, as we do from the Nativity of our Lord. At Medina he found the belief which had been refused him at Mecca. New adherents united themselves to him. Early friends, scattered from him at the time of his flight, gathered round him again. The Koreishites, indeed, still pursued him with implacable enmity, and many battles were fought with varying success ; these, indeed, being little more than skirmishes which grew out of the waylaying of caravans and similar marauding expeditions. But with all his cause was gaining ground, the number of his adherents increasing ; and when in 632 he expired, all Arabia recognized him as her prophet and her king ; and he who at the first had aspired, at the utmost, to the giving of a law, to his own people, did now, his horizon having widened with his success, bequeath to the Chalifs, his successors, the task of subduing the world to the faith which he had proclaimed. God, he said, had long tried gentleness, the meekness of Christ ;—for he did

not deny the divine mission of our Lord, nor yet that
of Moses, but always assumed these, and his own as
the complement of them ;—but now, wearied out with
the obstinacy of sinners, commanded that they should
either accept the true faith ; or yield themselves tribu-
tary to those who had accepted ; or, refusing both
these alternatives, should be destroyed as rebels
against the Lord of heaven and earth.   It was in effect
nothing less, it will be seen, than a war against mankind which he proclaimed.

The task which Mahomet thus left to those who
came after him to accomplish they prosecuted with a
zeal and a success which for a while seemed to threaten
the establishment of the faith of Islâm on the ruins
of every other religion in the world.   Terrible indeed
was the first outburst of the children of the desert from
regions where they had been cooped and confined so
long.   The two recognized powers of the East, the
Byzantine and the Persian Empires, each with an able
monarch at its head, had been weakening one another
by alternate victories and defeats, each in turn bringing the other to the very brink of destruction ; little
dreaming that a power was growing up in secret
which was watching them both, and in the end should
destroy them both, and one of them within a few
years.   On the Byzantine Empire, on some of the
fairest and most flourishing of its Asiatic provinces,
the storm fell first.   Exhausted by those long wars
with Persia, defended by ill-paid mercenaries, swarming with persecuted sectaries, with oppressed Jews,
with subjects disaffected from one cause or another,
and only too well pleased to change their master, that
Empire was wholly unequal to resist the shock.   Ten

years had not elapsed since the death of the prophet, and already Palestine and Syria and Egypt had accepted the yoke; already three out of the four famous patriarchates of Eastern Christendom—Jerusalem (636) and Antioch (638) and Alexandria (641)—if not actually blotted out, retained little more than a merely titular existence; and it wanted but a little that the fourth and last had shared their doom; for Constantinople itself, twice besieged by the Saracens (669, and again 716), with difficulty weathered the first violence of the storm, and, except for the opportune discovery of the Greek Fire, might have succumbed to Mahomedan arms, not in the fifteenth century, but the seventh.

The tide of conquest rolled onward. The Persian Empire ceased to exist (637-651). North Africa was subdued (665-709). Crossing over from this into Spain, the Arabs, or Moors as they were here called, from having assimilated to themselves the Moorish population of North Africa, overthrew in a single battle the kingdom of the Goths (711), surmounted the Pyrenees, planted themselves in Aquitaine, and threatened to make all France, and with France all Western Europe, their own. It was here at length that their proud waves were stayed. At the great battle called sometimes of Poitiers, and sometimes of Tours (732), one of the "decisive battles of the world"—for we must go back nearly three centuries, to the battle of Chalons (451), before we can find such another —Charles Martel encountered the armies of Islâm with the gathered chivalry of the West, and earned, or deserved to earn, his name of The Hammer, inflicting on them so crushing a defeat that for long centuries all their aggressive pressure upon Western Christendom was arrested, and indeed, has never again revived in its full strength.

How shall we explain these extraordinary successes, the going forth of this novel faith over the world, thus bringing the world to its feet? It is not enough to appeal, in regard of the conquerors, to their simple habits, their hardy training, their martial character; while many of the populations with which they were brought into conflict were unwarlike and effeminate, enervated by luxury and self-indulgence, torn by inner dissensions which they would not lay aside even in the face of a common foe; hating one another so much that the triumph of that foe seemed preferable to that of a rival Christian sect. This might explain something, but it would not explain all, or nearly all. We must look deeper than this. The Moslem hosts went forth in the confidence of a mission from heaven. Not Kaled only, but every Moslem warrior felt himself indeed to be "The Sword of God." Comparing what they now were with what they had been in the "times of their ignorance," when they worshipped dead idols, they felt that they had been brought into a new spiritual world, had learned now what was the true glory and dignity of man, namely, to be the servant of the one God, maker and ruler of all; that such servants they were; whose task it was to proclaim his power, themselves to submit, and to compel others to submit, to his will. What a truth was here, to have taken possession of a multitude of souls! No wonder that, in the strength of this, innumerable tribes, which had hitherto done little but mutually tear and devour one another, were presently knit together into a nation, and the worshippers of a thousand different and discordant falsehoods into that which bore some sort of similitude to a Church.

And then, if you would look further for an explanation, turn to the conquered. "Where the carcase is, there shall the eagles be gathered together." This is the law of God's dealings with men, with nations, and with Churches. Where they are abandoned by the spirit of life, and have thus become as a carcase, there the eagles, the executors of the divine vengeance, are at hand, who will presently remove out of the way that which, suffered any longer, could only taint the air and defile the earth. The Eastern Church was not altogether such a carcase, and therefore it did not wholly perish; but yet we must needs confess that it had grievously provoked those judgments which now fell upon it. How rent was it and torn with countless divisions; what mere strifes about words had taken the place of a zeal for holiness, and how fiercely were these debated; how much of superstition was everywhere; how much which, if it was not idolatry, yet played most dangerously on the verge of this. We can regard Mahomedanism in no other light than as the scourge of God upon a guilty Church. He will not give his glory to another. He will not suffer the Creator and the creature to be confounded; and if those who should have been witnesses for the truth, who had been appointed thereunto, forsake, forget, or deny it, He will raise up witnesses from quarters the most unlooked for, and will strengthen their hands and give victory to their arms, even against those who bear his name, but have forgotten his truth.

But it may be very fitly asked, does this negative

aspect of Mahomedanism exhaust its whole meaning;
had it no other purpose in the councils of God; was
it merely such a scourge? for if so, why has it been
permitted to exist for long centuries after this its
proper work was accomplished? The rods of God's
anger are for the most part, in the order of His providence, broken and cast aside so soon as ever his work
by them has been accomplished; but here it has not
been so. Before attempting to answer this question,
let us a little consider what is the worth of this religion, not as compared with that decaying form of
Christianity which it encountered, overcame, and sup-
planted in the East, but as compared with the Christian faith contemplated in its ideal truth and purity.
The name which the Mahomedans give to their faith
is Islâm, a word signifying the yielding of oneself
to God. Here, as so often, we have in the name
that which lies deepest and nearest to the heart of
the thing. The central idea of this religion in its
noblest aspect is just the surrendering of oneself
to God; but then it is the surrendering of oneself
to Him as absolute power, not as holy love. We
behold it here at once in its strength and its weakness; in its strength, inasmuch as it does preach
this yielding of self to God, the will of the creature to
the will of the Creator; in its weakness, in that this
surrender is but the surrender of the weak to the
strong. Power belongeth unto God—this truth the
Mussulman or true believer had grasped with all the
energies of his heart and soul; but he had missed the
truth which ought ever to go along with it, that this
absolute power is wielded by perfect love. The sense
of the difference and distinction between man and

God, the creature and the Creator, is mightily realized by him; and he has been God's fearful avenger
upon those who have dared to confound them; but the
fact of man's likeness to God, and union with God he
not only fails to make his own, but explicitly denies.
Man is for him God's servant, not his son. A mighty
gulf divides them, and shall divide them for ever.
The very title, Son of God, is blasphemy in his ears.
This name, first realized in the Everlasting Son, and
then in as many as have received adoption through
Him into a common family, this, which is the truest
witness and guard against all idolatry, he accounts
to be the worst and most hideous idolatry of all.

But Mahomedanism is not merely this falling back
from the blessed truths of the Gospel, it is a still
further retrocession in the spiritual history of mankind.
It falls short, not merely of Christian, but also of Jewish truth. It is a Judaism, not provisional; not looking
on to some better thing which it announces and pre-
pares for; not pregnant with a nobler birth, but a
Judaism stript of its prophecy and its promise, reduced
to a religion of nature, without a priesthood, without a
sacrifice even as it is without any deep consciousness
of sin, without a Messiah. It has no ideal of holiness
after which it invites its votaries to strive; and indeed
how should it, when the man who stands at its centre,
not without noble qualities, is yet so full of blots and
of bloodstains? You may read the whole Korân
through, without coming on words which in the least
resemble these, "Make me a clean heart, O God,
and renew a right spirit within me. Purge me with
hyssop, and I shall be clean; wash me, and I shall be
whiter than snow."

H

Or turn to it in its social working, as it has ap-
proved itself during the twelve centuries during which
it has been upon its trial.   It has all the faults, all the
narrowness of a local religion, which by strange unexpected successes has outgrown the region of its
birth, a region where it was not without its fitness,
and has obtained a dominion not limited but universal.   If in Christendom the attempt has been often
made to weave into one inextricable woof the kingdom of God and the kingdom of Cæsar, yet, as we
thankfully own, in the end the attempt has always
failed.   In Islâm it has completely succeeded, and
succeeded, not as the perversion of the Mahomedan
religion, but as the truest realization of all which it
was meant to be.   The despotisms of the East are
not accidents, but the legitimate outgrowths of the
Korân, and so long as this exists as the authoritative
book, they too must exist with it.   Then again, as has
been truly observed, in the very act of slightly allevi-
ating, the Korân has recognized and perpetuated the
two fatal social evils of the East, polygamy namely
and slavery.

But if all this be so, if Mahomedanism be this backward step in the religious education of mankind, if in
the long run it has no truth to teach the Church which
the Church does not itself already know much better
—for indeed it has nothing original about it, bastard
brother as it is, now of the Jewish and now of the
Christian faith—how shall we explain its continuance,
long since the work for which it was first permitted
has been done ?   Only, I believe, we shall understand
God's purposes in this, when we regard it in its relations, not to the religions which stand above it, but to

those idolatrous worships which stand beneath it.
Thus, as it is impossible to deny, how many of the
rude fetisch-worshipping tribes of Africa, sunken in
abject brutal superstitions, have been raised through
it to the worship of one God, to a certain measure of
order and morality, which, so far as we can see, without it they would never have attained. Such a process is even now going forward.

For the rest, it must be freely owned that as yet we
see very little of its service as a conducting medium,
as a religion of transition, a schoolmaster to Christ. Its
position is still one of fierce antagonism to the Gospel.
Shall it be so to the end? Is that mysterious re-ani-
mation of Mahomedan life, which for the last thirty or
forty years has been manifest to all thoughtful obser-
vers, no more than the quickening to a dread activity
of all the Anti-Christian elements in that religion, that
so it may challenge a mightier and a better to a last
struggle, and in that struggle may perish? Let us
hope better things. The end is not yet. Can it be
for nothing that so much of Christian truth was permitted to be wrought up into that fabric of error, that
the Son of Mary occupies the place which He does in
the Mahomedan theology? Not merely things good,
but also things evil, and much more than these, things
which, like that wherewith we have now to do, are
made up of both, a mingled woof of light and of darkness, they all serve God; and shall be shown at last
to have done their part for the working out of his purpose in the world; even as in Eastern legend other
spirits beside the good were compelled by Solomon to
take their share and do drudging work in the rearing
of the temple of God.

LECTURE V.

THE CONVERSION OF GERMANY.

The Medieval Church of the West found in the
seventh century an immense task before it to fulfil.
The fulfillment of this task was the performance of a
duty, but it was at the same time the conjuring of a
danger. How real and terrible that danger might
prove the Greek Church at this very time was giving
lamentable proof; from which one fair region after
another, the cradle lands of the Christian religion, was
being torn away by the Saracen misbeliever. Heathen Germany was hardly a less threatening peril to
Western Christendom ; and, even where it did not
positively endanger existence, was a constant annoyance, infesting and wasting the border lands. Pauses
in the conflict between the two there might be ; but
durable peace was impossible between races on such
different levels of culture, and so wholly antagonistic
to one another in the highest matters of all.

The missionaries who addressed themselves to the
enormous task of the conversion of Germany may be
conveniently divided into three groups—the British,
the Frankish, and, entering somewhat later into an
honourable rivalry with these, the Anglo-Saxon. A
word or two upon each of these groups. The British
—they include Irish and Scotch—could no longer find
a field for the exercise of their ministry in England,
now that there the Roman rule and discipline, to

which they were so little disposed to submit, had
everywhere won the day. Their own religious houses
were full to overflowing. At home there was little
for them to do, while yet that divine hunger and
thirst for the winning of souls, which had so possessed
the heart of St. Patrick, lived on in theirs. To these
so minded pagan Germany offered a welcome field of
labour, and one in which there was ample room for
all. Then there were the Frankish missionaries, who
enjoyed the support of the Frankish kings, which
sometimes served them in good stead ; while at other
times this protection was very far from a recommend-
ation in their eyes who were easily persuaded to see
in these missionaries the emissaries of a foe. Add to
these the Anglo-Saxons ; these last, mindful of the
source from which they had received their own Christianity, making it a point to attach their converts to
Rome, even as they were themselves bound to her by
the closest ties. The language which these spoke—
a language which as yet can have diverged very little
from the Low German of Frisia, must have given to
them many facilities which the Frankish missionaries
possessed in a far slighter degree, the British not at
all ; and this may help to account for a success on
their parts far greater than attended the labours of
the others. To them too it was mainly due that the
battle of the Creeds, which had been fought and lost
by the Celtic missionaries in England, and was presently renewed in Germany, had finally the same
issues there as in England.

It was not until near the opening of the seventh
century that the work of Germany's conversion may
be said to have fairly begun. One noble apparition,

for we can hardly call it by any other name, belongs to the close of the fifth, that, namely, of Severinus. Of other eminent missionaries we generally know something, who they are and whence they come, and in one way or another what spiritual descent they own. In him, as in another Melchizedek, all is shrouded in mystery, till we find him ministering as an angel of consolation, with a self-offering love which knows no bounds, to populations of southern Germany reduced by the frightful anarchy of the times to the lowest depths of misery and despair. I am afraid that the names of others who were the foremost to break up that hard soil, and to sow in its furrows the seed of everlasting life, well worthy as they are to be held in everlasting remembrance, must remain little more than names for you, so impossible is it for me to make more than briefest pause upon a few. Augustine had not yet landed on the shores of England, when already the Scotch and Irish missionaries were busy with the conversion of Germany. Columbanus (d. 615), a very strenuous worker, and mainly in the Vosges, who like another Baptist, could stand before kings and rebuke them; and Gallus (d. 646), his most illustrious scholar, called often the Apostle of Switzerland, whose name lives in the monastery and canton of St. Gall, lead up the van. Kilian, (d. 689), too, another Irish monk, must not be left unnamed; nor yet Eligius (b. 588, d. 659), goldsmith and saint, the St. Eloy of Chaucer's Prioress, and well worthy of any just honour, if not of that which she paid him. But he with Amandus, whose labours were on the banks of the Scheldt, into which many times he was flung by the heathen, and English Willibrord, who also toiled among the wild tribes of our modern Flanders and Brabant, belong to the Roman as contradistinguished from the Celtic group of evangelists.

These are but a handful out of the number of those whose names, with some notice of their lives, have reached us. Innumerable others there must have been, now forgotten of men, but whose names are written in the Book of life. When we call to mind the disappointment and defeat, with all of outrage and insult, of wrath and wrong, often even to death, which these must have endured from wild and savage populations before their work was accomplished, what grander fulfilment could we anywhere find of that prophecy of Christ, "I am come to cast fire upon the earth?" He had kindled indeed, and who but He could have kindled and kept alive in so many hearts a flame so divine?

At the same time, there were differences in the intensity and obstinacy of resistance to the message of the truth, which would be offered by different tribes. There was ground, which at an early day had been won for the Gospel, but which in the storms and confusion of the two preceding centuries had been lost again; the whole line, that is, of the Danube and the Rhine, regions fair and prosperous once, but in every sense wildernesses now. In these we may note a readier acceptance of the message than found place in lands which in earlier times that message had never reached; as though obscure reminiscences and traditions of the past, not wholly extinct, had helped to set forward the present work.

Behind this line, now reoccupied by the Church, there were populous regions in Frisia, in Hesse, in

Thuringia, in Saxony, into which a solitary missionary had hardly penetrated as yet; warrior races, which had never bowed to the superiority of Roman arts and arms, which had faintly heard of Rome, if they had heard at all; races animated by the deepest hostility against a Gospel of peace. The opposition of these was altogether different from any which had been encountered in the bringing to the obedience of faith those tribes which had already established themselves within the limits of the Roman Empire. The German races, which, when detached from their old seats, had so easily yielded themselves to the spiritual allurements of Christianity, which had received baptism and melted into the mass of Christian worshippers one scarcely knows how, offered a far more stubborn resistance when sought out in their own primitive haunts, among their own forests and morasses. It is not hard to see why. Established in lands which had been already won to the religion of Christ, and having left their own holy places, their own fanes and sacred forests, even their very priests behind them, they were surrounded, in a manner awed, by a Christian civilization so immensely superior to any which they before had known or imagined, by a worship carried on in stately temples and with magnificent rites. But in their native haunts all this prestige with which Christianity was encompassed was wanting. A band of wandering monks would often be the sole representatives to them of that invisible kingdom, which demanded of them that they should submit themselves to its laws, renounce all or nearly all in which hitherto they had gloried the most, and accept unknown mysterious benefits in return.

But despite of all difficulties in the way, much had been effected in advancing the frontier of Christianity, many successful aggressions had been made on the stubborn heathenism of Germany during the century which intervened between the missionary labours of Columbanus and the time when Boniface first put his hand to the plough. Yet for all this, and recognizing that in a certain measure Boniface entered on the labours of others, we need have no scruple in admitting the title of Apostle of Germany which has been often claimed for him. Winfrid or Boniface—whether Pope Gregory II. gave him this second name, or how he got it, is not clear—was born near Kirton in Devonshire, about 680. Fair prospects could not detain him at home, with so glorious an enterprise as the winning of Germany to Christ beckoning him to take his share in it. Some distinguishing features of his work are worth your attention. Thus all efforts for the conversion of Germany which preceded his had been more or less unconnected and desultory. With him the organization of the enterprise as a whole began; laying as he did first foundations, where it needed to lay these; building on the foundations which others had already laid, where such existed; strengthening what was weak and tottering; supplying things which were lacking; reviving things ready to die; recalling to Christian order and discipline populations which had relapsed into heathen practices; bringing the clergy together in synods, which were hitherto unknown, or which, having once been used, had fallen into desuetude and neglect; everywhere working upon a plan.

In nothing were the early missionaries more worthy

I

of note and imitation, than in their care to make sure, so far as this was possible, of the spiritual territory which they once had won, in the means which they adopted for impressing an abiding character on their work. They did not rely for this on any vague Christian sentiment which by their preaching they may have aroused among their converts; but, as conquerors, who not merely overrun but propose also to retain the lands which they have conquered, ever as they advance are careful to leave fortified posts behind them, so these were diligent, by aid of churches and schools and monasteries which they founded, to hold with a strong and permanent grasp all which they once had made their own. Among many eminent for this, Boniface stands out pre-eminent. What an unerring eye was his for the discerning of the fittest spot for a monastery with its cloistral school attached,—Fulda, so long the centre of the theological culture of Germany, and notably his choice, is a signal witness to this,—or for the dividing out of some land, newly gained to the faith of Christ, into dioceses, and selecting the spot where the Bishop's See should be planted. And what he saw as best, he was able as Apostolic Legate to carry out. Changed and modified as the ecclesiastical divisions of Germany have subsequently been, there is much in them which still attests his practical wisdom, his far-seeing out-look into the future. The Church has had few with a talent of organization such as his, fewer still who have had the opportunity of exercising this talent on so vast a scale.

It is very interesting to note other points in which the practical instincts of Boniface led him to adopt measures most closely resembling those to which the

great Missionary Bishops of our own times, such as
Selwyn and Patteson, have been led for the spreading
of the faith; and which, alike in his case and in theirs,
were crowned with signal success. He too sought to
win the confidence of heathen chiefs so far that they
were willing to intrust their children to be educated
by him. In these, trained in the school of Christ, he
found afterwards some of his most devoted and efficient helpers; while it not seldom happened that the
hearts of the fathers were in the end turned to the
children, the fathers through their children won to the
obedience of faith.

Let all of his somewhat excessive submission to the
See of Rome, excessive even for his own time, be freely
admitted; let it be admitted too that he profoundly
impressed the same, for good or for evil, upon the
Churches which he founded; let it be granted further
that with the gold, silver, and precious stones which he
brought to the spiritual building there were mingled
some hay, straw, and stubble, yet for all this the
foundation on which he built was Christ; and where
that is so, the true abides, the false perishes and passes
away. Then, too, God often makes the faults no less
than the graces of his own servants to serve Him; and
it may very well be a question whether at that epoch of
the Church's life, and with all which in the next centuries was before it, a national German Church, which
did not hold on to Rome, and to such learning and
light as could there and not elsewhere be found, was
possible. I have spoken on this subject already (p. 38),
and shall not repeat what I then said. It is only fair
too, before quitting this subject, to observe that there
was nothing servile in this submission of his.) Against

more things than one which he saw amiss at Rome he raised a clear and manly protest.

And a noble life had a not less noble close. Archbishop of Mentz—he would himself have preferred Cologne as the metropolitan See of Germany—he might have claimed a peaceful close for so stormy and laborious a life. But no ; he cannot forget how in his onward victorious march he had left behind him one fortress of heathendom untaken. His heart yearns after the Frisians whom in the early days of his mission he had sought to bring to the faith, but in vain. He lays down his dignities, is the simple missionary once more, revisits with a small band of fellow-workers the scene of his baffled labours in other days. Many are now converted, while others are the more embittered hereby, and at the hands of these he receives the martyr's crown.

Until within the last few years there was in the land which owed to Boniface so large a debt, a very hearty and unquestioning recognition of his work, and this on the part of Roman Catholic and Protestant writers alike. With some among the latter all this is now changed. Attacks of an inconceivable bitterness upon him and upon the whole character of his missionary labour follow fast on one another. Not the conversion of the heathen,—for about that, they say, he concerned himself very little,—but the overthrow of the Culdee or Celtic Churches in Germany, guilty of the unpardonable sin of declining to acknowledge the supremacy of Rome, was the life-task which he set before himself, and which he accomplished with only too fatal a success. Shameful intrigues at the Court of Charles Martel and his sons, which should help for-

ward this object, are laid to his charge, and this without a tittle of historic evidence to sustain the accusation, as the accusers themselves are compelled to own.
Even his martyrdom is denied. The authors of his
death, we are now told, were a wild robber horde ;
and Boniface only got what he merited, seeing that,
if he had not neglected his proper duties as a missionary Bishop, to curry favor at courts, these would
in all likelihood have been converted, have become
good members of society, and so have done him no
wrong. Surely it must be in other interests than those
of historic truth that all this is so persistently and
passionately urged.

At the death of Boniface the area of heathen Germany was very much contracted, as compared with
what it had been when his mission began. He who
once had so boldly struck and levelled to the earth the
oak of immemorial age, dedicated to the Thunder-god,
had indeed dealt a blow to Teutonic heathenism, from
which it never should recover. But there was still one
stronghold of paganism upon which little or no impression had been made. The Saxon swarms which
had passed over into England had submitted themselves for more than a century to the yoke of Christ.
Boniface himself was a living witness of the spirit in
which some of them had yielded themselves to Him.
But not so those that had remained in their native
seats, in a Saxony far wider in extent than any which
we know now by this name, and including a large
part of northern and middle Germany. Of Saxons
Tacitus in his muster of the tribes says nothing ;
Pliny too is silent. Some conclude from thence that

they rose comparatively late to numbers and power
and renown. It is more probable that the name only
was recent, and that we have here some of the most
famous of the tribes of old, the Cherusci and others,
but associated under a new collective title. The first
mention of Saxons which we have in books belongs
to the middle of the second century ; they do not actually appear on the world's stage till near the end of
the third ; a wild, fierce and stony-hearted race ; indeed, as some Latin philologers urged, they announced
as much in their name. Time was when the Saxons
and the various tribes which coalesced under the common name of Franks had dwelt side by side on the
banks of the Elbe and the Weser, and made common
cause together ; but since the Franks had risen to
such eminency of glory and power, above all since
they had accepted the religion of Christ, the strongest
antagonism had grown up between those who had
been neighbours and confederates of old.

It was not ambassadors of peace who " by the gentleness of Christ" should allure these to take his
yoke upon them. The task of their conversion was
reserved for the strong arm of the mightiest of the
Frankish Kings, even as the manner of the conversion was quite another. Seventeen years after the
death of Boniface the wars of Charles the Great and
the Saxons began. Again and again these last after
an obstinate resistance submitted ; again and again,
when Charles was occupied in some remote region of
his vast Empire, beyond the Alps or the Pyrenees, on
the banks of the Eyder or the Theiss, warring with
Lombards, with Moslem, with Danes, with Avars,
they threw off the yoke, renounced the baptism which

was to them the badge of servitude (and which, among its other consequences, entailed the paying of tithes, to which they had a rooted objection), and cruelly wasted the Frankish border-lands, only to be as often crushed after a while by his mightier arm.

The whole process of an armed mission, of which England had known nothing, this reading into the Gospel of a leaf from the Korân, and, in another sense than that in which Christ spoke the words, this compelling of men to come in, if judged without reference to the spirit and circumstances of the time, can only be absolutely and unequivocally condemned; and even with every such allowance may find excuses, but hardly a justification. Alcuin, with full knowledge of all the facts, did not hesitate to express to his royal friend and master how little pleased he was with what he was doing, did not fail to remind him that he might constrain men to baptism but not to faith. And yet it must be admitted that Charles' efforts were crowned with a signal success. After a struggle, which with brief intervals lasted for more than thirty years (from 772 to 803), through the larger part, that is, of his reign, he broke the Saxon obstinacy at the last. The chiefs who had led the resistance submitted, and now at length in good faith; and the people as usual followed in their train.

No doubt such conversion of nations in a mass must often and for the larger number have been a merely external form, with no internal reality to correspond. Indeed, it was often no better with their chiefs who led the way. Some of the most hideous perfidies, treacheries, and murders of Clovis belong to a period subsequent to his baptism; and his sons and grandsons, Christians by profession, do not seem to have unlearned a single heathen vice, or to have learned a single Christian virtue. Yet with the frankest admission of all this, it must not be left out of sight, that where this wholesale conversion was followed up, as it was in the case of the Saxons, with earnest conscientious efforts to bring the converts, not nominally only but in truth, within the Church's fold, much was hereby done, or was put in the way of being done. Public law was henceforward on the side of true religion. Idolatrous rites and practices were put down with a strong hand. Schools, churches, and monasteries were built; bishopricks were founded; in the present instance those of Osnabrück (803), of Paderborn (814), of Münster (805), of Bremen, with others, followed close on this pacification; there went forward a ministry of the Word and Sacraments. And even where the first generation, which had adopted the faith by compulsion or because others did, and with little or no sincere conviction, was slightly influenced or not at all, the next, growing up under fairer auspices,-would show that the training which from infancy it received had not been in vain. How soon the Gospel struck its roots, and how deep those roots were, in the once stony hearts of this Saxon race, is attested by the poem *Heliand* (=Heiland)—a versified life of our Lord which belongs to the reign of Lewis the Pious, Charles' son ; and which, springing up on Saxon soil, everywhere attests the religious feeling, deep and popular, out of which it grew, and to which it appeals.

The Eyder and the Elbe once reached, and Germany being, at least outwardly, brought to the acknowledgment of Christ, there was another group of tribes, nearly related to the Germanic, as their religion, their language, their whole manner of life attested, which was in like manner to be won for Him. But neither was the man wanting here. As Germany had its Boniface, so Scandinavia its Ansgar (b. 801, d. 865), "Apostle of the North," a gentler, tenderer spirit than Boniface; with a more introverted eye; less of a hierarch; but with less also of his practical talent, though not coming behind him in the faith which no perils could daunt, and no failures could dishearten. The one was a lineal spiritual descendant of St. Peter, the other of St. John.

It would be well worth the while to tell, but I cannot undertake to tell it, how the work of which he traced the first lines went forward after he was withdrawn; how Jutland and Denmark (1027), Sweden and Norway (1019–1033),—which last boasts in St. Olaf a very violent saint indeed,—how, I say, these one after another became obedient to the faith; Odin and Thor, and all the gods of the northern Walhalla, struggling fiercely but in vain to maintain their dominion, until by the end of the eleventh century all Scandinavia,— the isle of Rugen, last bulwark of Teutonic heathenism, and not converted till 1168, excepted,—was Christian; a result for it most blessed, but scarcely less so for the whole of civilized Europe. For just as at an earlier day the wild outbursts of the savage Hungarians ceased with their conversion (973), so now at length the intolerable ravages of the Danes (thus we name these destroyers, but their pirate hordes were recruited from all parts of Scandinavia), came to an end. These in their light ships infesting every coast,

K

sailing up every river, feared as far as the Adriatic,
where they encountered Saracen rovers from the East
on the same errand of rapine and wrong as their own,
had everywhere found something to destroy; while
yet their most fanatical hate had been reserved for the
church and the monastery, the priest and the monk.
What England suffered from them, and we know how
dismal and disastrous a page in her history this is,
almost all Europe was suffering as well.   But now at
length those perennial streams of wrath and bitterness,
which it had been impossible to staunch, were healed
at their source; and the dreaded Vikings, the Regnars
and the Hastings, or the like of these, with their deso-
lating hosts, sat down to peaceful occupations in their
own lands.   All this, with innumerable details of
interest, must remain thus slightly touched on and
no more.

As little can I follow at large the conversion of the
Slavonic tribes, with whom the Latin Church came in
contact so soon as ever the barrier between it and
them, that namely of the unconverted Teutonic races,
had been removed.   Before that removal the Greek
Church had made these the objects of its missionary
zeal.   This zeal, it is true, can at no time be said to
have equalled that which animated the Churches of
the West; while yet it is most unjust to charge the
Eastern Church with having wholly abdicated its
duties as a missionary Church, as a Church, that is,
holding the truth not for its own good only, but in
trust for all the world.   Cyril and Methodius, Greek
monks, brothers in blood as in toil, stand out the foremost, as Apostles of the Slavonic races.   A deep

obscurity, which later investigations have by no means cleared away, rests on the history of both, above all on their relations to the Roman See. Making no attempt to reconcile conflicting legends, or to choose between them,—for we are in a region here more of legend than of history,—I must content myself with observing that Bulgaria about 863 received the faith from Methodius; Moravia from Cyril; the Slavonic tribes owing to the latter, as to a second Ulphilas, an alphabet, and through that alphabet a literature.

The sacred fire spread from Moravia to Bohemia, from Bohemia to Poland. It might for some time have been a question whether these newly converted lands, or most of them, should not fall to the Eastern Church rather than to the Western; yet it did not prove so. Some indeed remained true to the mother from whose breasts they first drew the milk of the word; and others, like the Bulgarians, who, however, were not Slavonic by race, but Turanian, were long an apple of discord between East and West, as they inclined now to one and now to the other. The Wends of Pomerania and Mecklenburg, fiercely fighting for their idols, and allowing no peace to their Christian neighbours, were broken at length by the might of the Emperor Henry I. and the Ottos; while the Prussians, the most civilized of all the Slavonic races, were in the end rather exterminated than converted by the Teutonic Knights, an Order of military monks, like the Hospitallers and Templars; these, occupying their country, repeopled it with German colonists (1230–1283). Of the conversion of Russia, by far the most important exploit, in this line of things, of the Eastern Church, there is something which must hereafter be said.   For the present it will be sufficient to observe that, at the close of the thirteenth century, the receding wave of Moorish population in Spain, and a few outlying groups of Finns and Lapps, were all that remained in Europe not included within the pale of the Church.

LECTURE VI.

THE HOLY ROMAN EMPIRE.

AMONG the various Teutonic tribes which forcibly
occupied the different provinces of the Roman Empire, and made these their own, I have already mentioned the Lombards.   Their relations to the See
of Rome, as I then noticed, were almost always
unfriendly, their acceptance after a while of the Catholic faith doing little to abate an antipathy and remove
an estrangement, which might almost seem inborn, so
incapable did it prove of mitigation on the one side or
on the other.   The Lombards having taken Ravenna,
and destroyed the Greek Exarchate, and with this
the Imperial ascendancy in Northern Italy, were constantly seeking to extend their dominion in the
South as well, often threatening, and more than once
besieging, Rome.   The Roman Bishops might turn in
vain for help to their rightful protectors, the Eastern
Emperors, who still claimed their allegiance.   They
were far off; with embarrassments and perils more
than enough at home.   Unwelcome helpers at the best,
even if there had been any effectual help in them, they
were the more distasteful now as enemies of those
images which the Westerns had learned to honour,
and as branded with the note of heresy for this.   The
Popes looked round in their distress for a protector
more to their mind, and one who would not fail them

in their need.   No nation had shown such devotion to
the Papal See as the Franks, Catholic from their first
conversion, the mightiest of the youthful nations of the
Western world.   It was evidently the policy of Rome
to disengage herself for once and all from the falling fortunes of the Eastern Empire, and from the
ignominious servitude which the connexion with this
entailed, and to make common cause with abler and
more willing helpers at her doors.   To these she
betook herself now.

The alliance between the two had for a long time
past been preparing.   Much in the conditions of the
Western world was drawing them more closely together; and it so happened that just when the need
was most urgent, each was in a position effectually to
assist the other; so that the Roman Pontiffs did not
come merely as suppliants, asking much, but with
nothing to render in return.   There was that which
they, and they only, could give, which was of priceless
value in the sight of those whose assistance they im-
plored.   The Mayors of the Palace, the virtual rulers
of the Franks, counted that they had reigned long
enough in the name of the Do-nothing Monarchs of
the effete Merovingian race.   It was time that this
empty pageant of royalty should cease, that where the
reality of power was there should also be the name.
But it was not a light matter to set aside an ancient
race of kings.   A step such as this demanded the
highest religious sanction which the Church could
give ; only so could he who ventured upon it hope to
satisfy his own conscience or the conscience of his
people.   But, as men at that day esteemed, such a
consecration of the meditated revolution the Roman

Pontiff, as head of Christendom, alone could impart. Nor was this sanction withheld. Pepin, the son of that Charles Martel of whom we have heard something already, and father of a still greater Charles, of whom we shall presently hear much more, is crowned King of the Franks by Boniface, Archbishop of Mentz and Apostle of Germany, acting herein in the Pontiff's name (752). Henceforward Pepin makes the cause of the Church his own. The Lombards meanwhile, altogether failing to take a right measure of their own weakness as matched with the Frankish strength, are rash enough to provoke a conflict which issues in their defeat by him (755) ; and when somewhat later the provocation is renewed, Pavia, the Lombard capital, is taken, and the Lombard kingdom by the arms of Charles the Great overthrown (774).

This casting of the whole weight of the Frankish Monarchy into the Roman scale was one of the determining facts of medieval history. Charles, when he wrought this deliverance, already bore the title of Patrician of Rome ; this title, whatever it may have meant, having been first bestowed by a grateful Pope upon his father. But Charles' relations with the Papacy were destined to be more intimate still. "The new Constantine ;" as he was often called, he made over by donation to the Roman See large portions of the territory conquered by the Lombards from the Greeks, and now wrested by him from the Lombards. He was thus, with his father who had already done something of the same kind, though on a more limited scale, the founder of the temporal dominion of the Bishops of Rome,—the so-called patrimony of St. Peter dating back to this time. The lands thus con-

ferred upon the Pope he was to hold of the King, as of
his feudal superior, if we may thus anticipate a little
the use of this language ; for Charles had no intention
of setting up an independent state in the heart of his
own states—least of all one with such pretensions as
were inherent in the Papacy, and inseparable from it.
Those who in after times wrote in the interests of the
Roman Court have presented this act less as a free
gift upon his part, than as a restitution to the Roman
See of that which had been given long before by Constantine, but had since been violently rent away by
the Lombard arms, and was now restored to its rightful possessors.   But the whole story of the Gift of
Constantine, which first emerges in a letter of Pope
Adrian I. to Charles (775), but which there were
never wanting some even in the Middle Ages to denounce as a fable and forgery, is now acknowledged
by Roman Catholic writers themselves to be such.

More, however, than this was behind ; the alliance
between the Pope and King was destined to be closer
still.   On Christmas Day in the year 800, the Frankish Monarch was worshipping in the church of St.
Peter at Rome, when, as if by a sudden impulse from
above, Pope Leo III. advanced toward the King,
placed a crown upon his head, the whole multitude
present thereupon with loud acclamations hailing him
as Cæsar and Augustus, in whom the Empire, which
had been lost so long to the sight and desires of men,
was now revived and restored.   This incident was one
of profoundest significance. It is not too much to affirm
that it is the hinge upon which the whole history of
Western Christendom turned for long centuries to
come ; Emperor and Pope, they are the two centres

round which the whole medieval history revolves, the two poles which mutually complete one another. It has been often sought to represent what Leo did as a divine inspiration of the moment, and one which took Charles altogether by surprise. This suggestion is as old, or nearly as old, as the crowning itself. The King is reported to have said among his friends, that if he had known what was to happen, solemn as the festival was, he would not on that occasion have been present in the church at all. There may very well have been no distinct concert between the two chief actors on this ever-memorable day ; but it is hard to believe that they did not understand one another. Certainly the marvellous swiftness with which the multitude within and without the church at once comprehended, and by their acclamations adopted, this act as their own, if it does not betray previous arrangement, shows that the expectation of such an event was, so to speak, in the air. And who can doubt but that it must have been often in the mind of Charles himself, how mightily it would assist him in carrying out the grand designs of his life, if to all which he wielded of material power he could add the mysterious and yet most real consecration involved in this revival in his person of the Empire of the West ? We know that the moral fitness and political expediency of some step of the kind had been urged upon him by Alcuin and by others.

The idea of an universal theocratic kingdom as the divine idea of the government of the world, being one which the prophecies of Daniel did much to suggest and to nourish (Dan. ii. 31–45 ; vii.), exerted an immense influence on the imaginations of men during the Middle Ages. In Constantine, the first Christian

Emperor, and in his successors this idea had been realized for a brief while. It had now ceased to exist in any concrete shape for three hundred and twenty years; but it still walked the world as a mighty ghost, eager to clothe itself in flesh and blood once more; an august reminiscence; which men were the less content should abide as a reminiscence only, now that the Byzantine Emperors had forfeited by their crimes every claim to be considered as its rightful embodiment; and when, as the crowning outrage of all, a woman, namely Irene, that woman the murderess of her own son, and usurper of his seat, occupied the Eastern throne. Shadowy and undefined as might be the privileges and powers which this dignity conferred, yet this very vagueness had its advantages; and certainly it was not a small matter to stand out by the acknowledgment of all as the foremost man in all the world, linking the present with a glorious past, and so, it might be hoped, with a glorious future. Not, indeed, that the Emperor was the only gainer. "The Frankish alliance, the dissolution of the degrading connexion with the East, the magnificent donation, the acceptance of the Imperial crown from the Pope's hand, the visits to Rome, whether to protect the Pope from his unruly subjects, or for devotion, everything tended to throw a deepening mysterious majesty around the Pope, the more imposing according to the greater distance from which it was contemplated, the more sublime from its indefinite and boundless pretensions" (Milman).

Before we proceed any further, let us a little consider the man who thus bound up so closely his fortunes and the fortunes of his house with those of the

Church, who was willing to assume the official title of its "Devoted Protector and humble Helper," and to undertake the duties which this title involved; at the same time accepting from it in return such moral con- secration as it was able to bestow. Charles the Great (b. 742, d. 814), whose greatness is, in his French ap- pellation, indissolubly bound up with his name, great indeed in peace and in war, in arts and in arms, was immeasurably the foremost man of his age; nay, we must go back to Julius Cæsar or to Alexander before we find another whose figure so fills and occupies the canvas of history as does his. Gibbon, who has some- times an eye for greatness even when it displays itself in a Christian, as notably in the case of Athanasius, has no eye at all for the greatness of Charles: and it is not in his pages that you must seek an adequate appreciation of the mightiest man whom the Middle Ages produced. King of the Franks, by which we do not mean King of the French, for Germany had very much the largest part in him, while Aachen (Aix-la- Chapelle) and not Paris was the capital of his do- minions, he had carried his victorious arms as far as to the Eyder on the north of Europe, to Pomerania on the east, far into Hungary, to the river Theiss, on the south. All which the Lombards owned he had not very long before added to his dominions; while in Spain, despite of one severe but isolated check, which romance has made more of than history would war- rant, he had driven back the Arabs beyond the Ebro. Haroun Al Raschid, the Mahomedan Caliph, with whom Charles exchanged gifts and courtesies, was the only potentate who could even remotely compare with him in extent of empire, in glory, or in power.

But Charles deserved the title of Great by a better right than that of the extent of his kingdom, or the success of his arms. He was indeed the very ideal of a Teutonic chief, himself foremost in strength and prowess among his warriors. But he was much more than this. He spoke Latin; he understood Greek. The desire which lay closest to his heart was to rescue whatever remained of the Greek and Latin civilization, and of Christian theology and learning,—for all seemed in danger of perishing amid the confusions of the time,—to found schools, attaching them in most cases to cathedrals and monasteries, as the only hope of their permanence, and by aid of these to scatter and to repel the barbarism and darkness which were threatening to make everything their own. He saw, and saw truly, that in the Christian Church was to be found the one principle of all true culture for the nations under his sway. To the extending the influence of the Church—I do not mean by this the privileges and wealth of the Clergy; to the restoration of its prostrate discipline; to the raising up of strong barriers against any further pressure of the barbarous heathen on the civilized western world; to the turning, so to speak, the tables, becoming himself the aggressor, and blessing these against their will, bringing home to them benefits of which they knew and were disposed to know nothing; to the making of all who bowed to his sceptre partakers of the highest Christian culture which was then within reach,—to these as its central purposes his life was devoted. His contemporary biographer tells us that Augustine's *City of God* was the book which he was best pleased should be read to him at meals. The choice of that book was significant. Unutterably remote as was that kingdom over which he ruled from the true *City* or *Polity of God*, it was toward this that he was striving. The attempt, however faint, to realize this, he had accepted as the task for which he lived. Nor is it without its meaning that in the familiar circle of his intimate friends, in which each was called by some name, scriptural or classical, which he had assumed, King David was that by which Charles was willing to be known.

It has indeed been often urged in disparagement of him and of what he wrought, that in good part it perished with him, that the darkness, scattered for a moment, closed in again and swallowed up all. There is only partial truth in this statement. The cloister schools which he had founded lived through the tenth century, generally acknowledged as of the Dark Ages the darkest of all. In these schools were cherished, and from these proceeded, those new activities of the human mind which were to issue in the scholastic philosophy ; the University of Paris being in direct lineal descent from the Palatine school at Aachen, of which Alcuin was the founder. And if the reign of Charles does stand out as an isle of light with a night of darkness encompassing it on every side, so far from diminishing, this rather enhances the importance and significance of that brief season of refreshing, that breathing time thus obtained for arts and sciences, which might else have perished, unable to live at all through the dreary centuries which were before them.

But something more about Charles must not be left unsaid. The Chinese have a proverb, "Better a diamond with a flaw than a pebble without one." There were flaws and serious ones in the life of Charles which it is not for me to keep back. A just and merciful ruler in the main, he avenged on one occasion a Saxon revolt, under circumstances, it is true, of extreme provocation, with penalties of blood, which, as we read, seem to transcend all measure. Then too in the matter of marrying and putting away of wives he claimed a liberty, and in his private life a license, to which he had no more right than the meanest serf in his dominions. It is not therefore wonderful that, vast as were the Church's obligations to him, it did not see its way to make him partaker of the highest honours which it had to bestow; and when an Antipope, Paschal III., ventured on his canonization, the Church itself neither absolutely disowned, nor distinctly allowed what had thus been done, and had found favour with many.

We turn from these to the nobler aspects of his life; nor, when all is said, need we shrink from affirming that, if the Roman Empire was to be revived, Charles was well-worthy that it should be revived in him; if there should be again a Lord of the World, that he should be that lord. And yet for all this what a multitude of questions suggest themselves to us, when we seek to estimate the precise significance of this event, to define to ourselves with any clearness what the relations were in which Emperor and Pope should henceforward stand to one another. Thus, by what right did the Pope claim to revive in the person of Charles the Western Empire, or, to use the favourite language of a somewhat later day, to translate the Empire from the Greeks to the Germans; seeing that as yet the Popes did not arrogate to themselves

to be the givers or the takers away of kingdoms? If
not as Pope, was it as acting under an immediate
divine inspiration? Or was it as representative of the
City of Rome, even as the rabble of that City claimed
often in after times that the election lay with the Roman people, which people they styled themselves?
Was it clear to either or to both into what relations
they were entering, one with the other, relations of
mutual dependence, each in some sort owning the
other as superior? Thus the Emperor consented to
receive the Imperial crown at the hands of the Pope,
and only after this coronation to assume the Imperial
title; an arrangement so liable to misinterpretation
that already within little more than half a century
Pope Nicholas I. declared this crowning of the Emperor by the Pope to be a grant to him of the Empire
by the Roman See, an assertion in later ages repeated
again and again. Once more, could the Pope withhold this coronation on the ground of irregularity in
the election? or unworthiness in the person elected?
or on any other plea? could he, that is, hinder whom
he would from obtaining the Imperial dignity? or,
where there was a disputed election, did it lie with
him to determine which among the competitors had
been legitimately chosen? But then, on the other side,
the Emperor was not less Emperor at Rome than
elsewhere. The Pope was in a manner his vassal, his
man, swore fidelity to him, recognized him as the supreme Judge before whom he might be summoned to
make answer to charges brought against him. And
just as none might assume the title of Emperor, till
anointed and crowned by the Pope, in the same way
before a Pope, however canonically elected, could be

consecrated, it was necessary that the election should
be confirmed by the Emperor.

It must at once be evident that in this "Roman Constitution," as at a later day it was called, there were
innumerable unsettled questions, a very seed-plot of
occasions of strife, such as would be sure to spring up
so soon as ever the memory of mutual benefits had a
little faded away. Nor is it wonderful to read of
German armies continually crossing the Alps to redress some real or fancied wrong committed against
the majesty of the Empire, to compel the coronation
of an Emperor elect, unduly withholden, or to annul
the consecration of a Pope, which no due confirmation
had preceded. It was meant that the two powers, the
secular and the spiritual, should mutually sustain one
another, each with the weapons which were most properly its own; but suspicions, jealousies, conflicting
interests, incompatible ambitions did not fail to set
them very soon at division. The two swords, of which
we are to hear so much, were continually clashing;
and the story of this clashing of theirs constitutes a
large portion of the history of the Middle Ages. In
treating of this collision we shall find it impossible to
give our sympathy without reserve to the wielders of
the one sword or of the other. Both are right, and
both are wrong; or rather both contend for a right,
and with that right contend also for a wrong. But of
all this there will be other and frequent occasions
hereafter to speak.

LECTURE VII.

THE ICONOCLASTS.

Art had been so long and so completely in the service of the impure religions of heathendom, was so steeped in their spirit, had so often ministered to what in them was worst, that it is nothing wonderful if the early Church regarded it as something with which the faithful could hold no friendly relations, which they could only reject and condemn. It would be long to detail—and the story belongs to ages anterior to those of which we are treating—by what steps this extreme aversion little by little abated its intensity, gave way to other feelings, until, though not without struggle and remonstrance, Art won for itself a place first in the houses of men, and then in the house of God; and such a place in the end that the danger was no longer lest the Church should in a narrow spirit of intolerance exclude and ignore that which, kept within its proper limits, might render to her excellent service; but lest Art should abuse its victory, forget its proper subordination, and intruding into a region not its own, prove not a helper but a hinderer to any true worship of God in the Spirit. It would indeed be a mistake, and no where a greater mistake than in telling that story on which we are about to enter, to suppose that it was Art as Art, and for its æsthetic merits, which had won this acceptance. Rather it had done this, as being the

M   89

most effectual means by which supersensual things might be brought to the level of men's senses, and men relieved from the effort of lifting themselves up into a higher world, this higher world having rather been brought down to their level by aid of representations appealing first to the eye.

The time, however, at length arrived when excesses in this direction provoked a reaction, and a violent attempt on the part of some to return, not to the simple and naïve intolerance of the primitive Church, for that was impossible, but to a disallowance, forcibly imposed, of all those outward helps to devotion on which the faithful, for good or for evil, had learned to lean, and which through long use had grown into matters of necessity to many. In the Greek Church, as might have been predicted beforehand, the battle about the images, their abolition or retention, was fought out; the noise and wild tumult of this conflict, this tempest of wrath and wrong, filling for it the eighth century and reaching far on into the ninth. Not indeed that the Western was not continually drawn into the quarrel, which was fraught with immense and abiding consequences, theological, ecclesiastical, and political, for both; destined mightily to help forward the disruption of whatever ties still knit the West to Constantinople, and furthering to the same extent the birth and growth of a purely Latin Christianity. If herein there was gain, yet in other aspects it would be difficult to imagine anything more disastrous than this ill-omened struggle proved. Dividing as it did the East from the West, it embittered them in a thousand ways the one against the other; while the East, in addition to this separation, was itself

still further divided, torn by cruel intestine strife; some
of its greatest princes wholly alienated from their people, and the people from their princes; and this at a
time when all the forces of the East and West combined, would not have been too many, if any effectual
resistance was to be made to the Saracen invasion.

In a recent Lecture on the rise and early spread of
Islamism I dwelt on the marvellous successes which
waited during the first century after the death of its
founder on the Moslem arms. The controversy of
which we treat to-day is closely connected with these
events. The outer bonds which connect them may
seem very slight, but the inner are very real indeed. I
spoke in that Lecture of the hatred of idols which the
followers of the Arabian prophet deeply felt, and
missed no opportunity of displaying; of the strength
which they found in the proclamation of the unity of
the Godhead, and in the faith that they were raised up
—and in this surely they were not altogether mistaken
—as witnesses against the idol-worshippers of the
world, against all who in any shape or under any plea
gave to the creature the glory due only to the Creator.
They were still in the full career of victory at the beginning of the eighth century; Constantinople, twice
besieged by a Saracenic army and fleet (668, 716),
hardly escaping a catastrophe that would have abridged
by some eight centuries the course which the Eastern
Empire was destined in the providence of God still
to fulfil.

The principal agent in working out the second and
the most memorable of these deliverances was Leo
III., Leo the Isaurian as he is called (717–741), a
hardy mountaineer, who by courage and conduct had

raised himself from the humblest rank to be the founder of a new dynasty, and who offered in many ways
a singular contrast to the effeminate princes, " the
purple-born," who had gone before him; though resembling them only too faithfully in his inability to
distinguish the lines which divide temporal and spiritual power. We can scarcely be wrong in assuming
that he learned his abhorrence of images from those
with whom he had been brought into hostile contact.
He is taunted in the polemics of the time with having
taken the Arabs for his teachers ; and the taunt was
probably a true one. He had seen the strength which
the Islamites found in the one grand truth which
among so many falsehoods they held, and he thought
to make this strength his own. Probably he could ill
brook the title of idolater, which the Mussulmans, and,
where they dared, the Jews, cast in the teeth of the
Christians. He will be an ecclesiastical reformer ; he
will put down the worship of images (726) ; failing in
this, and angered by his failure, he will abolish them
(730).

In meddling thus, Leo does but follow the traditions of the Byzantine Cæsars. Almost every past
Greek Emperor had been a theologian in his way,
and generally a persecutor to boot. A rough soldier, bred in camps, he seeks to carry his resolution
through by courses the most violent and arbitrary;
while indeed the mischief, which was a most real
one, demanded to be dealt with in a manner the most
careful and considerate. Entwined as the error was
with so much which was not erroneous, it needed to
be disengaged from this with a firm, yet also with a
gentle and a reverent hand, with such care as men use

when they take down ruinous houses which adjoin to temples, lest the sacred should be involved in the same ruin with the profane. There was no such reverent heedfulness here. Doubtless the images often and in many ways ministered to superstition. Even those who were most earnest for their retention were compelled to allow as much. Men prostrated themselves, burned incense, before them, counted that prayers made at the shrine of one image were more prevailing than those made at the shrine of another; with much more, deplorable enough, in the same kind.

But the images,—which let me explain by the way were not sculptures or statues, for these the Greek Church has never allowed, but coloured portraitures on a plane surface or, more rarely, mosaics,—were precious to many, had endeared themselves to them by immemorial use, were associated for them with all which they had learned to hold the most sacred. Of all this however the reforming Emperor took no heed. The army was enthusiastically devoted to a leader who had brought back victory to its standards; and with the army upon his side he did not doubt that opposers and opposition might without much difficulty be trotten under foot. But he had not taken account of all with whom he would have to reckon. The Patriarchs of Constantinople were for the most part the passive instruments of the Imperial will; but now the aged Germanus resists; and another, more prompt for every servile and shameful compliance, must be chosen in his stead. His resistance indeed, and that of the tumultuary multitude of the city, might have profited little. Even the trumpet notes of John of Damascus, the most famous theologian of his time, who, dwelling at Jerusalem under Moslem protection and beyond the reach of the Imperial anger, incited the faithful by his writings as to a Holy War, might have sounded in vain, if it had not been for that other army which Leo had left out of account. In the monks he encountered opponents as rude, as resolute, and as fanatic as himself, men too whose interests as well as whose passions were bound up in the issues of the conflict, for it was chiefly from their workshops that the images proceeded.

Let us pause here and consider for a little what the monks, who found the violence, and the theologians, who found the arguments, said for themselves in reply to charges, of which the head and front was this, namely that in using and in defending the use of these images, they were breaking and defending the breach of the Second Commandment. Yes doubtless, they replied, such a commandment, and that to be taken in the letter, was given to the Jews, though even for them it admitted tacit qualifications. The Cherubin, shadowing the Mercy Seat, not a few things in Solomon's temple,—as the twelve oxen upholding the molten sea (1 Kin. vii. 25), and in his house the twelve lions beside the ivory throne (1 Kin. x. 20),—were each and all a modifying of the strict letter of this commandment. And then, in respect of that which offended the most, namely pictures of our Blessed Lord Himself, it was quite intelligible, they replied, that at an early stage in the religious education of mankind, men should be absolutely forbidden to make a likeness of Him whom no man had seen nor could see. But since the Incarnation, and by the

Incarnation, this all was changed. God had appeared, visible to the eyes of men, and had taken the human nature into personal union with Himself. The picture which we make of Him, they said, is a confession upon our part in act, as elsewhere we make confession in word, of the mystery of the Incarnation. You condemn this picture, they retorted on their accusers, because it is a setting forth of Christ in his humiliation ; but seeing that it was love which had brought Him to that low estate, it is indeed a setting forth of Him in his highest glory. So especially Theodore, Abbot of the Studion (d. 826); who, belonging to the latest period of this long struggle, is quite the most attractive figure in it, and the most notable theologian whom it produced. The defenders of the images further urged, though this was capable of receiving quite another turn, that the Iconoclasts were weakening the whole position of the Church as against its nearest and deadliest foes. What were they in fact affirming but that in all these matters the Arabian Anti-christ was right, and the Church of God wrong ?

It is only fair too to state that the most zealous favourers and promoters of this ill-directed homage always disclaimed with indignation the charge of offering to the images any reverence which did not differ in kind, and not merely in degree, from the worship which they offered to Almighty God, calling it by altogether a different name. We shall very probably feel that in these distinctions which they drew between the " honour " which they gave, and the " worship " which they withheld, there lay no slightest justification of that in which they allowed themselves ; but these distinctions acquit them of idolatry, and it is the merest justice to remember this.

Let me add a word or two more before resuming the historic thread of the narrative. No one, I am persuaded, who has studied with any care the questions which in this controversy were gradually brought into debate, but will feel, and will ever more strongly feel, that much larger and much deeper issues were here for determination than might at first sight appear. And yet for all this the whole theological struggle was only too characteristic of the Eastern Church. Assuredly the masculine common sense of the faithful in the Western would have chosen, even in the eighth century, some better field than this could ever prove, for fighting the battle of the Incarnation; or, if compelled to fight it on this, would have cleared the field betimes of all which encumbered it, which obscured or hid what was really at issue, and has rendered it impossible to give more than a most limited sympathy to those who believed that, as against their present foes, they were contending for the central truth of the faith.

I shall not attempt to follow the details of an unlovely struggle, in which all, if they had a right for which they fought, contrived also to put themselves wofully in the wrong; I shall pass quickly over the story of savage tumults more savagely repressed, of a throne shaken to its foundations, and a Church miserably torn asunder. Leo was succeeded by a son, Constantine Copronymus (741–775), as distinguished a soldier as himself, of a will as iron as his own. Fanatically resolved to carry through his father's work, he will yet give it the consecration which hitherto

it has lacked. It is not difficult for him to bring
together a Council, at which no Patriarch indeed, but
338 Bishops are present. What amount of freedom
reigned at this Council, which called itself the seventh
Council of Constantinople (754), may be guessed from
the fact, that by it the use of images was condemned
as idolatry without one dissentient voice. And now
every priest, every monk, every layman was required
to give in his separate and personal adhesion to
this condemnation. Multitudes yielded ; but not the
monks. No violence was spared—scourgings, muti-
lations, blindings, imprisonments, exiles, cruel mock-
ings, every device of insult and of wrong, all were
without stint employed to force their submission ; and
with so inexorable a purpose that, when the four and
thirty years of Constantine's reign were ended, it
might have seemed as if at last he had carried his
purpose through. A monk was no longer anywhere
to be seen. The monasteries had been turned into
barracks or stables. The images had wholly disappeared from the churches ; only, it is true, to be more
carefully cherished in the secret of the chamber and
of the heart. On the walls of the churches, where
used to be painted incidents from the life of the Lord,
or from the legends of the saints, there were now de-
picted landscapes, hunting scenes, vintage revels, the
profane temper of the destroyers, irreligious Puritans
we might call them, not caring to conceal itself any
more in this day of triumph.

Doubtless nothing has been lost in the telling of
the insolences, the outrages, the cruelties of which the
Iconoclasts were guilty. In the extreme poverty of
contemporary records, we are mainly dependent on

N

the adversaries who crushed them, and on these writing a full century after the events, for our knowledge of the acts and the actors; and such hostile reporters may very well have made in their narration that uglier still, which was ugly enough before.

But to return. It was but a shortlived triumph which the Iconoclasts could boast, and one destined presently to prove no triumph at all. An intriguing woman, the Empress Irene, finds herself guardian of her son, a minor, and craftily uses the opportunity to undo all which so painfully, and at a cost so enormous, had been effected. And now the Second Council of Nicæa (787) annuls all which the Iconoclast Council had decreed. It is true that under Leo the Armenian (813–820), the enemies of the images are again in the ascendant, that there remains one long and violent struggle more. But again a woman, Theodora, herself the widow of an Iconoclast Emperor, working with the spirit of the time, was strong enough to overthrow an edifice which only stood so long as the Court and army sustained it; but which, their support withdrawn, collapsed at once (842). The images in solemn procession are restored to their place in the churches; and the fury of the storm is now felt to have spent itself so entirely that a feast, called the Feast of Orthodoxy, is instituted to commemorate in all after time the final and complete triumph over the image-breakers which has been gained.

Throughout this protracted conflict the Church of Rome had thrown her whole influence on the side of those who sought to retain all the abuses connected with the images. This was inevitable. She was herself entangled too deeply in the superstitious use of these

to be able to give wise and moderate counsels to the
sister Church in the East.   But if not from her, it was
yet from the West that the wisest words came in the
end—from the Frankish Court of Charles the Great.
We may regard the Four Caroline Books,—so named
from him, and put forth in 790, three years after the
Second Nicene Council,—as his manifesto, and that of
the accomplished theologians, Alcuin the chief, whom
he had gathered round him. In this book a line is taken
alike remote from both extremes.   And first there is
in it a distinct condemnation of all religious homage
done to the image, or in and through the image to any
whom it may represent, let this homage be reduced to
what minimum it may, explained or explained away as
men will—a vigorous refutation. of the arguments by
which it was sought to justify such homage.   This is
the ground-tone of the book, the more worthy of note
as being directly in the teeth of the contemporary
utterances from Rome.   But so much thus plainly set
down, the author or authors can the more confidently
reprove the fanaticism of the image-breakers, who
would recognize no moral difference between these
images and the idols of the false gods of heathendom ;
who would not be content until they had made a clean
sweep of all wherewith little by little Christian men
had adorned and beautified their churches, or by which
they had sought to maintain and quicken a lively impression in their own minds or in others' of the sacred
events and persons of the past.   Man is not all soul,
it is here urged ; but body and soul ; and being thus
sensuous in part, may lawfully use sensuous helps.
Such is the tone and tenor of this very memorable
book.

I have not, you will have observed, invited you to
deplore very deeply the ill success attending a movement which was yet directed to the abatement of a
most serious mischief in the Church. That the
Church should have laid the axe at the root of this,
and with this, of other abuses, should have recognized the steps by which it had been unconsciously
drawn away from the simplicity of Christ, and thereupon should have retraced these steps, such a course
would have been a matter of most earnest thanksgiving. But what profit could accrue to a Church through
a reformation imposed by the arbitrary will of a monarch, and carried through with such violence and outrage and wrong as was this? A Pope virtually
claiming to be Emperor as well, a priest-king, is bad
enough, and this the history of Western Christendom
has abundantly shown; but an Emperor who demands
also to be Pope, a king-priest, this, which was the persistent claim of the Byzantine autocrats, is infinitely
worse.

And over and above this fault which clung to the
whole endeavour, namely that it was a violent intruding of the secular power into a region not its own,
there were other faults cleaving to it which gave sufficient evidence how barren of all good it would certainly have proved, if success had attended its efforts.
Reformations in religion can only be carried out to
any profit by those whose hearts God has touched, by
such as are themselves religious. There must at all
events be among the reformers a sufficient number of
these to leaven with some sort of higher leaven the
lump of the worldly, the self-seeking, the profane, who
will put themselves forward as sharers in the work.

But assuredly no one will affirm that the fierce princes
and their fierce satellites, the prime workers here, were
animated by any earnest love to Christ; on the contrary, the hatred of many for the images had passed
into a hatred of those whom the images represented.
No one will deny that, with rarest exceptions, all the
religious earnestness, all which constitutes the quickening power of a Church, was ranged upon the other
side. Had the Iconoclasts triumphed, when their work
showed itself at last in its true colours, it would have
proved to be the triumph, not of faith in an invisible
God, but of frivolous unbelief in an incarnate Saviour.

I can close this Lecture with no better or wiser
words than those which Milman supplies: "There was
this irremediable weakness in the cause of Iconoclasm:
it was a mere negative doctrine, a proscription of those
sentiments which had full possession of the popular
mind without any strong countervailing excitement.
The senses were robbed of their habitual and cherished
objects of devotion, but there was no awakening of an
inner life of intense and passionate piety. The cold
naked walls from whence the Scriptural histories had
been effaced, the despoiled shrines, the mutilated
images, could not compel the mind to a more pure
and immaterial conception of God and the Saviour.
Hatred of images, in the process of the strife, might
become, as it did, a fanaticism, it could never become
a religion. Iconoclasm might proscribe idolatry; but
it had no power of kindling a purer faith."

DENISON UNIVERSITY
LIBRARY

LECTURE VIII.

MONASTICISM.

A REHABILITATION—for this I believe is the word—of men and things, of some that might reasonably have despaired that such would ever include them, has gone forward of late years to a very remarkable extent. If you ask me what that unusual word means, I cannot answer better than by saying that it has been long, if not in English, yet in law-French, a word to signify the restoring and replacing in a position of esteem and honour, or, it may be, of authority, one who, rightly or wrongly, had forfeited such position, making him "habile" or able for this once more ;—or, not adhering so closely to the image which the word suggests, it might be described as a moral whitewashing of such as in men's sight were as blackamoors before. This rehabilitation has included men such as Tiberius, Nero, Richard III., Alexander Borgia, Marat, and Robespierre, has not excluded institutions such as the Spartan Krypteia and the Spanish Inquisition. But it has also included persons and things with better right to its benefits than any of these. It is nothing wonderful that medieval Monasticism has profited by the reopening of enquiries, which some on very imperfect information had too hastily assumed to be closed. Whether its rehabilitation will be complete, is another question. It may do much to explain and justify its

DENISON UNIVERSITY
LIBRARY

existence, to show the debt which the world and the Church owe to it, and yet fall short of this

With this much of introduction let us enter upon the subject before us, which is very far from an easy one. The whole medieval Church, with its grand features of devotion, of heroic self-sacrifice, with all its strivings after the highest, and then this same with its terrible aspects of evil, of evil which has often seemed as if it were inextricably bound up with its very existence, is a constant perplexity to the student who takes history in earnest, who is not satisfied with merely knowing that such and such things have been, but would fain know also why they have been, and to what ends they served; above all is it a mystery and a perplexity to him who regards the Church as a divine institution for good, and only for good, in the world. Some, attracted and awed by the noble aspects which the Church in those ages presents, have resolutely shut their eyes to all which was otherwise in it, have fallen down and worshipped, counting all succeeding ages a declension from ages of faith which have for ever passed away. Others, repelled and shocked by the frightful mischiefs of those times, have had no eye except for those mischiefs, and have refused to believe any good about them at all.

Now if the evil were separable from the good, so that, disentangling these the one from the other, we could approve the good, and condemn the evil, the perplexity would not be so serious; though it must be freely owned that this process of taking and leaving, allowing and condemning, is attended by very real dangers of its own in its reactive influence on the minds of them who thus become judges of men, it may be immeasurably greater and better than themselves. But in this woof which we are here considering the dark threads and the light are not capable of being thus disentangled the one from the other. This sense of an immense perplexity, of contradictions which it is impossible to reconcile, perhaps no where presses upon us so heavily as when we contemplate certain institutions which we cannot regard as accidents of the medieval Church, for they are of its very essence, not as the fringe of a garment, but as in a great degree the very garment itself. Imagine the Papacy, imagine the Monastic Orders, both, or either of them withdrawn, and, as a period of Church history with distinct features of its own, the Middle Ages would simply cease to exist. Of the Papacy I shall hope to speak by and bye. We have now to deal with Monasticism. We cannot abdicate our right to judge it. Every great moral phenomenon, and this was a very great one indeed, we are bound to have, or to endeavour to have, some judgment about, whatever the dangers may be which wait upon such judging.

To me it seems undeniable that so soon as ever the better moral forces, which even at the beginning were not the only ones, began to ebb, there sprung out of the Monastic system mischiefs the most enormous. To this we must stand, as by all history attested only too well; while yet again and again we ask ourselves concerning those ages of the Church, How could they have done without it? what substitute for it did they offer? The missioners who went as upon the forlorn hopes of the early Middle Ages, who wrought the conversion of England, of Germany, of Scandinavia, of Slavonia, had been trained in the cloisters of Iona, or of St. Gall,—centre of missions for all South-Western Germany, or of the Benedictine Abbey of New Cor-bey, of which it is not too much to say that the whole Scandinavian mission was fed from that single house, or of some other religious foundation of like kind.

And the same difficulty besets us, though not per-haps quite so strongly, when we contemplate other functions which the monasteries and the monks fulfilled in those long ages, sometimes so dreary, almost al-ways so tempestuous, which connect the ancient and modern world. Again and again we put to ourselves these questions, Who during those dark times would have kept alive the sacred fire of learning, if these had not been there? How would that remnant of the precious treasures of ancient literature which has escaped the shipwreck in which so many had perished, have reached us except for them? What would have survived of higher culture without the cloister schools? of art, if these had not cherished the sparks which might else have been quite trodden out?

Nor is this all. The world might have struggled on without literature and without art. But they were the monks who taught, not so much by precept as by example, that lesson of such surpassing worth, namely that in the labour of the hands there is dignity and not degradation. Immense was the gain when the Benedictines gave a religious consecration to the cul-tivation of the earth by the linking of this with prayer and the reading of Scripture, effectually and for ever redeeming this labour from the dishonour which sla-very in the old world had impressed on an occupation which was then regarded as the proper business of slaves. And never was there more urgent need of

O

such a moral glorification of labour than in those wild and savage times, when the earth, trampled, desolated, ruined by the march of successive barbarian hosts, its former tillers scared away or slain, required to be again, as from the beginning, subdued by patient toil to the service of man. We sometimes hear the ignoble observation—it used to be heard much oftener—that the monks knew how to pick out the best and most fertile spots for themselves; when indeed it would be truer to say that they knew how to make that which had fallen to them—it was often the waste or the morass which none other cared to cultivate—the best; but this by the sweat of their brow and the intelligent labour of their hands.

But freely admitting the debt and the greatness of the debt, can we help observing concerning the monastic ideal of the highest Christian life,—the separating off, that is, of innumerable companies of men on one side and on the other of corresponding companies of women, to live their lives apart,—that it is a human invention, running counter to a divine? Of the monks of the West must we not say that they shared with their Eastern prototypes the inevitable disease of seeming to be protesters against family life as gross and secular, witnesses that the sexes will be most holy when kept most asunder? Now, without gainsaying the accidental and occasional benefits which sprang from such an arrangement, yet such a witness, so borne, must have reacted most injuriously on the whole family life of Christendom, lowered its tone, and gone far to empty it of the beauty and consecration which according to the divine idea of the constitution of human society it should have borne.

What can we say to these things? What indeed but briefly this, namely, that He who is the King of Ages does in each age for his Church the best which the moral materials He has at command will admit. Men are free agents, with the choice therefore of working for God or working against Him. He who has willed to be served only by the free can only use the materials which He finds, whether these are absolutely the best or not. He will give partial allowance to much which is very far from being according to his perfect and highest will, shows Himself the one supreme and absolute Work-master, in that with materials and instruments so imperfect He brings about his purposes, making all things and, in one way or other, all men to serve Him; not suffering the evil which may have mingled with his good to defeat it; but rather causing the good to operate so effectually as often to rob what was not good of its worst power to harm.

Thus much said by way of introduction, let me sketch very shortly some aspects of Monasticism in the West, so far as it falls within the times of which we treat.

The first origins of Monasticism, how it took its rise in Egypt, where it was in a manner indigenous; how it spread over the neighbouring lands of Syria and Palestine; how it was brought by Athanasius to the West, found earnest resistance there at the first, but in the end an acceptance which should render it a mightier factor in the Church life of the Occident than it had ever been in the lands of its cradle,—showing itself far more flexible, far abler to adapt itself to new con-

ditions, to rise to novel heights; how it suffered by the
confusions and shared the disorders of the fifth and
sixth centuries, was reduced to some sort of order and
discipline by Benedict of Nursia (d. 543), who, intending to furnish a Rule for his own convent of
Monte Cassino, devised one of such practical good
sense that it was adopted over the entire West;—all
this belongs to a time anterior to that with which we
have to deal, and with this I have a right to assume a
certain acquaintance upon your parts.

In the disastrous times which followed the death of
Charles the Great and the failure of his scheme to re-
organize the Western world under a single head, the
discipline of the religious houses fell with everything
else; fell, not perhaps quite so soon, yet by the end
of the ninth century had fallen almost as low as it was
possible to fall. But here symptoms of a moral reaction showed themselves earlier than elsewhere. The
revival dates from 910, the year of the foundation of
the Monastery of Clugny in Burgundy, which was destined to exercise an enormous influence on the future
of the Church. While matters at Rome were at their
worst, there were silently training there the men who
should inaugurate a new order of things (see p. 119).
Already, so one said at the time, the whole house of
the Church was filled with the sweet savour of the
ointment there poured out. It followed that wherever
in any religious house there were any aspirations after
a higher life, any longings for reformation, that house
affiliated itself to Clugny; thus beginning to constitute
a Congregation, that is a cluster of religious houses,
scattered it might be over all Christendom, but owning
one rule, acknowledging the superiority of one mother

house, and receiving its Abbots or Priors from thence. In the Clugnian Congregation for example there were about two thousand houses in the middle of the twelfth century—these mostly in France; the Abbot or Arch-Abbot, as he was called, of Clugny, being a kind of Pope of Monasticism, and for a long time, the Pope excepted, quite the most influential Church-ruler in Christendom. The glory of Monte Cassino, which had been hitherto considered as the pattern on which other houses should fashion themselves, was eclipsed by the greater glory of Clugny; however it might retain, in the midst of all the novelties of this and of other younger competitors, a certain stately dignity of its own.

These religious guilds or corporations fell in with the temper of the time, and the eleventh century saw the foundation of several new Orders, as that of Camaldoli (1018), of Vallombrosa (1038), and more important than either of these, the Carthusian (1084). The Rule of this last exceeded in severity that of all which had gone before, while it hardly left room for any which should come after to exceed it. The eudemonism of the present age does not require to be flattered and fed; nor do men need, so far as one can see, to be warned against excessive severities; yet it is difficult not to feel that the austerities by this Rule imposed were to a great extent pursued and practised, not as a means to an end, but as an end in themselves, and as having an intrinsic value of their own. Neither should we here leave the Carmelites unnamed, though they belong to a somewhat later period (1156). These, tracing up their first origins to Elijah and Elisha, had their chief haunt and home

in Mount Carmel, until the loss of the Holy Land
compelled them to migrate to Europe. Other smaller
Orders there were, which claimed special works of
mercy as their own : of them, however, hereafter.

But one was founded at the close of the eleventh
century (1098), which should exercise a far stronger
influence on the Church's life than any which we have
named, the Clugnian perhaps only excepted. The
Cistercian, of which I speak, was, as all these new Orders, were, an attempt at reformation, this reformation consisting in a stricter observance of the Rule of
St. Benedict, with, it might be, here and there a drawing tighter of the Rule itself. But the Cistercian, besides this, was an attempt, in part successful, to make
Monasticism more of a quickening element of spiritual life, not merely for those within the walls of the
cloister, but also for the multitudes beyond. In this,
which was a certain anticipation of what was afterwards more fully carried out by the Mendicants, was
the main secret of its success. At first indeed the
new Order gave no promise of the magnificent future
which was before it, nursing mother as it was destined
to prove of so many Popes, of Cardinals and Prelates
out of number. Indeed at one time, as the first little
group of enthusiasts who founded the Order died out
one by one, and no other took their places, it seemed
likely that it would expire without having enlisted a
single novice, scaring these away as it did by the extreme severity of its Rule. It was in this precarious
condition when St. Bernard, the scion of a noble Bur-
gundian house, came to the rescue, drawing after him
some thirty young companions whom he had inflamed
with his own love of a life so rigorous and austere.

From him the Cistercians are sometimes called Ber-
nardines ; and this name does not more than express
the fact that he was their real, although not their nominal, founder. From Clairvaux, by him made famous
for ever, for some five and twenty years he ruled not
merely the Order which derived its chief lustre from
him, but, it is hardly too much to say, the whole
Church. Counsellor and admonisher of kings, trainer
and maker of Popes, healer of schisms, condemner of
heresies, author of a new Crusade, he was in every
aspect, save indeed that of high speculative theology,
the leading spirit of his age, even as he must be
owned to be the fairest flower which medieval Monasticism can show.

When this later embodiment of the monastic idea
began to compete for men's favour, and to show how
formidable a rival it was likely to prove, the older
Clugnian foundation had already seen two centuries of
existence; and the lapse of time, the world's admiration, and an immense prosperity which this drew after
it, had begun to tell upon it. We do not read of any
scandalous disorders there, though doubtless some
relaxation of the severe discipline of an earlier time
had crept in. Of the lavish offerings of the faithful a
part had been laid out on their own houses, which were
oftentimes of regal grandeur and extent, and on
churches, of which many were vast and magnificent.
To the splendour of these the whole aspect of the
Cistercian buildings was the strongest contrast, and,
whether so intended or not, a silent rebuke. There
were no splendours here, but everywhere an austere
simplicity, a puritan plainness; for costly tapestries
bare walls, for heaven-aspiring roofs low rafters; for

immense windows with their gorgeous wealth of stained glass, narrow openings sufficient to let in the day; for silver candelabra iron candlesticks, and of these only enough to give light: no gorgeous ritual, no elaborate music. Then too, while others, the Clugnians above all, gloried in their exemption from episcopal jurisdiction, a dutiful submission to this was an essential feature of the younger Order. You will not wonder that the glory of Clugny paled before a glory which exceeded, before the stricter discipline and severer living of Clairvaux.

But the rigour of the Cistercians themselves was in due time to thaw beneath the sun of the world's favour. Already in the thirteenth century their fall had begun. The Inner Mission had been taken out of their hands by the Mendicants, and they succumbed to that doom of declension and decay, to which, as it might appear, all were bound in; for indeed those Orders, wonderful at their beginnings, and girt up as to take heaven by storm, seemed destined to travel in a mournful circle from which there was no escape. Goethe has somewhere said, " When a man has done a remarkable thing, the world takes excellent care that he shall never do another." The words have their application to societies as well as to individuals. There was in these Orders zeal, and labour, and love, and self-denial at the outset; and these in so high a measure as to draw upon an Order the world's wonder, men admiring and by gift or by testament heaping lands, riches, boons of all sorts upon it. And then after a while prosperity did its work. The salt lost its savour, and the first love departed, and a revival in some novel shape of things ready to die became neces-

sary; which revival sometimes arrived, but not always,
—this also in due time to spend and exhaust itself, as
all before it had done. Fuller, at once witty and wise,
as is his wont, has put it well: "As mercers when their
old stuffs begin to tire in sale, refresh them with new
names to make them more vendible, so when the
Benedictines waxed stale in the world, the same Order
was set forth in a new edition, corrected and amended,
under the names first of Cluniacs—these were Benedictines sifted through a finer sieve, with some addi-
tionals invented and imposed upon them. . . . Secondly, Cistercians, so called from one Robert living in
Cistercium; he the second time refined the drossy
Benedictines."

With whatever jealousy the different Monastic
Orders might regard one another, or might all be
regarded by the parochial or secular clergy, they were
safe never to want the good will and protection of the
Papal See. The Church could not exist without its
Bishops and Pastors, who were by divine appointment
constituent elements of it. Yet it was not upon these
that the Papacy mainly relied, or in whom it looked to
find its chief support. This it found rather in the
Monastic Orders, which were its own creation, its
natural allies, and for which it reserved its choicest
favours and exceptional privileges. This preference
after all was not very wonderful, and had its measure
of justification. There was probably more real work
to be gotten out of the monks than out of the secular
clergy. If a signal emergency arose, they were the
readiest and the fittest to meet it. A new Order, allowed and favoured, was often a safety-valve to carry

P

off a perilous enthusiasm. That which, left to run its own course, and embodying itself in the form of a sect, might have gone far to wreck the Church, did in the form of an Order rather strengthen and sustain it. The Monastic Orders have been sometimes likened to the Schools of the Prophets; the secular Clergy, in their routine of fixed service, to the Levitical priesthood. The comparison is not altogether a fanciful one.

I shall fitly close this Lecture with a few words from two of the most accomplished defenders of the Monastic system in modern times, but two who looked upon it from somewhat different points of view. Montalembert, the latest of these, in his *Monks of the West*, repels with no little warmth and with some indignation the praise which Chateaubriand bestowed on the monasteries, namely that they furnished a refuge and retreat for the weary and sick of heart, for those whom the arrows of the Almighty had pierced, for the disappointed, the misunderstood, for multitudes who, so far as this world was concerned, could not boast of being "men who had succeeded," but might be regarded rather as having fought the battle of life and lost it. He refuses to see in these cloisters such hospitals for the sick as Chateaubriand describes them. They were rather in his judgment training places for the strong; where not what was feeblest, but what was most robust and most vigorous in the Church's life was to be found, where the men were formed and fashioned who should afterwards rule the Church or convert the world. There is truth in both statements, but doubtless in the best days of Monachism, and in the best examples of it, the verdict of Montalembert is nearer to the truth

than the more sentimental verdict of the other. Of
the qualifications with which either conclusion must be
accepted, of the abatements which must be made from
both, I have already said something, and cannot for
this present undertake to say more.

LECTURE IX.

HILDEBRAND.

So long as Charles the Great lived, it was not likely that there should be any serious collision between the spiritual power and the temporal. Few would have been disposed to provoke a conflict with one so powerful and predominant, so clearly resolved to allow no encroachment on the domain which he claimed as his own. He too upon his part recognized the limits which divide the two domains, and in remarkable contrast to the Byzantine Emperors and notwithstanding his own lively interest in the theological questions of his time abstained in the main from any undue interference with them, or, if he did interfere, so carried the Church with him, that none were disposed to resent the share which he took in her affairs.

But the Empire which Charles had won, it needed another Charles to keep together. His institutions had done something here, but his personal influence much more, and to this he left none to succeed. Through family quarrels and intestine wars, aided by the mutual jealousies of Teuton and Roman, the mighty fabric of empire which he had reared fell into fragments not very long after his death, and all attempts to piece these fragments together in new combinations came to nothing. The story is a deplorable one, but still we may deplore it overmuch. The throes and birth-pangs in which the new nationalities of Europe were born were terrible; but if at the cost of these Europe was saved from a second Byzantine Empire, they were not endured in vain. Nor was it long before the rudiments of future kingdoms, shaping themselves out of the general wreck and ruin, began to appear. For a century indeed or more the Imperial dignity was not absolutely tied to anyone of these kingdoms, but shifted from one to another, while oftentimes there was no Emperor at all, his supremacy and very name being alike in abeyance. In the end, however, the German kingdom, or kingdom of the East Franks, so transcended any other in power, that in the days of Otto the Great (936–973) it permanently annexed the Imperial dignity to itself. The consequences of this, alike for Italy and for Germany, above all for the former,—were incalculable. Throughout all the Middle Ages they stand in relations to one another the closest, and at the same time the most unhappy ; able to make one another miserable, but very rarely able to do one another any good.

The Popes meanwhile have used the partial, or what was often the total, eclipse of the Imperial power for the increase of their own ; and there is not wanting a brief gleam of glory to light up the Papacy during the Pontificate of Nicholas I., called, and not without some right, the Great (858–867). But close upon this there follows a time of very deep degradation. All which in the eyes of men is counted the holiest becomes the spoil of wild and wicked factions among the Italian nobility For fifty years and more (904–962) the election to the throne of St. Peter lay in the hands of three infamous women, a mother and her two daughters. Their domination has been often characterized by a word, which, though it veils its ugliness in Greek, I shall not care even under this veil to repeat. The moral outrages which this time beheld are not to be told, nor shall I attempt to tell them. Roman Catholic writers make no attempt to conceal the depth of desecration and dishonour which the Papacy then passed through ; nay, they seem rather to take a pleasure in making the worst of this, arguing that none but a divine institution could have sounded those abysses of infamy, and yet emerged with a glorious future before it. If indeed they had been content to urge from this recovery the profound roots which the Papacy must have had in the necessities of the time, there might be something in argument ; but more in this survival I fail to see.

Matters in the end had proceeded so far that even those who were most jealous of Imperial interference saw in this interference the only remedy for intolerable present ills, and besought the assistance first of the Emperor Otto I.,—from whom, as "Defender of Western Christendom," they had a right to claim this (963), —and when the old mischiefs gathered strength anew, of Henry III. (1046). The help thus sought was honourably rendered. A series of respectable Popes, all nominated by the Emperor, brought back some sort of credit to the chair of St. Peter. This help, it is true, was not very gratefully acknowledged, seeing that the most immediate use which the Papacy made of recovered strength and revived character was to get rid for ever of the necessity of obtaining the Imperial allowance of the Papal elections.

But while these Monarchs did something to reinvest it with some sort of reputation, it was more from within than from without that moral strength came to it again. The man who most effectually wrought for the lifting of it up to heights from which it might seem to have for ever fallen, for the giving to it a new lease of life, and a world-domination vaster than could have been dreamt of in the wildest dream (let us judge of him morally as we may), was unquestionably one of the few men who have made and moulded the history of their own and of after ages. Hildebrand—we know him officially as Gregory VII., but it is difficult not to call him by his proper name—was a Benedictine monk, trained in the famous monastery of Clugny. Clugny had already become a moral force in the Church, and one so great, that it is hardly an exaggeration to say that without a Clugny there would scarcely have been a Hildebrand; or, if such there had been, that, wanting zealous and trained instruments to work his will, he would have found himself for the carrying out of his purposes as helpless as alone. The name sounds German, but it is not recognized as such by German scholars; and there is no reason to doubt that he was an Italian by descent as well as by birth. Long before his own elevation, from the Pontificate of Leo IX. (1048), he had been more and more felt and acknowledged as the ruling spirit of the reforming party in the Church, had virtually named Pope after Pope, no less indeed than five; and under the shelter of their names had already begun the conflict, which, now that the time seemed ripe, he was prepared to wage more boldly than ever in his own.

It was not so much new ideas launched by him upon the world, as the energy with which he embodied old ones in act, that gave him his great position in history. All which he uttered had been uttered by others before him; but what others promulged and undertook with a certain timidity, presently stopping short as men terrified by that which they themselves had done, he carried out boldly and to the full. For him the source and spring of all the ills which afflicted, degraded, and threatened, unless arrested, to destroy the Church, lay in its bondage to the secular power. With its complete emancipation from this the sole hope for the future was bound up. The Church must be free; but for him it was only free when it had extinguished every other freedom but its own. Hildebrand could not so much as conceive a distribution of power which should assign to the Church and State severally a domain of their own, each sacred, each divinely traced out. For him the one was holy, having to do with the highests interests of men; the other profane;—Nimrod, the successful hunter of men, being in his eyes the true author and founder of that organized violence, the State. Here was a distinct advance on the views of his illustrious predecessor and namesake, Gregory I., who had been content to teach that the priesthood was of divine ordination, but the kingdom of human importunity (with reference, no doubt, to 1 Sam. viii. 6, 7); the one having been given by God, and the other extorted from Him. To one so minded, any other arrangement than that the Church should rule and the State should serve, must have presented itself as monstrous.

The first great reform by which he hoped to deliver

the Church for ever from shameful subservience to any worldly authority, was the revival and reinforcement of the laws compelling the celibacy of the secular Clergy,—laws which never since the time of their introduction in the fourth century had been universally obeyed, and which in his time had fallen, at least among the lower ranks of the Clergy, into general neglect. Our own Dunstan indeed, about a century earlier, himself in a narrower sphere and among a ruder people a prophetic type and harbinger of Hildebrand, had attempted what Hildebrand was attempting now, but with only temporary success. The hierarchical system which Gregory had at heart was essentially anti-national. It could only subsist by the absolute subordination of the interests of any and every particular nation to those of the Papal See. A celibate Clergy might consent to this, might labour for this, but certainly not a Clergy of which a large proportion were married. These ceased at once to be a militia in the heart of every land, upon whom as sure allies the Pope could under all circumstances rely. Their country, its honour, its dignity, its well-being were so much to them, that in any struggle they were at least as likely to be found ranged on the side of their native prince as on that of a foreign ecclesiastic.

Other motives, and of these some worthy of honour, wrought in the mind of Gregory. Doubtless he saw the danger, in those days a most real one, of the Clergy resolving itself into an hereditary caste; all the higher places in the Church preoccupied and handed down from father to son, or by other family arrangement. And with this he beheld a glory and chief strength for ever departing from it, namely its

offer of a free career to all, its placing what it had of
highest and best within the reach of the lowest and
the humblest, if only they showed themselves worthy
of it. Himself humbly born, the son of a carpenter at
Saona, he knew by his own experience what grand
opportunities it gave, and would fain preserve them
for others.

The issues which the battle against the family had,
need not surprise us. The married Clergy, without
organization, with many misgivings about the rightfulness of their own position, with the rule of the Church
plainly against them, however the law of God might
be with them, were no match for one who had no misgivings about the rightfulness of *his* position. Yet for
all this it cost him a mighty struggle to carry out his
purpose. The opposers were not overcome till he
had enlisted against them all the blind passion and
coarse manicheeism of the lowest among the people,
hounding on the rabble to insults and outrages of
every kind against the "Nicolaitans;" for in contests
like these there is nothing like fastening an offensive
nickname upon adversaries, and so this heresy of the
Nicolaitans was invented (with allusion, no doubt, to
Rev. ii. 15), and the married Clergy with their abettors counted guilty of it. Of the frightful evils which
sprang from the success which at length attended his
efforts, it does not need to speak more in particular.
Sufficient to say that Hildebrand's iron will and pitiless resolution triumphed in the end over all opposition. Milan, strong in her Ambrosian traditions,
attempted resistance, but with no other result than the
loss of ecclesiastical liberties which up to this time, in
the face of Rome herself, she had preserved; and

from the Pontificate of Gregory VII. dates, not the demand of the Roman Church that all who minister at
her altars should be unmarried, but any approach to
an universal observance of this rule. Henceforth the
Clergy became an exclusive body, not patterns to the
flock, models on which other Christians should fashion
the lives of themselves and their families, but a separate class, lifted above the rest of the faithful, and in
this central fact of their lives divided from them.

No sooner was it plain that from this struggle Gregory would come forth victorious than he followed up
this blow with another. In his determination to put
down the profane trafficking with holy things, and this
not merely in its coarser, but also in its subtler forms,
—to preserve the Church's *peculium* from being ab-
sorbed into the possessions of rapacious nobles and
kings, for the peril of this was immense,—he can only
have our sympathy, and, when we think of all the selfish and brutal forces which he challenged to the conflict, in a large measure our admiration. But, as we
shall see, he proposed to himself much more than this.
And now there comes to the front that which is known
as the struggle of the Investitures, a struggle which
was not to reach its settlement until nearly half a century after his death, and even then a settlement which,
as it turned out, was very far from proving an end of
strife.

There are some conflicts which, so to speak, are due ;
which may arrive a little sooner or a little later, the exact moment of their breaking out being determined
by accident, or by the action of some single will ; but
which in themselves are inevitable. This of the In-

vestitures, which, once begun, shook Western Christendom so long, in which pen and sword were alike so
busy, was one of these. It will not be very difficult to
explain to you its nature. In the eleventh century the
whole feudal system as it existed in the later Middle
Ages was rapidly shaping itself, and was so effectually
moulding European society to its own conditions and
requirements that the Church itself could not escape
its control. This system may be described as a complete organization of society through the medium of
land tenure, in which, from the king down to the lowest landowner, all are bound together by obligations
of service and defence,—the lord to protect his vassal,
the vassal to do service to his lord. This system,
which grew out of the conditions of the time, with all
its faults met the needs of the age; it was probably the
only one which then was possible. But it is manifest
that it could not stand, if one half of the land,—and in
many countries the Church was in possession at least
of this moiety,—had been exempted from the obligation
of those services which were everywhere else the condition of its tenure; or had been so held that the rendering of such services could not be enforced. The secular princes therefore demanded that a Bishop should
not enter upon the enjoyment of the temporalities of
his see, should not indeed be consecrated, until he had
done homage for, and had received from their hands
the Investiture of those temporalities; engaging himself
hereby to the fulfilment by himself, or, where this was
not possible, by proxy, of the duties corresponding.

There was a complaint of long standing on the
Church's part against the form in which this Investiture was made, namely, by the delivery of a crozier

and ring. As many as had any claim to be Churchmen at all were justly offended at the employment of
the sacred tokens, symbolizing as these did, not the
temporal rights and emoluments which were all that
the lay patron could confer, but spiritual gifts and relations; the ring the Bishop's marriage with his Church,
the crozier his commission coming direct from Christ
Himself, to feed the flock committed to his charge.
Whether so intended or not, this manner of Investiture was a practical denial of the spiritual character
of the Church; that it was a kingdom not of this
world, but from above : and they were altogether in
their rights,—Hildebrand the first and foremost of
these,—who required that Investiture should take place
in some other way. He felt, and felt truly, that spiritual power must be a divine power, not derived from
any mere man whatsoever; that no king nor kaiser
could be the source from whence it flowed; that either
the priest is nothing or is called of God to his work.

But he and the Churchmen who fought this battle
with him did not stop here. They were resolved to
get rid not of this fashion of homage or Investiture
only, but of the homage itself in any shape whatsoever. All the abuses connected with the obtaining
of Investiture from the lay-patron, simoniacal pay-
ments and the rest, frequent and flagrant as they were,
he was resolved by a single stroke to make for ever
impossible; and, more daring purpose still, by the
same stroke to release the Clergy for ever from any
and all dependence on the secular power. The property of the Church, now the desecrated spoil and
merchandise of princes, he would reduce within his
own dominion. Hildebrand was not the man to assert

a claim like this without seeking to put it through; and in a Council at Rome (1075) he deposed every Bishop or other spiritual person who had received Investiture from lay hands, putting them under an excommunication, till they should have renounced that accursed thing which by these wicked means they had gotten. The same excommunication he laid on Emperor, Prince, Potentate, whosoever he might be, that presumed to demand this homage, or to confer on any by Investiture the temporalities which belonged to his See, Abbey, or other benefice.

With claims like these, which, if admitted, would in fact have released from every obligation to the State the holders of half or more of the land therein, it could not be long before the two powers thus placed in opposition proceeded to measure their strength against one another. What arrangement was reached at length I may as well now relate, though in fact it was not till nearly fifty years after Gregory's death that the end arrived. The first Crusade, which followed hard upon that death (1097), drew men's thoughts away from the subject for a while. Before long, however, it occupied them anew; and various ineffectual efforts were made by means of some compromise to close the quarrel—Pope Paschal II. in the year 1111 going so far as to consent that the Clergy should renounce all possessions held by them on the tenure of homage. This arrangement would certainly have brought the quarrel to an end, seeing that then there would have been nothing wherewith to invest; but the German Prelates, not very unreasonably, refused to accept a settlement, which would have stripped their sees of their entire endowments; and they com-

pelled Paschal to go back from this undertaking.
After inkshed in abundance and bloodshed not a
little, a compromise was arrived at, which has since acquired the name of the Concordat of Worms (1122).
Both of the contending parties gave up something,
but one much more than the other ; the Church shadows, the State substance. The more important elections should be henceforth made in the presence of
the Emperor, he engaging not to interfere with them,
but to leave to the Chapter or other electing body the
free exercise of their choice. This was in fact to give
over in most instances the election to the Pope, who
gradually managed to exclude the Emperor from all
share in Episcopal appointments. The temporalities
of the See or Abbey were still to be made over to the
Bishop or Abbot elect, not, however, any longer by
the delivering to him of the ring and crozier, but by a
touch of the sceptre, he having done homage for
them, and taken the oath of obedience. All this was
in Germany to find place *before* consecration, being
the same arrangement that seven years earlier had
brought the conflict between Anselm and our Henry I.
to an end ; in Italy and in the kingdom of Arles within
six months *after* the same. Crozier and ring should
still be delivered, but not by any secular hand, even
as it was not any longer by these emblems that the
temporalities were conferred.

But we have put ourselves in advance of the times
of Hildebrand, to which we return. It was not long
before the Papal pretensions brought him and the
young German King, Henry IV., into mortal conflict.
It must be freely owned that if, in this first hostile
clash of arms between the kingdom and the priest-

hood, the Church was magnificently represented, such was far from being the case with the State. Henry IV., left an orphan at six years old, in childhood and youth submitted of a purpose to the most corrupting influences, having already alienated by tyrannous courses and driven into rebellion those on whose loyalty his throne should most have rested, displayed in the earlier stages of the quarrel none of those higher and nobler qualities which adversity revealed, if it did not create, in him ; and assuredly was ill to cope with the great and politic Pontiff, who had so dextrously selected not Philip of France, still less William of Normandy, but in their stead this dissolute boy for his antagonist; while yet, if he could humble him, the highest in worldly dignity of the Princes of the earth, he might be regarded as in some sort having humbled all.

Little by little the relations between the two became more and more strained : the Pope complaining of the King that he nominated Bishops hostile to the Roman See, that he retained among his confidential advisers excommunicated persons, that his rule was an intolerable tyranny, and his own life a shameful outrage on all decency ; and in the end citing him to make answer for himself in person to these charges. We have a glimpse here of the wonderful reversal which two or three centuries had brought about in the relations of Pope and Emperor that such a citation should have been possible. Henry understands what it means ; that the Pope is claiming the right to depose him; that in all likelihood he will exercise this right. He snatches at whatever weapons of defence are at hand. Hastily calling together a Diet, he hurls countercharges against the Pope, sorcerer, simonist, fautor of heretics,—this no doubt with reference to Berengar,—with whatever other accusations a blind rage can suggest ; and will prevent his own deposition by a declaration of the Pope's. And now the Church's thunders do not sleep. Henry is pronounced under ban ; to have forfeited his kingdom. This ban of the Church had not yet lost its terrors. Henry's adherents fall from him. He himself, as "a man forbid," loses heart and courage, makes abject submission (the well-known scene at Canossa); but, once restored to the Church's communion, repents his repentance, takes up arms again, and displaying energy and conduct for which none had given him credit, wins back the larger part of Germany by arms. An anti-Cæsar, raised up by Gregory,—such in these ages are almost as plentiful as antipopes,—perishes in battle ; Henry carries the war over the Alps, and, various causes helping, compels the Pope to abandon Rome, and to seek the protection of the Normans. Norman adventurers, as I shall have occasion again to observe, had recently founded a kingdom in South Italy, which on this occasion and on others proved an opportune refuge to Popes in the days of their adversity. Here, at Salerno, Hildebrand dies (1085), in exile and defeat ; to all appearance the vanquished champion of a lost cause ; but indeed, as the issue proves, not the conquered but the conqueror in that mighty duel which was now fairly begun, that tragedy in several acts, played now on Italian, now on German soil, and now on both, whereof this was the opening act.

But I have followed up to its close this struggle with Henry, which was indeed the main affair of Gregory's life, to the neglect of some other aspects of it which must not be altogether omitted. His restless activity, his high flying claims, brought him into collision with other of the kings of the earth. It was under a banner consecrated by a papal benediction that William of Normandy went forth to win the crown of England; and Gregory demanded homage from him for the kingdom which this benediction had enabled him to win. But when William refused, saying bluntly that he had promised nothing of the kind, that his predecessors had never yielded this homage to the Pope's predecessors, and that neither would he to him, Gregory let the matter drop. The same caution he displayed in the matters of Philip I. of France. Indeed, none was more wary than he was to know how far he might venture and with whom; and to let fall, for the time at least, claims which were likely to be seriously resisted. It is a characteristic of the man which the least favourably impresses us. One would gladly have seen in him a little less of cunning, and a little more of uncalculating fanaticism.

Lines and colours of the darkest have been freely employed in drawing the portrait of this Pope, not Hildebrand, but "Brand of Hell," as our homily has called him; "Höllenbrand," as not seldom the German Reformers. This is not very wonderful. With no misgiving but that his cause was the cause of God, he trampled without pity or remorse on human hearts and their strongest affections. Overthrowing one tyranny, but, unable to conceive of a free Church except under the conditions of a servile State, he reared high another, and a more intolerable in its room. Eminent statesman as he was, he yet was one in whom the serpentine craft left little or no place for the columbine simplicity. Peter Damiani, the man of his right hand, who knew him in his heights and in his depths, fondly calls him his *Sanctus Satanas*, his "St. Satan," or shall we render it, his "holy Devil?" and if this was more than half in jest, yet as we know, many a true word has been uttered in jest.

But we owe justice to all: and who can refrain from admiring the mighty energy of will which enabled him, against such oppositions, to bring the Church upon new lines, lines upon which for centuries it ran? "His conversation" (in all ages a rare grace among Church-men), was "without covetousness." Then, too, if stern to others, he was first stern to himself. Far off from him and from his Court, as it is almost needless to say, were those shameful disorders which had so disgraced the Court of some who went before him, and should disgrace the Court of others who came after. He took his place and his work in earnest. To be highest in dignity meant for him to be foremost in toil and first in danger. And when upon his deathbed he exclaimed, "I have loved righteousness and hated iniquity, and therefore I die in exile," let there have been what of self-righteousness there may in such an appropriation of words which only One had a right to make unreservedly his own, they were the utterance of his deepest conviction; and if this absolute identifying of his cause with the cause of God was his sin, it was also that which left pardonable the sin. Not to us the great Pontiff,—in my mind the greatest of all, for Innocent III. in the main did but reap what Hildebrand had sown, and fill in an outline which he had traced,—not to man, but to his own Master he must stand or fall. Whether he was one of the good it is not for us to determine; he was assuredly one of the great of the earth.

LECTURE X.

THE CRUSADES.

To understand the Crusades aright, we must travel
back and occupy ourselves a little with the history of
the Holy Land in the centuries preceding.   Jerusalem
had fallen at the first burst of the Mahomedan invasion
into the hands of the immediate followers of the Prophet (638) ; but had yielded under conditions which,
so long as they were observed, ensured a tolerable existence to the Christians who were content to remain
under the Moslem yoke.   Nor was the treatment of
pilgrims from the West on the whole intolerable.   So
far from this, the Saracens regarded with a certain
sympathy these devout visitants to spots which they
also counted holy.   It had, indeed, once been a question with Mahomet whether he should not select Jerusalem as the sacred City, the religious centre of Islâm.
This, with other similar baits, he had at one time held
out to the Jews, and only let them fall when he discovered that these were not by them to be won.   But
such fairer conditions did not last.   Great revolutions
in the East brought the Holy City and the Holy Land
under the dominion of a barbarous Turkish tribe (from
1073), recent converts to the Mahomedan faith, but
converts of the old fanatical stamp—at the same time
changing the position of Christian residents and
Christian pilgrims very much for the worse.   These

last, who were also much more numerous in the tenth and eleventh centuries than before, the zeal for pilgrimages having by this time much increased, brought back the most lamentable accounts of the treatment of their brethren in Palestine; of the outrage and scorn with which all places which Christians counted the holiest were treated; and, it would often be, of wrongs and insults which they themselves or their fellow pilgrims had endured. Men had listened to these stories long, and with an ever-increasing irritation; but as Western Christendom became more conscious of its strength, slowly there rose up in men's hearts the thought of winning back the land which the Redeemer in the days of his flesh had trod, the grave wherein He had lain,—for while all was holy there, this his Sepulchre was the holiest of all; and at the same time of avenging all this wrong, and securing for themselves and for all their brethren access free and undisturbed to the sacred places for evermore.

Long before the Crusades came actually to the birth, such a thought had been stirring in the hearts of many. Pope Sylvester II. (999--1002) had suggested a Crusade; but the time was not yet, should not be for nearly a hundred years. The great purpose came much more nearly to the birth in the time of Gregory VII., to whose heart such an expedition lay very near (1074); but what between quarrels with the Emperor, quarrels with the citizens of Rome, struggles with an antipope, he had made only too much of work for himself at home; and it was not till Urban II. was Pope, not, that is, till very near the close of the eleventh century, that Europe was actually afoot.

Where there was so much inflammable stuff as in

Latin Christendom had been accumulating for years,
a little spark was sufficient to kindle all into a blaze.
Peter the Hermit did not show himself a very capable
leader of a crusading host, nor, when it came to
blows, in any way a hero, but the furnishing of this
spark is usually ascribed to him.   Himself an eye-
witness of the wrongs which the Christians in the
East endured from the brutal and fanatic Turks, en-
trusted with letters from the Patriarch of Jerusalem
beseeching assistance from the faithful in the West,
he passed, with the Papal sanction, from land to land,
telling everywhere what things he had seen, perhaps
had suffered; and, gifted as he was with a rude but
popular eloquence, stirred the Western world to its
depths.   Such is in the main the generally accepted
version of the part which in the rousing of Christendom he played.   And certainly Peter and his ass have
so established themselves as recognized stage proper-
ties at this point of the wondrous story, that one
accepts unwillingly the results of later enquiries which,
stripping him of his legendary fame, leave him an
obscure fanatic with no influence whatever in the first
wakening up of the West; although, when this once
was accomplished, there were not wanting in him gifts
which enabled him to allure a huge unhappy multitude
to their ruin.

The leaders of the age did not seek to repress the
enthusiasm, but rather did all which in them lay to fan
it to an ever stronger flame; most of all the Pope,
who could not fail to perceive the immense increase
of influence which from such an enterprise must
accrue to him, the moral consecration of his power
which he must derive from placing himself at its head,

even as this headship would necessarily devolve on him. He saw that, as men in that day were minded, a devoted soldier of Christ meant also a devoted soldier of the Church, and this a devoted soldier of the Pope. Urban himself made early proof of the gains which were to be gotten from this movement; owing as he did his triumph over an antipope, Clement III., to it and to the leadership of the first Crusade which at once he assumed.

What motives wrought with others,—superstition, love of romantic adventure, sense of wounded Christian honour,—I shall seek presently to set before you. Let it suffice for the present to say that when, at a solemn Council at Clermont in Auvergne (1095), the Pope, in an impassioned discourse still preserved to us, set himself at the head of the Crusade, promised absolution from all their sins to as many as in a state of true penitence died while engaged in this holy warfare, there burst from the enormous assembly an universal cry, "God wills it!" "God wills it!" No time was given for colder calculation. All who offered themselves for the work attached at his bidding a cross to their left shoulder, sewn upon their garments, in token that they were Christ's soldiers, and prepared after a medieval and chivalrous fashion to fulfil his command, "If any man will be my disciple, let him take up his cross and follow Me."

And now the enthusiasm to take a part in this armed pilgrimage, to have a share in the delivering of the Holy Land from the yoke of the infidel, knew no bounds. Germany, it is true, was slow to kindle, though it kindled at last. England had not yet recovered the shock of the Norman Conquest, nor indeed in any case would William Rufus have found a Crusade much in his line. Spain had already on a smaller scale a Crusade of its own, which had lasted centuries, and was to last centuries more. It was thus inevitable that France should take the lead; indeed, this would any how have probably been hers, incomparably rich as at this time she was in saints, in warriors, in poets, in scholars,—foremost not in one movement only, but in all which were now beginning to stir as with a nobler life the heart of Christendom. It would have been impossible to repress, none tried to repress, the excitement. Fathers, mothers saw with joy the departure of their only sons on this perilous but glorious mission ; wives the departure of husbands whom they loved the best. Monks and other recluses, some with the leave of their superiors, some without it, forsook their cloistral retreats; women too, concealing their sex, were found in the ranks of the Crusaders. Few wished to stay behind, and fewer dared. Here and there, where some knight who in the general opinion might have gone had tarried at home, the ladies of the neighbourhood would send him the unwelcome present of a distaff, as the only implement which he was worthy to wield. So many pledged and pawned their worldly possessions to raise funds for their equipment, that the price of land fell immensely in the market ; while that of a horse, or of armour, or of ought which would serve a warrior's need, underwent a corresponding rise. Whole regions appeared to be depopulated, so vast a proportion of their inhabitants had been drawn into the ranks of the crusading hosts.

But the moral aspects of this marvellous agitation were the worthiest of regard. There will be dark colours enough in any truthful picture of the Crusades —but to look first on the brighter side.   Not a few who before had been bitterest foes now embraced and were reconciled, and as brothers in arms set forward for Palestine together.   Many who had hitherto been plunged the deepest in worldly lusts,—men violent, impure, profane, sacrilegious, with hands steeped in blood,—seemed suddenly to be awakened to a nobler life, to leave their former selves behind them, and, set-ting forward to the earthly Jerusalem, to have become pilgrims also to that Heavenly whose towers and pin-nacles shone as it were through and behind those of the earthly City.   This was eminently the case, St. Bernard tells us, with the Knights Templars, a valiant Order of soldier-monks, founded for the defence of the Holy Sepulchre ; and in the main recruited from men such as these ; so that, as Bernard with perhaps a faint touch of irony observes, the world was not less bene-fited in losing than the Church in gaining them.   Let me note by the way that he is sometimes spoken of as their founder, which is a mistake; but certainly with-out his enthusiastic allowance of them and the conse-cration—for the word is hardly too strong—which this approbation gave them, they would never have grown to what they did.   Their rule too, which was that of St. Benedict, but this adapted to the new conditions of a military Order, they owed to him.

A mighty tempest of elevating, purifying emotions swept over Christendom.   It is not easy for those who have never known, to understand what it must be for an age receptive of noble impressions to have a pur-pose and aim set before it, which claim all its energies, meet all its peculiar conditions ; while at the same

s

time, lifting it above the commonplace and the mean,
they are far loftier than any which men's minds have
hitherto entertained. Such a purpose and aim were the
Crusades during well-nigh two centuries for Europe;
and the answer which Christian Europe made to the
appeal is a signal testimony of the preparedness of
the Middle Ages for noble thoughts and noble deeds.

I need hardly say that in presenting the Crusades to
you under this aspect, I would not, as I have hinted
already, lead you to suppose that all was thus elevated
and grand about them. Every page in their history,
not to say the final issue which they found, and which
must be taken as the divine judgment about them,
would bear witness against me. The false was mingled
in large proportion with the true, the dross with the
fine gold. All did not set forth to Palestine, no, nor
yet nearly all, single-minded warriors of the Cross.
Some, on the contrary, drawn along with the crowd,
and unwilling to stay behind when so many went;
some out of a mere love of adventure, and weary of
inaction at home; some hoping to find that wealth
and position in the East which were denied them in
their own land,—to carve out a domain, or it might be
a kingdom, for themselves with the sword; others,
again, that they might escape their debts and leave
their creditors behind them,—for so long as they were
engaged in this holy war none might disquiet them in
person or property, nor did the interest of debts accumulate; others that they might relieve themselves
from heavy penances which they had incurred, the
Church accepting the Crusader's vow as a discharge
in full of whatever censures a man might have come
under. All these and many other such motives helped

to swell the crusading armies. The atrocities of which too many among them were guilty,—the massacre of Jews on the way to Palestine being accounted by many nearly or quite as laudable a work as the slaying of infidels in Palestine; the dissolution of morals; the extent to which multitudes succumbed to the temptations of the East; all this made it only too plain that the fire which in many bosoms had been kindled, was not fire from heaven; that in any true sense Christ's soldiers and servants they were not, since, whatever victories over the infidel they might win, they had not won the victory over themselves.

I must pass over with only the briefest notice the mighty acts which on both sides were wrought, and mightier the world has never beheld—the battles, the sieges, the prosperous and adverse fortunes, the frightful calamities inflicted, the frightful calamities endured; which do not properly form part of a Church history at all. It will be enough to remind you that this precipitation of Europe upon Asia, beginning in 1097, lasted on for the larger part of two centuries, during which time Jerusalem was twice won and twice lost again; that, not to speak of the stream of pilgrims, armed and unarmed, which was continually setting eastward, there were during this period seven great expeditions,—expeditions in which, not to speak of kings and princes of a second rank, three Emperors took a personal share,—which are styled the seven Crusades; though it is not difficult to count them, as some have done, at fewer or at more. As a little help to memory, I will attach to each of these one or more of the most notable persons or most signal features connected with it.

Of the first you have heard something already.   It was the Knights' Crusade, no Emperor or King gracing it with his presence ; but Tasso sung it. It issued in the taking of Jerusalem (1099), and the founding of a Latin kingdom, on the pattern of the feudal kingdoms of Western Europe, under Godfrey of Bouillon ; although he, noblest and worthiest of this first band of Christian warriors, refused to be styled King, or to wear a golden crown, in that city where his Lord had worn one of thorns. But that Latin kingdom, though constantly recruited by new accessions from the West, though sustained by the knightly valour of the two military Orders, the Knights of St. John and the Knights Templars, in whose members the character of soldier and of monk was so strangely blended, utterly refused to take root ; and in less than fifty years another Crusade became necessary (1147) for the propping up of an artificial edifice, which, undermined by vices, jealousies, quarrels from within, and hard-pressed by the gathering forces of Islâm from without, was already tottering to its fall. Edessa, one of the minor principalities which the Crusaders had reared, and the main outlying bulwark of the kingdom, had already fallen (1144). Of the second Crusade St. Bernard stands out as the principal figure, even as he was its animating spirit.   It was he who, leaving his beloved retreat at Clairvaux, and passing through Germany and Switzerland and the Netherlands, everywhere roused by eloquence of speech and letter the chivalry of the West, that they should hasten to the aid of their brethren; persuaded Conrad III., the first of the Hohenstaufen line, not to fall short of so grand an occasion; invoked a divine

benediction on their arms, and promised them a success which never came; for, as the event too plainly
proved, the gift of prophecy was not among the many
wonderful gifts which were his.   This Crusade, thanks
in part to Greek treachery, in part to miserable dissensions among the Crusaders themselves, proved a disastrous failure.   Its leaders, a French king and the
German Emperor, return home having effected
nothing, and bringing back with them hardly a wreck
of the magnificent armies which they had led to defeat
and dishonour (1147--1149).

If the dreaded catastrophe which this Crusade should
have averted did not arrive at once, it was only de-
layed for a season by the dissensions of the Mahomedans among themselves.   When indeed the tidings
came at last that the Holy Sepulchre was again in the
hands of the infidel (1187), a cry of anguish went up
from all Western Christendom; quarrels at home
were made up for a while, and the armed knighthood
of Europe girt itself for one mighty effort more, which,
as it was fondly hoped, should be the last that was
needed.   And now two Crusades, the third and the
fourth,—for it is best to count them as two,—were
both on foot at the same time; one mainly German,
the other English and French.   Great names, and
names more or less familiar to us all, are connected
with both.   Frederick Barbarossa, indeed, the grand
Hohenstaufen, is less familiar to some of us than he
should be, and we do but faintly estimate the loss
which his death, drowned as he was in crossing a little
river in Asia Minor (July, 1190), entailed on the crusading hosts,; but Philip Augustus (1180–1223) and
Richard Cœur-de-Lion (1189–1199) on one side, and

the royal-hearted Saladin on the other, are something more than the mere ghosts and shadows which so often are all with which the past is peopled for us, if indeed it be peopled at all; though for this better acquaintance many among us may thank Sir Walter Scott and *The Talisman* rather than any proper studies of our own. Not the winning back of Jerusalem, but only some precarious privileges accorded to the pilgrims were all which by these mighty efforts were obtained.

What should have been the fifth Crusade (1204) and what by some is reckoned as such,—though I shall not count it a Crusade at all,—did not so much as attempt the recovery of the Holy City. It issued in the capture of Constantinople by the Latin armies, under the plea of restoring a rightful Emperor to his throne; and when he was slain, in the setting up of a shortlived Latin Empire in the East. False and treacherous the Greeks, from the Emperor downward, had been from the beginning, embarrassing, thwarting, and betraying the Crusaders, and for these ends oftentimes in secret league with the infidel; yet this was a shameful diverting to objects of selfish greed and ambition,—such a diversion as became only too common at a later day,—of armies gathered for quite another purpose.

In the fifth Crusade, which lasted some fourteen years, there stand out two principal figures; at its opening Innocent III, who by his earnest appeals did much to revive the old crusading spirit; at its close the Emperor Frederick II., grandson of Barbarossa, and one of the most enigmatic characters in history, of whom I shall have to speak more by and bye. A Crusade was indeed a strange enterprise for the Imperial

free-thinker ; and yet was crowned with so much success, that what others had failed to win by utmost
efforts of arms he obtained by negotiation, namely the
cession of Jerusalem with some other towns, as Bethle-
hem and Nazareth, dear to the Christian heart (1229);
which, however, did not remain long in Christian
hands; nor did it fare better with Jerusalem, which,
falling once more into the hands of the infidel, has
never been wrested from them again.

The passion which animated Western Europe was
now very nearly spent; nay more, there were voices
of earnest remonstrance lifted up here and there
against such expeditions at all. For all this there
must be two more Crusades, three, if we include
among these the expedition of Richard, Earl of Cornwall, King of the Romans and brother of our Henry
III., (1240), which, however, hardly rose to the dignity
of a Crusade. I count therefore but as two those
which were still to come before the end should arrive;
these two, moreover, the result of one man's high-
hearted devotion to that which he believed to be the
cause of God, rather than to impulses stirring still the
popular mind and heart of Christendom. They were
both exclusively French, and the nobility of France
who followed St. Lewis followed out of loyalty to their
sovereign, rather than out of any lively sympathy of
their own for the work which he had in hand. In the
first of these Lewis lost his liberty (1249) ; in the second, undertaken after an interval of more than twenty
years, his life (1270).

This last abortive effort closed the list of the Crusades; and no wonder, for who could hope to succeed,
where the saintly King had so signally and disas-

trously failed? It was quite time that they should end.
Whatever work they could do was done; whatever
benefits Europe could derive from them, and these I
believe had been many, they were already obtained.
A new Crusade might still figure in the Papal programme as often as a new Pope came to the throne;
he might announce, as did Pope Pius II. (1458–1464)
that he would himself be the leader of it; princes, as
our own Henry IV., might assume the Cross, and profess themselves bound, so soon as more urgent affairs
at home would permit, for the Holy Land; contributions might still be demanded from the faithful, and, indeed, it was sought to levy a permanent tax upon them,
"Saladin's tithe" it was called, to meet the expenses
of these coming expeditions; nay, the rudiments of
fleets and armies destined for the East were more
than once gotten together, at Venice, at Genoa, and
elsewhere.   But these were faint umbrages and no
more.   All these preparations came to nothing.   Men
did not mean what they said, or at all events did not
mean it with a whole-heartedness strong enough to
overcome hindrances which, in giving actual body
and shape to their purpose, they were sure to encounter.

The crusading passion had fairly worn itself out.   It
could hardly co-exist with what I will not call the
money-making spirit, for I have no wish to find fault
with it, but the commercial spirit which was beginning
to pervade Europe, and which these very expeditions
had done much to arouse.   If the enthusiasm revived
for a moment, when the fall of Constantinople (1453)
revealed to Christendom the nearness and the greatness of the danger which threatened it from the Otto-

man arms, this enthusiasm never embodied itself in the shape of an eighth Crusade; and those who tried to quicken it again were doomed to discover the truth of the homely proverb which says that it is no use to flog a dead horse.

On the first blush of the matter the Crusades present themselves to us as a lamentable failure; and such failure in one and in a very real sense they were. After all that prodigal expenditure of life and treasure, after nearly two centuries of toil, during which the winning back of the Holy Sepulchre had been the darling project of Christendom, for which no sacrifice had been counted too costly, "the world's debate" had ended, but ended leaving all as it was at the beginning. The miscreants—for we owe that word to the Crusades, and it meant at first no more than mis-believers—still kept the spot where the Lord of Glory had lain. The Christians of the East still groaned under the yoke of their Mahomedan oppressors. The pilgrims from the West were as much exposed to insults and outrages as ever. The petty Latin states which still survived in the East dragged out for a while a feeble existence only through the jealousies and discords of the Moslem enemy; till with the fall of Acre (1291) the last fragment and wreck disappeared of structures so dearly and painfully reared, to which generation after generation had so lavishly contributed their prayers and toils, their tears and blood.

And yet this is not the whole story. The balance sheet of history does not offer all this loss upon one side, and zero in the way of gains upon the other. Of some gains which Christian Europe made I have spoken already. Let me before we leave this theme

T

speak also of some other. Assuredly if Europe found not what it sought, it found much which it had not sought. I will not dwell here on the new roads which commerce discovered for itself, the manifold arts and inventions which were brought back from the East; nor yet on the rise of a middle class through the impoverishing of the nobles in these costly expeditions. These were secondary, but at the same time important, benefits which grew out of the Crusades. But other benefits were more important still. Europe, emerging from the anarchies of the earlier Middle Ages, owed to the Crusades, and to the bringing together of the nations of the West in one common enterprise, its first vigorous consciousness of constituting one body, one Christendom. Inner divisions there might be many in it; but as against all external foes henceforth it was one. Nor may we forget that, if the tide of Mahomedan invasion was not rolled back, yet for two most critical centuries it had been effectually arrested. To the Byzantine Empire were given three centuries of existence more than it would have otherwise enjoyed —a respite not without significance for the whole Western world. This arrest of the onward progress of Mahomedan arms might as a political necessity have been proclaimed for ever, but would have been proclaimed in vain. No appeal merely to the reason, but only such an one as this, addressing itself first and chiefly to the feelings, the passions, the imagination, the devotion of Christendom, would have profited at all, or roused the nations to a common resistance. The struggle with Islâm has so long ceased to be a life-and-death struggle for the moral and spiritual possession of the world that we find it most hard to believe that such it ever should have been ; and yet, let us for a moment bethink ourselves of what, despite this check, was the tremendous pressure of Mahomedan power upon Western Christendom for centuries more, up to the Reformation and beyond it, and we shall own that the Crusades could very ill have been spared.

And then to them, to the high thoughts which they kindled in so many hearts, to the religious consecration which they gave to the bearing of arms, we are indebted for some of the fairest aspects of chivalry, as it lives on a potent and elevating tradition to the present day. Thus to them we owe the stately courtesies of gallant foes, able to understand and to respect one another, with much else which has lifted up modern warfare into something better than a mere mutual butchery, even into a school of honour in which some of the gentlest and noblest of men have been trained. *The Happy Warrior* of Wordsworth could never have been written, for such an ideal of the soldier could never have been conceived, except for them. What Europe gained by them we may best measure by considering what it evidently lost by their ceasing. It is not too much to say that with their ceasing the whole physiognomy of the Middle Ages changed, their romantic, poetic, ideal aspect in the main disappeared. To a thirteenth century, with all which it had of grandeur and beauty, a fourteenth with its meanness and poverty succeeded.

And lastly, we may well believe that in contact and conflict with the Unitarians of the East, the faithful discerned, as they never had discerned before, what treasures of wisdom and grace were laid up in the

Church's faith; in her faith who is Unitarian indeed, but this in a far higher sense,—confessing as she does a divine Unity, but in that Unity, a Father, a Son, and a Holy Ghost, the Spirit of both.

We may be content then to leave to Lord Chesterfield and to others like-minded to pass their judgment on the Crusades, namely that they were "the most immoral and wicked scheme that was ever contrived by knaves, and executed by madmen and fools against humanity;" and we may thank God that at all events history is now so written, and the past so judged, that we are not even tempted to such ignoble verdicts as these.

LECTURE XI.

THE PAPACY AT ITS HEIGHT.

FEW thoughtful students of Ecclesiastical history, or indeed of any history, can have failed from time to time to put this question to themselves, Was it by divine providence, or by divine permission, or, to put it somewhat lower still, by divine patience, that the dominion grew up in the Church which we call the Papacy? It is a question not easy to answer; being made the harder from the fact that the lines which divide the providence from the permission, and the permission from the patience, can often only with difficulty be drawn. An analogy has been sometimes suggested between the coming up and continuance of this power, and the coming up and continuance of the kingship in Israel; that earlier dealing of God with his people being adduced as helpful and supplying a key to the understanding of the later. In one aspect, it has been urged, that setting up of a kingdom in which God ceased to be the only King was the outcome of the people's sin; in another aspect it was made by Him to fit into his scheme for the moral training and discipline of his Church. It was the outcome of the people's sin; for where would have been the need or the want of a king, if only the people had held fast to the glorious truth that God was their King, and that therefore in all their dangers and necessities the shout of a

King was among them? And as sin this request of theirs was regarded by Him: "They have rejected Me, that I should not reign over them" (1 Sam. viii. 7). Nevertheless, having asked a King, He gave them the King that they asked, and wove this kingship into the grand providential scheme of his grace. Something corresponding to this, remotely corresponding one cannot help observing, has been traced in the later story. Where, it has been asked, would have been the need, or where the desire of a visible representative of Christ upon earth, if Christ Himself, the personal, ever and everywhere present, Lord of his Church, had not for most men receded very far into the distance? But this human world-centre, in place of the divine world-centre, having once been set up, God bore with it in his infinite patience, was content to use it, so far as it was capable of being used, for his Church's good; not indeed as the everlasting order there, but rather as that provisional arrangement which, allowed for a time, should be, and was, set aside so soon as a better order was prepared to occupy its room.

But leaving this for what it may be worth, and with no further attempt to look within the veil and to read what may have been passing there, let us a little consider the main circumstantial causes which, converging, wrought together for the giving to the Papacy during the Middle Ages, a pre-eminence and preponderance so vast and so enduring,—one which still haunts and sometimes disturbs the world with memories of what it has been, with forebodings of what it yet may be. It is of these secondary causes, and these only, that I propose to treat.

First then I will draw your attention to the fact that the Church of Rome was the sole Patriarchate of the West, towering so far above every other occidental Church that none of these so much as dreamt of disputing her rank and precedence. Not indeed that the Pope in the high days of his power much affected this title of Patriarch, shared by him with four others, as compared with that of Pope, which from the days of Gregory VII. was absolutely his own, and might not be given to any other, or taken by him.

But if no Western Bishop could venture to dispute the pre-eminence of the Bishop of Rome, it was not less certain that, in any rivalry or competition with him, the Eastern Patriarchs would discover that they had to do with a stronger than themselves. Before the day of their worst trouble came, they had forfeited much of their prestige by unworthy disputes among themselves; not to say that presently three among them, Antioch, Alexandria, and Jerusalem, if not wholly blotted out by the victorious advance of the Moslem arms, were reduced to merest ghosts of what they once had been, and henceforth subsisted only by Mahomedan sufferance. Constantinople alone remained;—but this New Rome fighting at an immense disadvantage the battle of "Who should be greatest?" with the Old. All the reasons which she could adduce in her favour were purely mundane:—as that she was the Residence, the seat of Empire, the city of the amplest wealth, wherein was treasured up the best that remained of the arts and learning of the world, with more of the same kind. All this could not profit much when it was urged for the other Rome that she was founded by one Apostle, even by him to whom Christ's great promise had been made, and watered by the blood of two.

Once more, the Bishop of Rome found an immense advantage in this, namely that his spiritual throne was not overshadowed by a secular and Imperial throne, set in immediate nearness to it. The Emperors of the East may have wished to treat him, and from time to time they may have actually treated, as they constantly treated the Patriarch of Constantinople ; but distance did much to restrain and limit their interference, and in the ninth century it ceased altogether. Neither did the peril which had thus been escaped in one shape come back in another. Charles the Great, genuine Teuton as he was, did not care to make Rome the centre and capital of his dominions ; while all the fantastic schemes of Otto III., including this, his darling project of all, were cut short by his premature death. German armies might from time to time cross the Alps, and might succeed, or might not succeed in imposing the Imperial will on a recalcitrant Pope ; but attempts of this kind, desultory and intermittent, were very different from a dwelling evermore under the baleful shadow of Eastern Cæsarism. The occupant of the Papal Chair enjoyed a freedom of self-development, an escape from the miserable and often disgraceful intrigues of the Palace, such as was altogether denied to his less fortunate rival in the East, who was now the partner of these intrigues, and now the victim, and not seldom both.

The superiority which in this matter the Old Rome possessed was long ago felt and understood. Thus Dante describes Constantine as founding the city in the East which is called by his name, that so " he might give the Shepherd room." So much indeed is very clearly expressed in the forged Gift of Constantine itself, and on that no doubt the assertion of Dante rests. I need hardly say that it is a mistake to ascribe this motive to Constantine; but the words express admirably well the result of the transfer of the seat of empire from the banks of the Tiber to the shores of the Bosporos. The Latin Shepherd, and mainly through this transfer, obtained the room which to his Greek rival was denied.

But there were other superiorities which belonged to Rome, and in which she left behind, not merely that remoter rival, but every other city in the world. It was much that from her, the ancient mistress of the world, this claim to an universal empire should proceed. We feel at once how impossible it would have been for a Bishop of Ravenna, or Milan, or Aquileia, to make good a similar pretension, even if it had entered into his heart to conceive it. But the world had been drilled and disciplined for so many centuries to the taking of its commands from the City on the banks of the Tiber, that there needed other centuries almost as many before it could unlearn this lesson of a submission which had well nigh become to it as a second nature. The new domination of Rome, "that ghost of the deceased Roman Empire sitting crowned upon the grave thereof," as Hobbes has so strikingly called it, with only such inevitable changes as the changed world-order demanded, seemed the natural, almost the necessary, continuation of the old. Rome might sink to the rank of a second-rate provincial town, all her significance might appear to have gone from her—so more than once it had—and yet in mysterious ways

U

this would all come back to her, as to one who could not abdicate her position though she would.

With all their unlikenesses, with this fundamental difference between them, that one asserted a dominion over the bodies, the other over the spirits of men, the resemblance was wonderful between the earlier and the later Rome, till it seemed impossible to exorcise the spirit of statesmanship, which still haunted and would not quit the City of the Seven Hills. Christian Rome did not disdain to learn from heathen; to walk in the lines which that had traced out; to wax great by the same methods. From Rome secular she learned how to mix herself with the affairs of her neighbours, to play the part of a mediator or umpire, to take the side of the weak against the strong:—breaking down, for example, the power of Metropolitans by her support of Bishops in their conflicts with them, the Bishops, when their natural leaders were gone, falling an easy prey in their turn. In this and in other like ways she knew how to obtain a footing for herself, which, once gotten, was not lost again, to advance pretensions which, if the time was not ripe for them, might remain dormant for a while, or, where this seemed safer, might be withdrawn altogether. If heathen Rome sent out her proconsuls, Christian Rome could boast that she too had her legates to carry her behests through the world, that for her the prophetic words of the Psalmist were fulfilled, "Instead of thy fathers thou shalt have children, whom thou mayest make princes in all lands."

It is impossible to say of Rome secular how early the thought arose in her heart, that let her only be true to herself and she should in due time be the queen of the world ; yet a dim prophetic instinct may have very early stirred within her that she was thus predestined to a mighty doom. As little can we tell how early in other hearts the idea of the Papacy, of an universal spiritual kingdom, with the Bishop of Rome as its priest-king, arose. Certainly it obscurely wrought, claims being put forth inconsistent with the liberties of other Churches, at a very early date,—not first during the Pontificate and in the heart of Leo the Great (440–461), however much by his abilities and his virtues he may have done to prepare the way for results which in his time were still many centuries in the distance.

Then too there was a claim on the part of the Roman Bishop that his should be regarded as the court of final appeal, and he the supreme judge and arbiter before whom all arduous or important causes might be brought,—this "might" at a later day being changed into a "must." It was a claim which dated from a time anterior to that of which we are treating, and found this much to support it, namely, that at the Council of Sardica (347) there was by the Council attributed to the Bishop of Rome a power of revision, so that, if any Bishop was dissatisfied with an ecclesiastical sentence, he might demand of the Roman Bishop to institute a new investigation : — I need hardly observe that the setting up of such a Court of Cassation was purely an ecclesiastical arrangement, and was never supposed at the time to rest on any divine right. At the same time it is easy to perceive how much there was to nurse that claim into ever greater strength, when once it had obtained partial acknowledgment and allowance. It was inevitable that in instances out of number the party worsted before some other tribunal would attempt to mend his position by a course which might better, but which could scarcely make it worse; for on one thing an appellant could securely count, namely that there would be a certain predisposition to regard him with favour. Neither, coming for help to Rome, was he likely to be under very strict self-restraint in the language which he used. He would declare that he came to that tribunal which was the last refuge of the oppressed; that his sole hope was in the justice of the Roman Pontiff, who, and who only, had authority to redress the wrong which he had endured. It was not in the nature of things that suppliants such as these should be repelled. We know that they were not, but were in every way encouraged; that no injury at Rome was resented more keenly than the putting by any secular power of hindrances in their way.

Then, exactly when they were needed the most, in the earlier half, that is, of the ninth century (about 845), the famous Decretals, falsely ascribed to St. Isidore of Seville, made their appearance. Decretals (*Litterœ Decretales*), let me say, were decisions by the Pope of questions brought before him, which thenceforth constituted part of the law of the Church. Such collections, with their falsifications of history more or less daring, there had been before, and have been since. But these supplied exactly what was then wanted. The fatal fault and flaw in the whole Roman pretension lay in its unhistoric character; in the fact that so much which was now confidently claimed had not been even heard of in the first three or four centuries. Some have tried in our own time to remedy this flaw by aid of the doctrine of development—with what success, each may judge for himself. This ingenious scheme had not then been devised, at any rate not elaborately wrought out. But here was all which was needed. Here were letters of the early Popes, beginning from Clement; decrees of early Councils, all of them bearing out and sustaining to the full the latest and largest pretensions of Rome. If only these were authentic, there was no authority, pre-eminence, jurisdiction challenged by a Pope of the ninth century, which had not been challenged and allowed in the first or the second. Now the Popes, I believe, may be acquitted of any share in the forgery, for forged these Decretals have long since on all sides been acknowledged to be; when too they appealed to these—Nicolas I. was the first who did so (858),—they did this in good faith, being deceived, as all the world was deceived. I am aware that it has been recently urged that these Decretals were not originally thrust upon the Church with any purpose of setting forward Papal pretensions; and ingenious explanations of their primary intention have not been wanting. But let these have what truth they may, the Decretals did not the less effectually do their work; and, most remarkable of all, the complete demolition of their authority failed to shake in the slightest the huge fabric which had been gradually built up on the assumption of their authentic character.

But professing to enumerate the chief causes which, working together, enabled the Church of Rome to leave so far behind her all the sister Churches of Christendom, it would be unworthy to pass over some of a different character from those on which hitherto

we have dwelt. Assuredly we should not leave out
of account, as having wrought to this end more than
any other of these causes, the succession of states-
men, and these of the very first order, who, often at
the most critical moments, and just when they were
needed the most, occupied the Papal throne. We
may form what judgment we will about them in other
respects, but none, I think, can deny this title to Leo
I., to Gregory the Great, to Nicolas I., to Gregory
VII., to Alexander III., to Innocent III. ; not to speak
of many others who, if they may not take rank with
these, yet did each contribute his stone to that wondrous edifice which thus grew from age to age, till it
seemed that its top was to reach even to heaven.

As little should we omit as an element of Roman
power that the Church of Rome had taken the side
which finally triumphed,—in other words, the right
side, in almost all the principal controversies which
had agitated the early Church. It did so notably in
that with the Arians ; so also,—with two memorable
exceptions on the part of Vigilius (540–555) and Honorius I. (625–638), but these sufficient to defeat the
claim to Infallibility,—in the long and confused struggle with Monophysites and Monothelites, which followed the Council of Chalcedon ; until it grew to a
popular conviction that the side which Rome took
was the side which would triumph in the end.

Nor were other moral forces wanting here. It
would have been little to the honour of Christendom,
if it had bowed ·the neck to a yoke which had not
been something better than simply a yoke of power.
Who can doubt that in ages of such savagery and
violence, times in which all laws of God and man

were so recklessly trampled under foot, it was much,
and it was felt to be much, that there should be one
man in the world, who could, and who sometimes did,
rebuke without fear or favour the strongest and
proudest of the wrongdoers, the men of the earth,
who were fain to persuade themselves that everything
was permitted to them?   Amid all the tyrannies and
oppressions with which the earth was full, how often a
deep cry and an agonizing question must have gone
up from the hearts of men, Is there anywhere in earth
or heaven a father, one with a father's heart? is there
anywhere a king the sceptre of whose kingdom is a
right sceptre? And here was one claiming to be all this,
a King ruling in righteousness, the immediate image
upon earth of the Universal Father in heaven.   And
righteous interferences in the world, such as in their
measure might justify these titles which he claimed,
were not wanting upon his part.   Thus, on more than
one memorable occasion the sanctity of the marriage
tie was upheld and vindicated by him against the wan-
ton caprice of princes and kings, who would fain have
made the laws of God to bow to the lusts of men.

It is true that this aspect of the Papacy as the re-
dressor of wrongs, the upholder of right, has in our
own day sometimes been pressed much farther than
the actual facts of history would warrant; and, if we
would at all arrive at a truthful balance sheet, then
over against the interferences on the side of right
must be set others on the side of wrong: the unrighteous wars which Rome fostered or directly
brought about; the subjects whom she released from
their allegiance, and invited to rebellion against their
lawful lords; the sons whom she encouraged to wage

unnatural war against their fathers ; the princes, as
for instance Charles of Anjou, whom by some huge
bribe she induced to seize what was not hers to give,
nor theirs to take ; the Papal mantle of allowance
thrown over hatefullest deeds of cruelty and wrong,
as for example the judicial murder of the Templars.
Setting these against those, the balance sheet of
history will present results very far different from
such as we are sometimes invited to accept.

The whole notion of Western Christendom in any
age as a complex of States, all recognizing the Roman Pontiff as the umpire of their quarrels, all inviting and all acquiescing in his decisions, and indeed
the whole dream of a golden age, brought by those
wicked Reformers to a violent close, is a fancy picture,
to which actual history presents no corresponding
reality.   There never was a golden age for the
Church, and there never will be, till Christ, her Lord,
shall come ; but every age will be full of scandals and
shames : none were more crowded with such than
those of which we are treating now. Doubtless in
every quarrel it was always well worth the while for
either of the contending parties to have Rome on its
side ; and one or other, and not seldom both, sought
to secure this advantage. Where they did not invite
interposition, and anything was to be gained by inter-
posing, she would push her way unsolicited into the
strife ; and claiming to act as umpire, would throw her
weight often into the right scale, not seldom into the
wrong.   That from time to time she effected something, which no other could have effected, for the
keeping or for the restoring of the peace of Christendom, for the substituting of a higher law between na-

tions than the brutal law of the strongest, no one who knows the facts and deals honestly with them will deny; but all this in a very imperfect, in a very human way, with faults of temper, of greed of gain, of lust of dominion, and other faults innumerable, which continually marred the very best which she did.

Let us consider a little the Papacy as Hildebrand left it. It gives some sort of measure of the rapidity with which new claims were pushed ever in advance of old, that the Decretals, so effective in their own time, were already felt in his to fall quite behind; very inadequately to express the rights and prerogatives of him who inherited the throne and the authority of St. Peter, so that new historical supports had need to be found to sustain the new pretensions; the same thing happening again when in turn Innocent III. had filled in much which Gregory had left only in outline. In the finding of these historical supports there was indeed no sort of difficulty. What was wanting was always forthcoming, or if not forthcoming, there were always the Canonists ready with new law, or with new interpretations of old, whereby anything and everything could be justified. It is true that in one sense the Papacy of Hildebrand was hardly capable of any further development. It was scarcely possible to advance loftier claims than he had advanced. But much had yet to be made good; much had been sketched by him, but waited to be filled in by some other hand; much existed in theory, but had not yet been embodied in practice. Herein lies the difference between his position and that of Innocent III. But so far as claims could go, all was already his own. The Pope who at first had been content as Vicar of

St. Peter to be recognized as the foremost in rank and dignity among the Bishops of the Church, demanded now as Vicar of Christ to be acknowledged as in some sort its only Bishop ; making no scruple to name himself Universal Bishop, a title which Gregory the Great had repudiated as inconsistent with the rights of the other members of the Episcopate. Not to the collective Episcopate, as was now declared, but to him alone had the government of the Church, with the authority to bind and loose, been confided ; for to Peter alone had it been said, "Feed my sheep," "Feed my lambs." All other Episcopal authority was but an emanation of his. He might invite others to a participation of the toil, but the plenitude of the power remained still with himself.

That the Pope only could canonize—this, which was claimed first by Alexander III. as his exclusive right, and is sometimes charged against him as a usurpation —as matters stood, was reasonable enough. If there was to be such a spiritual peerage, and the idea is a very grand one, the creation of it could scarcely be in any other hands save his. But the Pope alone could call Councils ; and even a General Council, when called, could do no more than advise. He could dispense with every law of the Church which was not divine. Somewhat later there were not wanting those who in their frantic sycophancy affirmed that his word, who was as a second God upon earth (*quasi alter Deus*), could make right out of wrong, justice out of injustice ; that he could dispense with every law ; that any concordats or other agreements into which he was pleased to enter were binding on the other party, but were not binding upon him.

It was only at a later day that, as against this theory of the Pope as the sole depositary of spiritual power, another theory was advanced, whereof the famous Parisian Doctors, of whom by and bye, were the main upholders. According to this, so far from one man absorbing all Church authority in himself, and merely dividing off to others such portions of this as he pleased, the parochial Clergy were the lineal successors of the Seventy, the Bishops of the Apostles, and the Pope of St. Peter, Prince of the Apostles; all those others having as direct a commission from Christ as he had, and having indeed received a power, as it was pointedly described, *under* the Pope (*sub Papâ*), but by no means *from* the Pope (*a Papâ*). I shall have to tell you before long what little permanent effect these Doctors were able to give to this or any other theory of theirs.

It is generally allowed that the medieval Papacy attained its highest pitch of splendour in the time and in the person of Innocent III.; that he approached nearer to the realizing of that idea after which it was striving than any who went before him, than any who followed after. True to my scheme of bringing a few of the prominent persons in Church history before you, rather than seeking to fill the scene with many who are not prominent, and who only serve to obscure those that are, I will dwell a little upon him and his Pontificate; which done, I shall bring this Lecture to a close.

Cardinal Lothair, of a noble Roman family, was only thirty-seven when, in view of the struggle with the Hohenstaufen Emperors, which was only half fought out and sooner or later must revive again, he was called by the unanimous voice of the Conclave to the post of highest dignity and authority in the Church (1198). Let me here observe how important a step it had been when the election of a Pope was taken out of the hands of the Roman Clergy, magistrates, and people, in whom at one time it had resided, and was transferred to the College of Cardinals. This significant change was effected in 1059 by Nicolas II., acting under the influence of Hildebrand, Pope already in all but name. It is very easy to see how much in unity of aim the Papacy must have gained, delivered as it thus was from gusts of popular passion and caprice, and able to continue and carry through a policy which had once been determined; and, if it incurred new and untried dangers through this close election, how many old dangers, of which it had abundant experience, it thus left behind it. On the present occasion there was hereby brought to the front the ablest men whom the Church possessed.

There is much to provoke a comparison between him and Hildebrand, who alone among all the Popes is comparable with him,—points of likeness as of difference. Innocent was quite as strongly the hierarch as Gregory had been; he advanced claims quite as extravagant. He could say, "The Lord bequeathed to Peter not merely the government of the Universal Church, but the whole secular estate," and the other could not have said more. And on the faith of this he acted. Thus there was hardly a monarch in Europe whom he did not make in one way or another to feel his hand, "binding their kings with chains and their nobles with links of iron;" measuring himself not with petty kings alone, of Portugal, of Leon, or of

Aragon, but with the mightiest potentates on earth. Philip Augustus of France after a fierce resistance was by him compelled to take back the wife whom on some frivolous pretext he had put away; and we are all more or less familiar with the shameful story of our own King John, how he was brought to acknowledge himself "the Pope's man," resigning to him his crown and sceptre, and receiving these back from him to hold, he and his successors, as the Pope's vassals henceforward (1207–1213). Of Innocent's share in the struggle with the Hohenstaufen Emperors I speak elsewhere.

But in him the hierarch did not swallow up the Chief Pastor. Innocent was diligent in preaching. "The just shall live by faith" was the text of his sermon at his own consecration. It may be monkish piety which his ascetic writings breathe, but piety it is. He had, I am persuaded, the removal of the monstrous scandals in the Church which drove so many into wildest opposition to her, quite as much at heart as any among these; although his position made it many times more difficult for him than for others to discern the true character of the evils which demanded a remedy. His letters do not deal merely with questions affecting the honour, glory, and worldly prosperity of the Church, but not seldom with the redressing the wrongs of the humblest; and attest that, if he regarded himself as the Judge of all the earth, he accepted also the toil and responsibilities implied in this name, the terribleness as well as the grandeur of such a pre-eminence.

Pope Innocent's was in outward aspects a splendid Pontificate. No antipope, challenging his right to the

tiara, entangled him in miserable disputes where success was almost as ignominious as defeat.   If once at
the beginning of his reign he found it convenient to
withdraw from Rome, yet no popular tumult chased
him, as it chased so many before and after, from an
insurgent city.   Magnificent above all was the close
of that Pontificate, when at the Fourth Lateran Council
(1215), the so-called Twelfth Œcumenic, the representatives of two Emperors, all the Eastern Patriarchs
in person or by proxy (for it was the time of the brief
Latin kingdom), seventy Primates or Metropolitans,
more than four hundred Bishops, and eight hundred
other Prelates, all acknowledging him as their head,
took counsel with him for the interests of Christendom,
or, to speak more accurately, received the law from
his lips.

Some dim presentiment that this gorgeous pageant
was about soon to dissolve, that the end was very near,
may have moved him to appropriate, in his opening
address to the Council, words of an infinite solemnity,
and such as it required not a little boldness even for
him to make his own : "With desire I have desired to
eat this Passover with you before I suffer" (Luke xxii.
16).   And the end *was* near, even at the door.   A
few months had not elapsed, and all the mighty pro-
jects, the new Crusade, a reformation in the morals
alike of the Clergy and of the laity, the extirpation of
heresy, must either fall to the ground, or be accomplished by other hands than his.   Innocent died in his
fifty-fifth year (1216), but not before he had reaped to
the full that harvest of greatness which Nicolas I.,
Gregory VII., Alexander III., with many more, had so
patiently and so boldly sown.

And yet, let me say in parting from him, that, if time would permit, it might be well worth while, over against all which he accomplished, to set all which he failed to accomplish; or which it would have been much better if he had failed to accomplish; or which, so soon as ever he was withdrawn, reverted at once to its former tracks: even as failure in carrying out an idea such as his was inevitable; seeing that to realize this nothing less than omnipotence, and this wielded by omniscience, was required. In the absence of these it remains "the grandest and most magnificent failure in human history."

LECTURE XII.

THE POPES AND THE HOHENSTAUFEN.

THE antagonism between the spiritual and the secular head of Western Christendom, as I have already more than once observed, went farther to shape medieval history, and to give it its peculiar character, than any of the other forces which were then working, potent as, no doubt, were some of these. The antagonism itself was inevitable, and not less inevitable that it should force itself to the front, and to refuse to be remitted to the sphere of abstract opinions about which men might consent to differ. "These two powers, the Empire and the Papacy, had grown up with indefinite and necessarily conflicting relations; each at once above and beneath the other; each sovereign and subject, with no distinct limits of sovereignty or subjection; each acknowledging the supremacy of the other, but each reducing that supremacy to a name or less than a name. The authority of each depended on loose and flexible tradition, on variable and contradictory precedents, on titles of uncertain signification, Head of the Church, Vicar of Christ; Patrician, King of Italy, Emperor. The Emperor boasted himself successor to the whole autocracy of the Cæsars, to Augustus, Constantine, Charlemagne; the Pope to that of St. Peter, or of Christ Himself." (Milman).

The contention on the part of the spiritual power, as

it uttered itself by the Pope, was as follows: "Men's souls are more precious than their bodies. The heavenly life is much more than the earthly. The training for that heavenly life has been committed to my charge, and I can suffer no interference with it. And first and chiefly the ministers of this higher kingdom must hold of me, must own no allegiance which may compete or interfere with this prior allegiance to me. Touch not my anointed, and do my prophets no harm. If they need correction, let them be remitted to me for this." We know what the answer was. Our Henry II. uttered it with all clearness; not without many faults in the manner of his utterance, but with a true sense that there must be one law in the realm, and that to this all must be submitted. "These," he replied, "whom you claim to belong only to you, belong also to a mundane order of things of which I am chief minister, and if they violate that order they shall suffer for it as any other. Kings are of God as well as Popes ; and criminous clerks shall receive at our hands the due reward of their deeds no less than criminous laymen." Impossible as it is to deny the justice of this answer, or to take our stand where Becket, as representing the Church's claim, took his, there was in that twelfth century far more to be urged in its behalf than at first sight might appear. License on the part of the Clergy to do evil without being duly punished for it, this assuredly was not the object for which our great Archbishop contended and died. The untenable nature of his position and of the arguments by which he defended it we can now see clearly enough; but it was very far from being then so clear.

If I do not enter at full into this struggle, this will

W

not be as underrating its significance; but it is in truth such a thrice-told tale, has in these last times been told so often and by such masters in the art of narration, that I shrink from going over the ground again. You upon your parts can scarcely have escaped some acquaintance with it; while I for mine shall gladly devote the time thus gained to the setting forth some other less familiar aspects of that same struggle, as it wrought itself out upon a larger stage.

Your attention has been already called to the first grand collision which grew out of the irreconcilable pretensions of the kingdom and the priesthood, the civil and the spiritual power. You have heard how the quarrel, provoked by Gregory VII., not without a measure of right upon his side, seemed to have found its settlement in the Concordat of Worms. But the compromise which goes by this name was a truce and no more; the prologue, or perhaps more properly, the first act of a portentous drama, which was not nearly played out. Two other acts were to follow; the second closing with the Treaty of Constance (1183), the third with the final extinction of the House of Hohenstaufen (1268). It is quite true that this struggle, in its second act and its third, was not so predominantly one for spiritual objects as that of the Investitures had been. There were fair kingdoms of this world which would prove the prize of the victor, with other earthly things precious, whereon Pope and Emperor had alike set their heart. It will be my aim to put before you to-day some of the leading features of the conflict, the several aids and alliances with which the combatants entered upon it, the alternations of victory and defeat, and then the close, and its results.

This conflict, let me say at the outset, had features of its own, which distinguished it alike from conflicts that went before and from others that came after. It was a struggle not for victory upon some one point, but upon all; such as should for ever determine who should reign and who should serve; and, with all the fair words which from time to time passed between the combatants during the treacherous pauses of the battle, there was no self-deception upon either side as to its real meaning,—that it could only end with the complete subjugation of the one or of the other. It has been called, and with a certain justice, the struggle of a hundred years. But you must not be misled by these words as though they implied open hostility, the raging of a war without disguise, for all this time. There was nothing of the kind; but every possible variety of relation, the actual clash of arms being rather the exception. Thus there were times, although these were brief, when, having some identical objects and interests to promote, Emperor and Pope were in real alliance; when they hunted heretics in couples, and in other ways played into each other's hands. Thus the first Frederick delivered Arnold of Brescia, a most dangerous innovator, as men esteemed, and that alike in Church and in State, to the will of the Pope (1155); while the second Frederick, probably believing nothing himself, sent heretics and unbelievers by scores to the stake. There were times of simulated friendship, each watching and waiting his opportunity to do the other a mischief, each in secret correspondence with the other's mortal foes. And lastly there were times when the mask was dropped, and it was war to the outrance, each of the contending powers rallying all the forces and means of annoyance which it had at command, and openly employing these for the inflicting of deadly harm on the other.

There is another mistake which you must not fall into; for it would be a mistake to suppose of these two powers, locked as they so often were in a mortal embrace of hate, that either sought the entire destruction of the other. What each sought was the other's submission; that the grand question running through all medieval history, "Which should be greatest?" should be decided in its own favour. Neither desired, nor indeed could have so much as conceived, the total disappearance of the other; the world-king and the world-priest belonging alike to the eternal order of God's moral universe. What, moreover, would have been the value of a Pope's triumph, if there had been no Emperor whom he might keep starving in the cold at his gate for days, or on whose neck he might literally or figuratively plant his foot? What, on the other hand, would an Emperor's complete success have been worth, unless there had been still a Pope whom, as a kind of chief chaplain, he might order about at his will like any other official of his Court? It was in the drawing of the boundary line which separated the several jurisdictions, and in the attempt so to draw it that all substantial power should remain on one side, that the never-dying source of contention lay.

It was mainly, but not exclusively, on Italian soil that the long struggle which came to a head in the time of the Hohenstaufen monarchs was fought out; —Italy, dowered as she was with her fatal gift of beauty, being doomed to suffer intolerable outrages and wrongs from the rude German hosts which trampled on her as their victim and their prey. But what she suffered in one shape she could inflict in another. Intrigues first set on foot at Rome were only too successful in stimulating the anarchy of Germany. The Imperial dignity, tossed from one princely House to another, from Frankish to Saxon, to Suabian, to Bavarian, resisted all attempts to compel it for any length of time to continue in one stay. It was indeed a leading object in the policy of the Roman Court, and one of which it never lost sight, to hinder the Empire from becoming hereditary in any single House; and thus to avert the knitting of the German races into a single nation, which might so easily have followed if once a ruling family could have been founded. On more occasions than one this seemed likely; but in the end by one fatality or another all hopes that so it might prove invariably came to nothing. The task of perpetuating the weakness by maintaining and multiplying the divisions of Germany, was only too easy. Each new election might safely be trusted to leave behind it many disappointed ambitions, one or more defeated competitors prepared to head an opposition, sometimes an open revolt against successful rivals, so that an anti-Cæsar was never very difficult to find.

By the very necessities of her position, Rome was in a manner driven to this activity of intrigue against the peace and prosperity, above all, against the unity of Germany. But apart from this, it was not a small misfortune that so many among the noblest of the German monarchs, instead of addressing themselves to the reducing to some sort of order the anarchy of their own realm, should again and again be drawn aside to the pursuit beyond the Alps of objects

shadowy, remote, unattainable, or having no real
worth even if for the moment attained; that in this
same pursuit the flower of German youth, from generation to generation, should whiten the battle-fields of
Italy with their bones, or perish by deadlier though invisible foes, by the fever and the malaria, which then
as now brooding over the land, girdled Rome above
all as with a very girdle of death.

But what the Popes of the twelfth and thirteenth
centuries dreaded perhaps even more than German
unity, was the meeting of the Imperial Crown and
that of the Two Sicilies on a single head. With the
Norman adventurers who had planted their foot in
South Italy, and little by little had founded principalities, and in the end a kingdom there, there had been
hostile collisions at the first; but the Pope and the
Normans perceived after a while that they needed
and could effectually help one another, so that these
Norman settlements, instead of a menace to the Papacy, had become rather a support and a defence.
But in the event of the meeting of the Crowns on one
head, the case would be very different. Cooped and
confined,—with an enemy, it might be, on either side,
—set as between two fires, what room would there be
for the Pope to breathe ? Or should matters come to
the worst, what avenue of escape from his foes would
be open to him ? This union of the two crowns upon
one head, dreaded so much, actually came to pass
during the course of this struggle, when Henry, son of
Frederick Barbarossa married Constantia, the Norman
inheritress of those fair southern lands. But it did not
draw after it that accession of strength to the Empire
which its friends had hoped, and its enemies feared.

Let me briefly sketch the course which the actual conflict took. I observed in a former Lecture that the Empire was very inadequately represented in the first grand clash of arms between the two powers which divided the world,—Henry IV. being ill to match with Gregory VII. The same could not be now affirmed. The battle was a battle of giants, but of giants not all ranged on one side. How grand, and at times how pathetic, are the actors who now sweep across the historic stage ; for we are now in the heart of the Middle Ages, and they are yielding their might-iest and most wondrous births. On the one side there are the two Fredericks. And first Frederick Barbarossa, or Red Beard, as the Italians with their fondness for nicknames derived from personal pecu-liarities, called him ; greatest Emperor since Charles, unless indeed Otto I. should dispute the palm of greatness with him ; great-grandson of Henry IV., in-heritor therefore of an unfinished feud ; one of the noblest figures of medieval Europe ; as profoundly convinced that he wore the Imperial Crown by the grace of God, that he was God's second Vicar upon earth, as ever Pope was convinced that he sat by immediate delegation from Christ in the Chair of St. Peter. Frederick, I believe, always meant to be just; but his justice not seldom hardened into severity,—that we call it by no harsher name,—when he had to do with those whom he counted rebels and revolters from the authority by God committed to him. Gen-erous he was, and word-keeping; of unstained private life ; able, when the battle was won, and, harder still, when the battle was lost, to forget and to forgive ; so that one does not praise him overmuch who has recently styled him "the noblest type of medieval chivalry in many of its shadows, in all its lights." "The Xerxes of the Middle Ages" Sismondi has called him, but wholly misapprehending the man and his work. It is not merely that there was nothing of the effeminate Sultan in him, who did not sit upon a throne and look on while others were fighting for him, but who was ever to be found himself in the "high places of the field." Plainly, however, it is another charge which this comparison is intended to convey,—namely, that as Xerxes was the lawless invader of Greece, so Frederick of Italy. He came thither, no doubt, in arms, but as claimant of strictly legal rights. That as King of Italy and wearer of the iron crown, he possessed some rights, even those who opposed him the most admitted, only contesting the extent and character of those rights. It might have been better if he had recognized that, in the altered conditions of the world, those rights were growing into wrongs, and had abstained from urging them; but it is somewhat too much, when this, namely that he did not thus renounce them, is laid against him as a crime.

The great commercial and manufacturing cities of Lombardy, rapidly growing into sovereign and independent commonwealths, could ill brook the resuscitation of claims which seemed to them to belong to a dead past. These cities, or the richer, stronger, more populous among them,—Milan above all,—were allies upon whom the Pope, if it came to the worst, could securely rely; even as he found it well worth his while to appear as the champion of their liberties, to play the part of chief demagogue of Italy. Inner bonds might be few between him and them, but so far as those who have the same enemies are allies and friends, they were such; and it is hardly too much to say that if the Papacy was able to bring this tremendous struggle to a victorious close, it owed this triumph quite as much to the Lombard League as to its own spiritual weapons, excommunication and interdict; upon which, indeed, it was very far from exclusively relying.

When Frederick crossed the Alps to revive claims which, through the internal troubles of Germany, had been long in abeyance, it might have seemed at first as though all which he demanded would be yielded to him, without his needing to have recourse to arms. The Lombard cities, indeed, stood sullenly aloof, but did not at once make up their minds to resistance. Pope Adrian IV.,—he was the only Englishman who ever wore the tiara,—accepted with the best grace he could a visit which he was unable to avert, and set the golden crown of Empire on Frederick's head. At the same time it is curious to note the vein of suspicion which from the first ran through the intercourse of these two, their inability to refrain from petty slights and irritations of each other. Thus the Emperor, according to a custom as old, some averred, as Constantine, did upon certain great occasions lead the palfrey of the Pope, and hold his stirrup when he alighted. The complaints were loud upon Adrian's part that this mark of respect was turned into an insult, Frederick having held the left stirrup when he should have held the right; to which the other thought it enough to reply that the Hohenstaufens had not much experience in the duties of a groom, and that thus the mistake was not very wonderful. Other

X

complaints too there were, grounded in the main on small breaches of etiquette, although not without their significance. Nor was the Emperor without his counter plaints; but on these I cannot enter.

Resistance began in the Lombard cities. They could not accommodate themselves to the new order of things. Pope Adrian, whose griefs were not all so fantastic as one which I have just related, was drawn before long, by the inevitable drift of things, to the taking part with his natural allies; and thus the long woe began. In this first shock of arms, a shock which lasted for some two and twenty years (1154–1176), victory, which at first inclined to the banners of the Emperor, was not always true to these. Seven German armies had crossed the Alps at his bidding; Milan he had twice taken, once razed to the ground, but only to see it rise from its ashes more powerful than ever; while his son's son was to learn what a harvest of undying hate he had thus sown in Italian hearts. Defeated at Legnano (1176), one of the battles which are the turning points of history, he accepted the inevitable, renounced by the treaty of Constance (1183) all save a few shadowy and well-nigh nominal rights over the Lombard cities; and, yet bitterer humiliation, recognized Alexander III., against whom he had raised up three antipopes in succession, as the true spiritual chief of Christendom. With all this Frederick was formidable still, and had by no means renounced his hope of bringing back the relations of Pope and Emperor to what they had been in the time of Charles and the Ottos. But his part was played. The tidings of the actual fall of Jerusalem (1187) suspended for a little the quarrels of the West. The

grand old warrior King girded himself for his latest
task, and died as he would have wished to die, leading a crusading host to the rescue of the Sepulchre
where his Lord had lain (1189).

His son and successor Henry VI. inherited none of
his virtues, but he did inherit his energy of purpose,
his far-reaching designs; and these never seemed
nearer their accomplishment than now. Alexander
III.,—a great pontiff, though he may not quite take
rank with the greatest, and we see him at his weakest
in his relations to Thomas of Canterbury,—was no
more. Against Henry, in the full vigour of his youth,
was arrayed a feeble nonagenarian, Cælestin III. But
deaths altogether unexpected more than once during
the course of this struggle brought safety to the Papacy; and, when matters seemed at the worst, changed
in an instant the whole aspect of affairs. So was it
now; Henry, dying in his thirty-second year, left behind him a son of two years old (1197). Pope Cælestin, swiftly following him to the grave, was succeeded
by Pope Innocent III. Where there was strength before, there was weakness now; and where weakness,
there was strength.

Henry's infant son had been already elected King
of the Romans, but this election was now set aside.
And yet, strange to say, it was with Innocent's active
good-will and favour that the young Frederick, some
fifteen years later, being then only seventeen years
old, aspired to the Imperial throne, and took it, so to
speak, by storm. The Pope, confident in his strength,
and nothing doubting that he could mould to his will
the stripling who had grown up as his ward, little
guessed that this second Frederick should prove a

more dangerous foe than ever the first had been. It was he whom his wondering contemporaries hailed as the *Stupor Mundi*, the " Astonishment of the World." This title, or one very closely resembling it, had been already given to Otto III. ; but he, " inheritor of un- fulfilled renown," died too soon to show how far he had deserved it. Poet and scholar, legislator and war- rior, busy with manifold speculations about manifold things, Frederick was in many ways far in advance of his age, which may have resented this superiority of his, and in its judgments of him may possibly have wronged him ; he, if this was so, offering, as it must be owned, not a little provocation for any injustice that it did him.

By his mother's side Italian blood was in his veins ; and all his sympathies were Italian. Not in rugged Germany but on the sunny shores of the Mediterra- nean, most of all at Palermo, he loved to keep his Court, so brilliant, dissolute, and refined. Cruel he was, as voluptuaries so often are, though not as his father had been ; shocking too the public opinion of Christendom by the familiar terms on which he lived with his Saracen subjects,—by the mocking words, the shafts of scorn, which, as men reported, were launched by him against holiest mysteries of our faith. Dante, Ghibelline as he was, must have given credit to these reports; for he places Frederick, and him alone among the Emperors, in hell, and among the heresiarchs there.

Fair words and friendly offices were exchanged at first between Innocent and Frederick ; but it was not long before the inborn antagonism between Pope and Hohenstaufen revealed itself once more ; and the open conflict between them, inevitable from the first, was

close at hand, when the death of Innocent deferred its
outbreak for a while.   Honorius III. (1216–1227), a
man of peace, would have fain patched up the quarrel,
but this could not be.   Not so Gregory IX., who on
the first provocation, flinging the scabbard aside, addressed himself to the conflict with an energy which
seventy-seven years, for so many he numbered at his
election, could not abate ; no, nor yet the ninety and
more which he numbered when he bequeathed the
conflict, still undecided, to his successor.   Frederick in
an unlucky hour had taken upon him the Crusader's
vow, which yet he showed no readiness to fulfil, aware
probably of the advantage which would be made of his
absence from his dominions.   It was a terrible hold
which he had given to his foes, and they did not fail to
make the most of it.   Excommunicated again and
again, for not going to Palestine according to his engagement, for going without the Papal benediction, for
returning without the Papal leave ; every place which
he profaned with his presence stricken with an Interdict ; heaven and earth fighting against him,—for so in
that age it must have seemed to most, sometimes perhaps to himself,—there yet were no signs of yielding
in him.

One deceitful truce calling itself a peace might follow upon another ; negotiations might go forward even
in the midst of arms ; but the distrust on both sides
was too profound, the enmity too strong, for these
ever to lead to anything.   New griefs on either side
were urged ; and then presently it thundered and
lightened from the ecclesiastical heaven ; new excom-
munications against Frederick being piled upon the
old, as though it had been impossible to curse him

enough. But indeed there was no weapon on either side which was not snatched at, if only it could work effectual harm to the other. Pope Gregory in a circular to the prelates and potentates of Europe solemnly denounced Frederick as the beast rising out of the sea, and full of the names of blasphemy. But the Apocalypse was not to be interpreted all on one side; and the Pope was proclaimed in a counter-manifesto of the Emperor's as the great Red Dragon, deceiving the whole world; the second Balaam, speaking lies for reward; the personal Antichrist; the Angel from the bottomless pit. To such a white heat of fiercest mutual hate had matters between these two arrived, who according to the original idea of the kingdom and the priesthood should have been a mutual strength and support the one to the other.

So all-absorbing was the animosity between them that the frightful inroad of the Mongol hordes, whose triumph would have been fatal alike to both, could do nothing to allay or even to suspend it. These, having wasted the better part of Asia, had just at this moment burst upon Eastern Europe (1240), inflicting upon it all of worst which the Hungarians had inflicted three centuries before; but neither Pope nor Cæsar could lend the slightest help to the noble leader who with his scanty host stood in the breach and died there; and who, vanquished though he seemed, did yet at Liegnitz set bounds to the further advance of this hideous chivalry;—Tartars indeed, as men in the anguish of their fear proclaimed, for they were the very brood of Tartarus or hell.

Whether, if Frederick had lived, he would not have found the Papacy and the Lombard League and the

Mendicant Friars, which last never served the Papacy better or more zealously than now, too strong for him ; whether, notwithstanding many partial successes, the battle which raged in every corner of Italy and in much of Germany was not going against him, may very fairly be a question ; but with his untimely death (1250),—for he had but reached his fifty-sixth year,— the Imperial or Ghibelline cause was lost. The struggle, it is true, did not end for years to come ; it could not indeed end so long as a Hohenstaufen was in life; but the issues of it were virtually determined. I cannot follow it further ; only I must spare a few words for the epilogue to this long tragedy, itself in some sort more tragic than all which had gone before.

Certainly Rome could not boast that she scorned to war with the dead. She pursued with inextinguishable hatred all of that detested Suabian House. Frederick left several children, legitimate and illegitimate, behind him. But a weird was upon him and his race. An evil destiny pursues them ; they perish one by one, and by strange dooms ;—until, last male scion of that Imperial family, comes

> " wandering by
> A shadow like an angel, with bright hair
> Dabbled in blood."

It is the young and beautiful Conradin, grandson of Frederick, least guilty—humanly speaking, the one unguilty of a guilty race,—who yet, as so often happens, gathers up in himself all the curse and the punishment which was due to all, and, paying the things which he never took, attests how impossible it is to dissociate the members of a family from each other. He was safe in Germany ; but would fain win back the kingdom of the Sicilies, which by right of inheritance he claims as his own. Defeated in this attempt by Charles of Anjou, whom in a disastrous hour for Italy the Pope had invited to take that kingdom in possession, Conradin stoops his neck to the headsman's axe at Naples (1268).

And now the end has come : the Hohenstaufens have perished from the face of the earth ; and the Papacy issues forth visibly triumphant from this long and terrible struggle—not unscarred, yet never greater, or indeed never so great. It has encountered the one power which could pretend to dispute the world with it, and has overcome it. "With Frederick fell the Empire. From the ruin which overwhelmed the greatest of its Houses it emerged, living indeed and destined to a long life; but so shattered, crippled, and degraded that it could never more be to Europe or to Germany what it once had been " (Bryce). What is known as the Long Interregnum succeeded,—three and twenty years of frightful anarchy ; until Rodolph of Hapsburg, at length chosen Emperor (1273), brought some sort of order into Germany again. But now the armed pilgrimage to Rome for the obtaining a coronation at the Papal hands fell so far out of use that more than sixty years elapsed before Henry of Luxembourg attempted to renew it ; and his brief career, so big with unfulfilled promise, being ended (1313), a new interregnum left the Italians ample leisure to dissolve whatever ties still attached them to Germany. Meanwhile the French monarchs, conscious of the growing power of France where all was knitting together into a compact military monarchy, while in Germany all was loosening and dissolving,

took up the policy of opposition to Papal pretensions which had dropped from German hands. The
grander features of the conflict do not produce themselves again ; but when we come to the time of Boniface VIII. there will be occasion to speak of the immense consequences which from this resulted. It will
then perhaps be seen how "the art, the policy, the
tyranny of France from this period inflicted deeper
wounds upon the dignity and authority of the Papal
See than the haughty hostility of the Hohenstaufens."

Y

LECTURE XIII.

THE EUCHARISTIC CONTROVERSIES OF THE MIDDLE AGES.

IT was very graciously ordered by Him who orders all things for the good of his Church, that the leading outlines of its teaching should, in almost all main particulars, have been traced and authoritatively fixed before that general break-up overtook the Western world, of which the invasion by the Northern tribes was the immediate cause. It thus came to pass that the faithful, notwithstanding the darkness and ignorance of the ages which followed, found themselves in conscious possession of precious results which, with the scantier helps at their own command, they could never for themselves have attained. Things which would have been too high for them had not been too high for the well-trained and accomplished theologians of the fourth and fifth centuries; and upon their labours the Church of the next centuries thankfully entered. Nor can there be any more signal evidence of the completeness with which the Church of the Fathers had done, and not for itself only, the work of defining the truth which it held, had drawn accurate lines of demarcation for the separating of this truth from the errors upon either side which it denied, than this, namely the few struggles involving questions of doctrine which agitate the Middle Ages. Whatever the early Church had settled, it was very rarely that any endeavour was made, or any desire shown, to disturb the settlement. There was a feeble effort at the close of the eighth century (794), on the part of some in Spain to revive, though with a difference, the Nestorian heresy; but, this excepted, there was no attempt, and perhaps no intentional one here, to go back from the decisions of the Four Great Councils as touching those cardinal truths of the Christian faith on which they had definitively pronounced. Full of speculative activity as the men of those ages were, the questions which stirred them belonged to their own times, and were not those of an earlier period brought anew into debate. Such were looked at as having received their final solution.

But strangely, and, as it proved, most unfortunately, there had been one omission. The doctrine of the manner of Christ's Presence in the Holy Eucharist, of the relation in which the consecrated elements and the Body and Blood of Christ stand to one another, had never come into serious debate during those times, and thus had never been the subject of authoritative definition. Men had been content with the blessing, and had not cared to define it. The leading Doctors of the Church, it is true, had almost all uttered themselves upon it, but this by the way: not under the special responsibilities which are so solemnly felt, when some actually existing error needs to be condemned; nor with that careful weighing of every word which can hardly fail to find place, when some precious but imperilled truth demands to be affirmed, and the frontier lines laid down which shall divide the truth from the error that would fain usurp its room or encroach

on its domain.   That Christ was really present in the
Sacrament, that in that sacred feast He fed the faithful
with the precious food of his own most blessed Body
and Blood, in this all the Fathers of the early Church
were agreed.   But, starting from this and always remaining true to this, they expressed themselves further
with a grand and careless boldness: as those upon
whom no heresy, watching to make its gain of any
random word, had imposed necessities of caution; as
those, too, who felt that the most rapturous words
would not be too rapturous for a worthy magnifying
of that central mystery of the faith, and of the gift in
it made ours.

But matters could not always continue in this state.
It was inevitable that sooner or later the Church would
have to pronounce what it meant by this Presence,
which evidently might mean so much or so little.
When men once began to give an account to themselves of this, how near, on one side, lay the peril of
refining that Presence away into mere words which,
seeming to mean something, yet in fact meant nothing,
or assuredly nothing with any right to so august a
name.   How near, on the other side, was the danger
of a degeneration into a coarse materialism, the supersensual truth which that word embodied being drawn
down from its spiritual heights, adapted to the meanest
capacity and the least spiritual mind, with all the true
mystery gone from it.   How certain it was that sooner
or later extravagances on this side or on that, if not on
both, would need to be repressed and condemned.
And so it proved.

Paschasius Radbert (b. 786, d. 865 ; but both these
dates are doubtful), a learned monk, well skilled in all

the theological lore of his age, put forth his world-famous treatise *On the Sacrament of the Body and Blood of Christ,* with which the conflict may be said to have begun, in 831. It was the first regular and comprehensive treatise on the Holy Eucharist which had ever appeared, at all events the first of which any notice has reached us. Thirteen years later, and having in the meantime recast the book in a more popular form, he published it again. Coming as it did now from one who occupied a foremost position in the Church of France—he was Abbot of New Corbey—it attracted the attention which at first had been denied it. There is nothing wonderful in this. It fell in with many tendencies of the age, with the direction of popular thought and feeling which was more and more craving after an outward and visible embodiment of the inward and spiritual. It gave form and consistency to that which was already the floating belief of multitudes, who were delighted to find elaborated all round, and with a certain theological justification, that which hitherto they had obscurely and more or less unconsciously held. What Paschasius taught and claimed to be the Church's teaching was this, namely that in the Holy Eucharist, by virtue of the priestly consecration and the operation of the Holy Ghost which goes along with this, the substance of bread and wine is changed into the substance of the Body and Blood of Christ; yet so that the accidents, as they were called—in other words, the form, colour, and taste of the elements—still, for the better exercise of faith, remain. The word " transubstantiation " does not appear in the book, indeed does not appear till a much later date ; but all which the word implies is here. The outspokenness of the book was a real power. Many had taught before that Christ feeds the faithful with his own Body and Blood, but their words had been more or less open to a figurative interpretation,—had not at any rate absolutely excluded this. He was resolved that, if he could help it, there should henceforth be no mistake in the matter.

The immense embarrassments which ensued so soon as ever, virtually or formally, this was accepted as the Church's teaching; the enormous difficulty of weaving this into one coherent and consistent whole with other accepted articles of the faith,—of dealing with all the consequences which it involved and which on it must follow; the infinite ingenuity which has been expended in attempts of the kind; all these are matters sufficiently familiar to theological scholars. I cannot undertake to treat of them here. Only I will observe that now it might be seen how immense a misfortune it was that the Church had not long since been called dogmatically to declare what she held, and what she condemned, in a matter so high and so difficult. The inevitable conflict had not been escaped; it had only been adjourned, and adjourned from favourable times, those of the great early Doctors, to other far less favourable; for assuredly it was not the ninth century which one would willingly have chosen for the coming up for discussion of a mystery so sublime.

Great as was the favour which this treatise found with the many, there were also not a few who were offended. The theological leaders of the age were divided into opposite camps. Hincmar of Rheims sided with Paschasius, and Remigius, of Rheims as well; so also did Ratherius of Verona;—names such as these attesting the strength with which the spirit of the age was setting in this direction. But on the other side was Rabanus Maurus, a scholar of Alcuin, and perhaps the most distinguished theologian of his time. Better known to us now, at least by name, is Ratramn (d. 868). Bertram he is often called, but by mistake;— his book, which has a literary interest no less than a theological, being sometimes ascribed to a greater than he, even to Scotus Erigena (see p. 208), who, as there is reason to suppose, did write against Paschasius, though his work has not reached us. These, and others with them, denounced his teaching on this matter as novel and erroneous; yet did not always in their resistance to it observe the golden mean: they might be sometimes likened to the woodman who, in his eagerness to disengage the oak from the ivy which is strangling it, incautiously wounds the tree itself. The conditions of the struggle were, indeed, in every way unfortunate; above all unfortunate in this, namely that what Paschasius taught of error attached itself closely to what the Church had always held of truth, might only too easily be confounded with this, or mistaken for it; even as numbers to this day confound any Real Presence with Transubstantiation, and, in their zeal to get rid of the superstitious accretion, are intolerant of the truth on which this has been superinduced.

In the two centuries which intervened between Paschasius Radbert and Berengar of Tours,—among the dark ages two of the darkest,—little or nothing was done for the scientific working out of the immense problems with the solution of which the Church had burdened itself when it adopted the teaching of Paschasius for its own. In using this language I do not imply that there had been as yet any authoritative allowance of his teaching or condemnation of that which it excluded; but only that such as would not receive it were growing to be more and more regarded in the judgment of the many as of questionable rightness of faith; the popular sentiment which anticipated, and at the same time prepared the way for, dogmatic definition, pronouncing itself ever more strongly against them. But they were not to be silenced without one struggle, one vigorous protest more. When indeed this was made, it did not fail to exemplify the danger which was most to fear. The Charybdis of Transubstantiation was effectually avoided; but in efforts to keep clear of this it was often forgotten that there was a Scylla of mere spiritualism on the other side.

From Berengar (born about 1000, and called of Tours to distinguish him from others of the same name), the protest came. Following in the footsteps of Ratramn, but with clearer insight into what he was doing and a more definite purpose, and probably under the spell of a mightier spirit, that namely of Scotus Erigena,—he renewed the opposition to Paschasius which had well-nigh died out. But, while rejecting the gross carnal error of Paschasius, he rejected with it, so it seems to me, a portion of the truth on which that error had fastened itself; the true doctrine of the Eucharist meanwhile retreating out of sight, there to tarry until better times should come round. A letter of Berengar to Lanfranc, Archbishop of Canterbury that should be, and at that time Prior of Bec in Normandy, —a letter which there may fairly be a question whether Lanfranc was justified in allowing others to make use of,—first brought him into trouble. He was condemned by Pope Leo IX. in a Council at Rome ; again in the same year at Vercelli (1050). "Would God," exclaims Luther, "that all Popes had borne themselves so Christianly in all things as this Pope in the matters of Berengar,"—his hatred of sacramentaries proving for the moment stronger than his hatred of Popes.

Berengar, though condemned, had many powerful friends ; these, however, by no means all or nearly all agreeing with him. Among them was no less a man than Hildebrand, at this time Cardinal Legate in France, and the coming Pope. Having succeeded in persuading Hildebrand of the soundness of his faith,—for Berengar was prepared to sign a declaration, "The bread and wine of the altar after consecration are the Body and Blood of Christ,"—he ventured to appear before a new Synod at Rome, where it was intended that he should clear himself (1059). But, as will often happen where a public assembly has to be reckoned with, matters did not take their course according to the programme designed. As many as counted Berengar a heretic, and a shifty one, were resolved there should be no mistake, no escape for him under shelter of equivocal statements ; and there was put before him for his acceptance quite another palinode, with no vague generalities or convenient creepholes. This, not for a moment believing (for so he tells us), but overborne by multitudes, and in fear of immediate death, he signed. No sooner, however, had he put the Alps between himself and his enemies than he recanted his recantation, and openly bewailed the weakness out of which he had set his hand to the document forced upon him. Entangled before long in angriest controversy with Lanfranc and with others,

z

he reaffirmed all which for the moment he had re-
tracted ; and so filled Western Christendom with his
doctrine that Hildebrand, now Pope, was compelled to
cite him to make answer for himself (1078).

The great Pontiff, who was an eminent Church-ruler
rather than a highly trained theologian, and who had
no desire that the existing freedom should be restricted
by a new dogmatic definition, would fain have helped
Berengar again, and by the same means as before.
Some correspondence, only recently brought to light
and published in 1850, reveals how much had passed
by letter between them on the subject. Obtaining
from Berengar a new and somewhat more explicit
confession of faith, Gregory avouched himself at an
assembly of Bishops satisfied with it, and would fain
have had others satisfied as well. They were *not* satisfied, and made him clearly to understand as much.
And he now, who on occasion could set his face as a
flint, evidently did not count that such an occasion was
here. Prepared to go far, he yet was not prepared to
go all lengths, in Berengar's behalf. He had another
work and that a far mightier in hand ; nothing less
than the complete elevation of the spiritual above the
temporal, of the successor of St. Peter above the successor of Cæsar. It was a task for the putting through
of which it was absolutely necessary that his own orthodoxy should be above the breath of suspicion.
None must be able to cast in his teeth with any show
of truth that he was a fautor of heretics. But his enemies were even then making use of the evident favour
with which he regarded the heretic already twice condemned ; and when Berengar was rash enough to appeal to him as in a certain sympathy with himself on

the matter in dispute, Gregory at once threw him over, demanding from him instant subscription to the form of recantation from which he shrunk the most. It was again to be manifest that Berengar had not what we have lately learned to call " the courage of his opinions." After a faint struggle he signed; willing, as he subsequently avowed, to commit himself to the mercy of God rather than to theirs into whose hands, as an obstinate and relapsed heretic, he would otherwise have fallen. Deeply wounded in conscience, feeling that he had secured his safety at the cost of his Christian honour, likening himself to Aaron and to Peter,—they also both of them unfaithful to God through the fear of men,—he spent the long years which yet remained to him (for he did not die till 1088), in retirement; indebted, no doubt, to the potent protection of Gregory that, despite of a third retractation, he was not molested any further.

A word or two more concerning the man and his teaching. And first concerning the man. Who is there that would not fain adopt, if he might, Coleridge's judgment of Berengar, so glorious in its charity? Who is there that is not disposed to feel and think somewhat worse of himself, when he is not able to make this judgment his own? And yet such is my condition. I have no choice but to say that, as it seems to me, there has been a disposition to overrate Berengar, and this both intellectually and morally. An adroit dialectician, when such were rarer than half a century later they became, a scholar of very various accomplishments, gifted with a singular power of drawing and attaching friends, he was from the beginning restless and vain, ill content to walk in old paths, eager to make a figure in the world, and in the end making one only too notable. Incapable he plainly was of taking the true measure of himself, for else he would not have twice challenged dangers from which at the decisive moment he shrunk. Incapable he also showed himself of taking the true measure of others. When one considers what was the relative calibre of Lanfranc and of him, the insolent tone of superiority in which he addresses the Italian scholar and theologian, and this before any personal antagonism had sprung up between them, can only, as one reads, fill with a painful astonishment.

Then too there is a passionate feebleness about him. He scolds like an angry woman. A much smaller man than Abelard, who will presently appear on the scene, he shares with him in a very unpleasant trait, namely that he cannot conceive of any opposing or even disagreeing with him, except as impelled to this by ignorance, or dishonesty, or personal malice. His adversaries are "savage wild beasts;" a Bishop of Padua, who was not on his side, is "the Paduan buffoon;" another is "the Pisan Antichrist." If he has to speak of Pope Leo, "that holy lion of yours," he observes, "is very far from being the Lion of the tribe of Judah." As the conflict deepens, he over and over again assures Lanfranc, and in every variety of language, that he lies, or, slightly varying the charge, that he speaks against the testimony of his own conscience. Certainly his own writings leave an impression about him as of a man singularly wanting in self-restraint, with little sense of personal dignity, grievously deficient in that unfailing mark of true nobleness, the power of doing justice to a foe.

So much for the man. But his doctrine, was it a timely protest against errors and exaggerations of Paschasius which the Church had adopted and virtually made her own? or was there danger from his teaching lest both should go, the error and the truth, —lest with that which it would be gain to lose, there should be also lost that whose loss would have been irreparable? As I have said already, it seems to me the last, and that his success would have been a calamity. No doubt the truth of the Sacrament was in his time dangerously overlaid, but it was not lost; and all experience has shown that in these matters it is far easier to take from the too much than to add to the too little. Superstition sometimes guards the truth which it distorts, caricatures, and in part conceals. Putting all things together, I am unable to share in the sympathy with which this revolt of his against the prevailing dogma of his time has often been regarded. It presents itself to me in the light of a feeble and ill-concerted insurrection, which so mixed up objects desirable and undesirable, that those who could wish its success for some reasons could only deprecate and dread this success for others; an insurrection which, having been presently put down, had for its only consequence the fastening of the yoke more firmly than ever upon their necks, in whose behalf and for whose deliverance it had originally been planned. At the same time it is not easy to affirm what the doctrinal results of success on his part would have been; neither does an increased acquaintance with his own writings make it easier. Since Lessing's discovery, something more than a century ago, in the library at Wolfenbüttel, of Berengar's latest answer to

Lanfranc, and its publication in 1834 by Neander, it cannot be said that we are compelled to derive from others, and those for the most part adversaries, our knowledge of what his doctrine was; which to a considerable extent was the case before. But the difficulty remains. There are statements of his which satisfy all just demands; but then again there are others in which he seems " to hedge," and which would leave the words of Consecration a trope, and the Sacrament itself little more than a commemorative meal. There will be always, I think, a difference of opinion as to which is the truest voice of the man.

A few words before we leave this theme. It is certainly a thought of infinite sadness that this Sacrament,—the very bond of innermost communion of the faithful with their Lord, and through Him with one another,—should have thus proved so often, and, in times which this course of Lectures does not reach, will be found to prove still more, a source and spring of strife and debate, dividing Churches, and then dividing again the divided. And yet from the bitter of this thought a sweet may be extracted. There is comfort even here. How priceless it and its benefits must have been felt to be, before men would contend for it as they have done, counting it as the very apple of their eye, so that he who wounded them here wounded them in a part at once the tenderest and the most vital; willing to set all upon the hazard, to taste all bitternesses, in exiles, in prisons, on scaffolds, at the fiery stake, for what they felt to be the truth of God in this matter. And no wonder. In the Sacraments, above all in this Sacrament, is the great abiding witness in the Church, a witness not in word only but also in act, against all merely rationalistic explanations of our relation to Christ and his to us. We are herein and hereby brought into real and direct contact with the whole Christ, and He with us; translated out of a spiritualistic world of shadows into a true kingdom of realities.

And another comforting thought may abate the sadness with which we contemplate the endless differences with which men have learned to regard this holiest mystery of all. No doubt there can be but one truth about it, and all which is not this is wrong. But those who miss this absolute truth, we are sometimes tempted to think of them as missing the blessing of that which they underrate, or—I will not say overrate, for that is impossible—which they wrongly rate. Let us be reassured. God is greater than our hearts. Many a one who, under imperfect teaching, has come to this as no more than a commemorative rite with some vague ill-defined solemnity clinging to it, has gone away strengthened and inwardly nourished, as he only shall fully know and understand in that day when Christ shall quicken the mortal bodies of his saints. God's purposes of grace are not so lightly defeated, the ordinances which He has appointed are not so easily robbed of their blessing, as we too often assume. Let us devoutly thank Him that the condition of receiving the grace of this heavenly feast does not lie in holding what Paschasius Radbert held about it, or in denying what Paschasius Radbert held about it; in being a Berengarian, or in being an anti-Berengarian. There are things which may be too high for us, too high for our understanding, but not too high for our using and enjoying; and of such things this is one, and the greatest.

LECTURE XIV.

THE EARLIER SCHOOLMEN.

THE passion for the Crusades and for the Scholastic Theology may be regarded severally as the outer and inner expression of one and the same movement in the heart and mind of Western Christendom. As by the Crusades men avouched that they would no longer be satisfied merely to hear of that land which the Son of God had hallowed by his presence, by his life, and by his death, but must have the very land itself in possession, not walking in this matter merely by faith when it was free to them to walk also by sight, so fared it presently in another region as well. There were as adventurous spirits, as chivalrous hearts in the cloister as in the camp. These too will not be content until they have grasped—not by faith only, but with every faculty of their being, and therefore intellectually no less than morally and spiritually,—that entire body of truth taught by Christ and by his Church. What they have taken upon trust, upon the Church's word, they have so taken in the fullest assurance that it would justify itself to the reason as well. And that it can so justify itself throughout, that the *auctoritates* and the *rationes*, as severally they were called, were in perfect harmony with each other, the Schoolmen made it their task to show.

But the Schoolmen,—what exactly do we mean

when we speak of these? who were they? The name, which oftentimes implies so much, reveals so much, does not help us here. A *scholasticus* in medieval Latin might be a teacher, or he might be a learner; all which the word affirms is that he has something to do with schools. We must then look further for an explanation of what the Schoolmen were. Persons, some will reply, who occupied themselves with questions like this, How many angels could dance at the same instant upon the point of a needle? or with others like to this. Never having read a line of their writings, absolutely uninformed of the conditions, moral and intellectual, of Western Christendom which gave birth to these Schoolmen, and which at the time left room for no other birth, they have no hesitation in passing their judgment of contempt upon them. Thus, if Albert the Great is named,—Albertus Magnus as he is more commonly called,—their ignorance about him may be absolute, but they will not let him pass without observing, and with a perfectly gratuitous contempt, that there was nothing great about him but his name. So, not long since I read.

This contempt, it is worth remarking, is very far from being shared by the more illustrious thinkers of the modern world,—not, for example, by Hegel, or Alexander Von Humboldt; the latter characterizing the disquisitions of that same unfortunate Albertus on the subjects with which he, Von Humboldt, was chiefly conversant, as "admirable beyond expression, for the period in which he lived;" while Von Raumer declares, under like reservations, that "he might be called the Aristotle or Leibnitz of his age." And only a few years ago one lost too early to the English

2A

Church, wrote as follows:—" Through two eventful centuries which witnessed, as they passed, the formation of nationalities, the establishment of representative government, the birth of vernacular literature, and the grand climacteric of ecclesiastical power, the philosophy of the Schools held on its way, not only commanding with an undisputed sway the intellect of those restless times, but elaborating its system, extending its influence, and drawing into its service some of the highest minds that the Christian world has produced. For two centuries longer, though spent in vital energy, it continued to rule on, till with the fifteenth century came the resistless onslaught, which with the revival of classical letters broke for ever the spell of its dominion " (Shirley).

I must add a personal reminiscence. Once when as a young man I made with Arthur Hallam a pilgrimage to Highgate to have the privilege of hearing Coleridge talk, he occupied himself for nearly an unbroken hour with the intellectual greatness of the Schoolmen. The revived interest in patristic literature which was so marked a feature of that time suggested his special theme, which was this, namely, the much larger amount of profit which might even now, in his judgment, be gotten from the Schoolmen than from the Fathers, whose frequent " nugacity," for I am afraid he used that word, he denounced. The manner in which Aquinas had anticipated and met nearly all the later assaults on the miracles, and the greatness of the speculative genius of our English Occam, with the perilous lines on which his speculation was travelling at the last, were the special subjects of his discourse, or at all events are those which, after the lapse of so

many years, still survive the most clearly in my
memory.

Let me seek to explain to you, so far as I myself
understand, how this Theology arose; what the objects were which it proposed to itself; and how far it
can be said to have accomplished these. When in
the eleventh century the reviving activity of thought,
the fresh life which was everywhere stirring, sought
some material on which it might exercise itself, with
the exception of that which theology and the Church
supplied, such was nowhere to be found. All other
sciences in the troubles and tumults of the centuries
preceding had either wholly perished, or had been reduced to the barest and most meagre elements. The
classical treasures of antiquity, though not all or
nearly all irrecoverably gone, were mostly hidden out
of sight for the time. Papal Canons, decrees of
Councils, treatises of the Fathers and such like, were
apparently all which had survived the mighty wreck.
In these, and in these only, was to be found the nour-
ishment for the mental craving of the age. If any
new intellectual edifice was to be reared by aid of materials which the past supplied, here and here only
were those materials to be obtained.

But whatever edifice was reared, it must conform
to certain conditions. Thus, there was no general
desire at this time to overpass the limits of thought
and speculation which the Church imposed. These
were felt to be, and, as compared to what any
free-thinking in that age was likely to prove, they
were, blessed restraints. Whatever intellectual revolt
against the Roman system might be covertly brooding in other hearts, there was none such among the

builders here. With a very few exceptions they wrought in the interests of Rome; always intended to be, and for a long time were, her most devoted champions.

Here then were causes and conditions of the rise of this Scholastic Theology:—In the first place a great mental activity; a young world, conscious of its powers, and eager to exert them. And then secondly, the absence of any material on which to exercise a shaping, moulding power, save such as the Church furnished;—no classical literature, no independent ethics, no natural philosophy; a comparatively narrow basis which compelled men to build high rather than broad. Some words of Fuller are here to the point: "As such who live in London and like populous places, having but little ground for their foundations to build houses on, may be said to enlarge the breadth of their houses in height (I mean increasing their room in many stories one above another); so the Schoolmen in this age, lacking the latitude of general learning and languages, thought to enlarge their active minds by mounting up; so improving their small bottom with towering speculations, though some of things mystical that might not—more of things difficult that could not—most of things curious that need not—be known unto us." And thirdly, there was the wish to put forth these activities only within such limits and under such restraints as the Church laid down, without the calling in question, or even the evading, of any dogma or decision of hers. It was the "how" and the "why," never the "what," of the Church's teaching which the Schoolmen undertook to discuss. *Doctores* they claimed to be, not *Patres;* not, as fathers, productive; not professing to bring out of their treasure things new, but only to vindicate and establish the old.

Under limitations such as these, there was only one great work which was possible for the human intellect. It might organize the vast, often unshapely, mass of materials which lay before it into one symmetrical whole; adjust the relations of the several parts to one another; atone, or put in the way of atonement, apparent, or it might be, real contradictions; it might, in short, systematize theology, a work which was still waiting to be done. The more illustrious teachers of earlier periods of the Church had found each his own special and peculiar work to perform, his own position to make good. Occupied with this, they had not found the inclination or the leisure for a deliberate oversight of the whole field of theology; they had not mapped it out as it demanded to be mapped out. It was to this that the Schoolmen addressed themselves, —to the organizing after a true scientific method the rude undigested mass which lay before them.

But this was not all. The arranging and marshalling in due order of the enormous amount of materials which the Medieval Church had inherited or acquired, adjusting parts and proportions, bringing in the end complete "Sums of Theology" to pass,—this was neither all, nor nearly all, which these new champions of the faith took in hand as a task worthy of their best endeavours. This much patient industry could have accomplished; but their aims were higher and more ambitious. What the Schoolmen set before themselves was nothing short of an attempt to justify to the reason that which had first been received by faith.

Observe, they did not say, We will only believe that which we have first understood. Such shallow rationalism would at once have put them in conflict with the Church and with Scripture. But what they did say was this, The truths which we receive by faith can never be unreasonable. They may be, they often no doubt will be, beyond and above our reason; they can never *really* be contrary to it; and it cannot be displeasing to God, who has given us these reasoning faculties, that we reverently seek to understand not merely *what* He has done, for that is the object of faith, but *why* He has done it,—in the search of which last reason must serve as our guide.

This reconciliation of faith and reason by the giving of its due rights to each, this inauguration of a supernatural rationalism in the Church, was certainly a glorious undertaking; I speak of it in its ideal perfection, and not as, in the carrying through, it was more or less marred by the fault of men. Such a reconciliation was not indeed then and by these for the first time attempted; for it has always been recognized as a principal office of theology. But the Schoolmen set the attaining of this object before them with a more perfect consciousness of what they were doing, and strove to carry it out through the whole region of Christian dogma more systematically, than any before them had done. Nor did these spiritual freemasons leave off until there had risen up under their hands structures as marvellous in an architectonic completeness of their own, as the magnificent domes and cathedrals which at the self-same time were everywhere covering the face of Europe with novel forms of grace and beauty.

There was, it is true, a fault cleaving from the first to the task which they had thus undertaken. It was a fault which never left it;—which planted in it germs of dissolution and decay, such as, in due time unfolded, should prove fatal at the last. The fault was this, namely, that the Schoolmen started with the assumption that all which the Church in their own day held and taught, all the accretions and additions to the pure faith of Christ which in successive ages had attached themselves to it, formed a part of the original truth once delivered, and were as such to be justified and defended. The Knights Errant of the medieval theology, they were prepared to hold the lists against all comers; claiming for that vast complex of doctrine to which the Church more or less was committed, that it was in every detail defensible, and avouching themselves ready to defend it.

St. Anselm (b. 1033, d. 1109) is generally regarded as father and founder of the Scholastic Theology in the West; and rightly, so far as this title can be ascribed to any single man. But even he was not without forerunners. In the first place there was a very wonderful apparition in the ninth century of a profound and original thinker, Scotus Erigena, whose writings on their better side,—for there was a worse and pantheistic,—anticipated much of what was most characteristic in the Schoolmen   Lanfranc too, Anselm's own teacher and his predecessor at Canterbury, had used the same dialectic weapons ; but what Lanfranc did reluctantly, driven to the use of these weapons by Berengar's employment of them, Anselm did of free choice, and with full consciousness of the significance of the step which he was taking. I have referred already, but very briefly, to his conflict with our Norman kings, William Rufus and Henry I., in the matter of the Investitures ; but it is as a theologian that we must speak of him now. " The Augustine of the Middle Ages" Anselm has been sometimes called; and hardly any name of honour would be too honourable for him. Nor is this one without its special fitness ; for in him, as in Augustine, there met a singular dialectic dexterity and subtilty of intellect, with the profoundest humility, the most ardent piety, and the most absolute affiance on the merits and righteousness of Christ.

" I believe that so I may understand" (*Credo ut intelligam*), this was his favourite motto, even as he loved to fall back on the words of Isaiah, " Except ye believe, ye shall not be established." Nor did he reckon that this seeking to harmonize the two, namely, faith and reason, was merely permissible to us ; he counted that it could not be left unattempted without sin. Thus in one place he says, "As the right order demands that we believe the deep things of the Christian faith before we presume to discuss them by reason, so it appears to me a piece of negligence if, after we are confirmed in the faith, we do not seek also to understand what we believe." A very significant token of a new theological era beginning is a little work of his, in which all is characteristic, but its name, the most characteristic of all. It is called "*Cur Deus Homo?*" or "Why did God become man?" In this ever-memorable treatise, so small in bulk, and which yet has affected the after-speculation of the Church in the matter of the Atonement as no other book has done, he does not stop short, as hitherto the positive

theology had stopt, with teaching that in some way or
other Christ's death was substitutive and accepted in
the room of ours, but goes on to seek the reason of
the fact, the inner moral necessity that, if our sins were
to be forgiven, Christ should take our nature and die
our death; and to show that Christ having so done,
the forgiveness followed as a necessary consequence.
The fact of the worth of Christ's sacrifice every faithful member of the Church had at all times acknowledged; but what it was which gave to this sacrifice
its transcendant worth, and how the obedience of one
overweighed the disobedience of millions, all this is
here for the first time reduced to a systematic and
scientific form, and cleared of excrescences which
sometimes clung to it in the earlier Church.

But the vindication of the rational character of all
supernatural truth, if only the first approaches to it
are made from the right quarter, from that, namely,
of faith, the position that in the end theology will be
found the true philosophy, and philosophy the true
theology, this has dangers, as is evident, which lie
very near to it. It might resolve itself only too easily
into an almost exclusively intellectual treatment of
mysteries which should be first and chiefly the objects
of devout affections, of adoration and prayer, and
which can never, without grievous mischief to those
who occupy themselves about them, forego their character as such. Investigations safe in the hands of an
Anselm, how soon and easily might they degenerate
into something very different, where the true balance
between the activities of the intellect and those of the
heart was wanting; where the one was overbusy, and
the affections of the other hardly called into play or

not at all. And then, what intruding into things not seen and which never can be seen, what seeking to weigh in scales of reason that which in its nature was imponderable by them, would follow. So fared it here. Before long the simple faith of many was offended. Holiest things, as it seemed to them, were needlessly forced into debate, and in this debating profaned.

The first to call forth such remonstrances was Peter Abelard (b. 1079, d. 1142), a teacher of theology, immensely applauded, and with all the world going after him, in the University of Paris. Probably no person of the Middle Ages has awakened so lively an interest in modern times as he has done; there are few known to us so well. No doubt he is a very significant figure in the times to which he belongs; but it is quite possible to rate him too highly. Vain, "ignorant of nothing in heaven or on earth save only of himself" (this at least is St. Bernard's description of him), sadly wanting in moral earnestness,—for he could endure all that applause as a teacher of things divine while living in deadly sin,—he owes his reputation not a little to his misfortunes, and to the fact that in these a woman of a far nobler type of character than his own was entangled: something also to the surprise, —a welcome surprise to many,—with which men recognize in him not indeed a rationalist, but one with a very unmistakeable vein of rationalism, a champion of "free enquiry" in the ages of faith. A favourite maxim of his, "We must not believe what we have not first understood" (*Non credendum nisi prius intellectum*), reveals to us how wide the gulf was which divided him from Anselm; while his theology of the

Atonement, which begins and ends with the benevolence of God, is in the same direct opposition.

Silenced, and condemned to cast into the flames with his own hand the book of his which had offended the most, he became before very long the rallying point once more for all the most advanced spirits of the age. The condemned book, slightly altered, reappeared; and at length St. Bernard counted that he could not keep silence any longer. It was not as an enemy to enquiry, or as one denying that it was man's privilege and prerogative to know the things of God, that he thus entered the lists. What was mainly now in dispute was *the way* of this divine knowledge; whether man by searching could find out God; or whether any true knowledge of Him was not *given* to holy and humble men of heart, the violence of prayer rather being the only violence which profited here; while others were more blinded than illuminated by the light toward which they presumptuously soared.

The Church in again condemning Abelard,—for it did condemn him (1140), and adjudged to a cloistral seclusion which endured to his life's end,—had no intention of condemning thereby the Scholastic Theology itself. This, so long as it kept within its own limits, and in the main it showed no desire to transgress them, was capable of doing service too essential to allow that it should be alienated or repelled. The extent to which it had taken possession of all Western Europe is strikingly illustrated by the fact that there is almost no great nationality of those times which cannot boast some famous Schoolman of its own. Thus Abelard, as we have seen, was a Frenchman; Albertus Magnus was a German, Aquinas and Bona-

ventura Italians, Alexander Hales and William of
Occam Englishmen, Scotus Erigena and Duns Scotus
Celts. There are occasions when to keep these nationalities in mind will not be unhelpful for the better
understanding of the men and of their teaching. Such
an occasion we just have had.

I must hasten to the end. The two tendencies, the
scholastic and the mystic, which had been in implicit
opposition in St. Bernard and Abelard, arrived before
long at a thorough reconciliation, completing not excluding one another, in the illustrious school of theologians who are named from the monastery of St.
Victor, near Paris, of whom Hugh (b. 1097, d. 1141)
and Richard (d. 1173) are the chief. These scholastic
Mystics of the twelfth century, it may be well to state
in parting, must not be confounded with another band
of German Mystics who appeared in the fourteenth
century, and of whose merits and faults something
must be said bye and bye. These mystic Scholastics
of whom we are treating now, felt, as has been well
said, "the influences of the time in which they lived,
so that, while by their writings and teachings they
helped to check the excessive subtlety and speculation
of the period, by keeping in view the more practical
contemplative aspects of Christianity, they were themselves preserved from that degenerate mysticism
which ends in a vague and feeble Pantheism because
it neglects the scientific aspects of religion and decries
all creed-statements." The later fortunes of the
Scholastic Theology, which are so closely bound up
with those of the Mendicant Orders that there is no
choice but to consider the two together, I reserve for
a later Lecture.

LECTURE XV.

I SAID in my opening Lecture that he who would read the story of the Church aright, for better and not for worse, should, as far as might be, read it as a story of the Wheat, and not of the Tares. Yet this after all can only partially be done; for indeed there are tares everywhere; and that field of the Lord, toward which our eyes are now turned, abounding as it does with the best and with the worst, will inevitably be the very spot where the tares will be found in rankest luxuriance;—neither until the consummation of the present Age shall these, with everything else that offends, be removed from it. All which being so, that would assuredly be a very-one sided, and thus untruthful, representation of things, which should take no account of these, should strive to conceal their existence or the multitude of them. My Lecture to-day will have to do with the tares.

The attempt to give in a brief compass any intelligible account of the sects of the Middle Ages is one beset with difficulties which might well-nigh drive the most confident in himself to despair. In the first place, if we except the Waldenses, whom I shall not include in this Lecture,—for they deserve better than to find themselves mixed up with such very questionable company,—we know them almost wholly by the report

of their adversaries, who have good reason to blacken
the character of those whom they did not count worthy,
whom often they did not suffer, to live; and whose
memorial has for the most part perished with them. I
do not mean that it is impossible to arrive at a knowledge, accurate in the main, of what the various sectaries really held, and what was erroneously imputed
to them; but much care and caution are necessary
here. Then too, while we watch in a spirit of generous
fairness to do them right, there are also temptations
to do them more than right; above all, in a just indignation at much which Rome was doing in these ages,
we are tempted-to make antagonism to her to cover a
multitude of sins. There are not wanting some who
are prepared to accept as true brethren in the faith
any who can be shown to have been in vigorous opposition to her, as though distance from Rome was
itself a pledge of nearness to the truth. What an example of this, pushed to an extreme, we have in the
persistence with which some, in the face of evidence
the most overwhelming, are still prepared to assert
that the Albigenses (of whom presently), occupied the
same doctrinal ground as the Waldenses, and were
fighting, as these were, the battle of scriptural religion.

Other difficulties beset this task which I have to-day
undertaken. Thus, consider the infinite confusion
which reigns in the mere nomenclature of the sects :—
some sects going by many names; in each several
locality known by a different one; many sects confounded under a common name, applied ignorantly
and almost at random to them,—Lollard is an example
of this. In the case of those diversity is suggested,
where there was none; in the case of these it is kept

out of sight, where it really existed. When, too, we address ourselves to the names themselves, and ask them to give up their secret and to tell us what they mean and why they were originally imposed,—for to know the secret of a name is always to know something, is often to know everything concerning the bearer of the name,—in very many instances they absolutely refuse to reveal from whence they are, or what they signify, or indeed anything certain about themselves. Take names as frequently recurring as the following, Paulicians, Patarenes, Publicans, Picards, Beghards, Beguines, Lollards, there is not one of them about whose origin there has not been some dispute.

And then, too, while truth is one, error is manifold. It is not one labyrinth, in which we have patiently to find our way, but many; each upon its own plan, and each with intricate and tortuous paths of its own. There was indeed one bond between all the sects— namely that the dominant Church was for them a Church utterly apostate, such as had wholly let go and lost the faith, the mystical Babylon, the Synagogue of Satan, and the Pope the Great Antichrist, the centre and source of all falsehood and corruption ; that, as they counted, not in this Church's reformation, but only in its destruction root and branch, was there hope for the future, or could room be made for the true kingdom of God. They differed from the heretics of an earlier time in that those called in question some single doctrine of the Church ; while these called in question its whole existence. It was for them an incarnate lie. Not less did they differ herein from those whom we may call the Reformers before the Reformation, of whom I hope to speak hereafter ; who did not refuse to recognize a Church, although one deformed by manifold corruptions, and needing above everything else a reformation in its head and in its members. The writers against the sectaries were never weary of comparing them to the foxes which Samson caught and sent among the corn-fields. Whatever way the faces of these might look, their tails were tied together into a common knot (Judges xv. 4). It did not fare otherwise, so their adversaries said, with the heretics. Utterly discordant they might be each from the other; looking in the most opposite directions; but a common enmity to the Church of God was as the knot which tied all their tails together; in this enmity was the bond of their union.

Again, there was this which the greater number of the sects, but not all, had in common, being indeed the same which we have already noted, pushed a little further,—namely, that they wholly ignored what we may justly call historic Christianity. In a false spiritualism they resolved all the main facts of our belief into allegories of the Christian life; changed its objective realities, which have the warrant of God's Word, into subjective fancies with no other warrant but such as they themselves might lend them. The Sacraments, as a matter of course, and Baptism most of all, as abiding witnesses for God's acts as against men's imaginations, were special objects of their hate.

Among all the sects of the Middle Ages, very far the most important in numbers and in radical antagonism to the Church, were the Cathari, or The Pure, as with characteristic sectarian assumption they styled themselves. Albigenses they were called in Languedoc; Patarenes in North Italy; Good Men by them-

selves. Stretching through central Europe to Thrace
and Bulgaria, they joined hands with the Paulicians of
the East, and shared in their errors. Whether these
Cathari stood in lineal historical descent from the old
Manichæans, or had generated a dualistic scheme of
their own, is a question hard to answer, and which has
been answered in very different ways. This much,
however, is certain, that in all essentials they agreed
with them. They sought, like them, an explanation
for the moral riddle of the world in the opposition between matter and spirit ; completing this with that
which had always gone with it, a rejection of the Old
Testament and of the Sacraments,—a denial of any
but a phantastic Crucifixion, of the resurrection of the
body, and of other facts of the kingdom of God.
Certain inner differences they had among themselves ;
but of these I cannot undertake to speak : nor do I
profess to understand the mighty attraction which
these doctrines,—in part Gnostic, in larger part Manichæan, by the Church already proved and rejected,
and as much opposed to sound reason as to Scripture,
—exercised just at this time on the minds of so many.
Very strange is the satisfaction even for their religious
instincts and cravings which some must have found in
them ; for I suppose Baxter's estimate of the Albigenses—" Manichees with some better persons mixed "
—is in the main a true one.

The Manichæan view of all matter as essentially
impure, of the body as a mere sinful prison-house of
the soul,—the devil, as these Cathari expressly taught,
having made the one and God the other,—worked
here, as it never fails to work, in two opposite directions. There were who counted that this sinful flesh

could never be punished enough,—in their excessive and extravagant asceticism denying everything to it; there were those who reckoned as a point altogether indifferent to what uses so vile a thing was turned, and who thereupon proceeded to turn it to the vilest; while there wanted not others who veered from one extreme to the opposite, and who, affecting to live above angels, descended presently to a life below beasts. First attracting notice in the latter half of the eleventh century, they multiplied with extraordinary rapidity, so that in many districts they were in the next century more numerous than the Catholics. St. Bernard, who undertook a mission among them, describes himself as having found the churches of the Catholics without people, and the people without priests.

As the Cathari disappear from the scene,—which they begin to do toward the close of the thirteenth century, unable to stand against the tremendous organization of Rome, and her inexorable application of the means of repression at her command,—the Beghards and Beguines, of whom we heard little or nothing before, come to the front. These at the beginning were free guilds or associations, the first of pietist men, and the second of pietist women, who, without vows and without the Papal allowance, associated themselves for works of piety and love. But though these might refrain from constituting themselves into societies hostile to Rome, it was not very long before others found their way among them, and sought to take possession of their name and their organization for purposes of their own—and above all the extreme Franciscans known by many names, as Zealots (*Zela-*

tores), Little Brethren (*Fraticelli*), and Spirituals (*Spirit-uales*). I must here anticipate a little, for I have not spoken of St. Francis, and reserve the most which I have to say about him for my next Lecture. Let me satisfy myself with observing here that, already in his lifetime, there had been attempts on the part of some of his followers to relax the extreme severity of his rule of absolute poverty; while after his death appeals were made to Rome to sanction this relaxation. That one Pope after another, Gregory IX. (1231), Innocent IV. (1245), should have favoured this appeal was not very wonderful. They must have been well pleased to abate, though ever so little, the enormous contrast between the poverty of the Orders, and the wealth, splendour, and magnificence with which they were themselves surrounded. But the concessions to human weakness by them allowed were profoundly resented by the party of rigour in the Order of St. Francis, who saw in them the abandonment of its fundamental principle, and a treason done to its founder, who for them was hardly less than a second Christ.

Little by little these drifted into a position of open antagonism to the Church. All the floating prophecies against the Papacy,—and the air was full of them,—they adopted and made their own. There were writings in highest esteem among many, apocalyptic visions and such like, by Joachim, an Abbot in Calabria, wherein he had spoken plainly of the corruptions of the Church, and prophesied a new and better age which was coming. These they appropriated, adding to them others in which no terms were kept with Rome. She was for them the Great Babylon, doomed to a speedy and utter destruction; for the "Everlasting Gospel" beheld by the Seer in the Apocalypse (Rev. xiv. 6), a new and last revelation, and one which should throw all that went before into the shade, was at hand. The dispensation of the Father had closed with the coming of Christ; that of the Son was just on the point of closing; when that of the Holy Ghost, the Everlasting Gospel, would begin;—the faithful in the first age, the age of St. Peter, having been the servants of God; and in the second, the age of St. Paul, the sons of God; but presently in the third, the age of St. John, and with allusion to John xv. 15, to be the friends of God. Some attempts at reconciliation, but these unsuccessful, were made; until at last, under John XXII., it was war, which could only end in the destruction of one or the other, between them and the Papacy. But if they fought, by aid of prophecies and apocalypses, against a heretic Pope, for as such they regarded John, he fought against them with the scaffold, the prison, and the sword, delivering them over to the Inquisition to be burned in heaps as often as he could lay hands upon them; and these the weapons of his warfare proved in the end the most effectual; so that long before the end of the fourteenth century we cease to hear of these sectaries any more.

Among the most noticeable but least commendable of the medieval sects were the Brethren and Sisters of the Free Spirit, as they called themselves; of whom and of whose teaching we shall have more to say when we come to speak of the German Mystics. These made their first appearance in and about Cologne early in the thirteenth century. They had emancipated themselves not merely from the yoke of

Rome, but from the obligations of the moral law, justifying the freedom which they claimed by an appeal to
words of Scripture, "Where the Spirit of the Lord is,
there is liberty,"—words which they made to cover
all their libertine doctrines and deeds. Consistent
pantheists, they denied the distinction between good
and evil. All was good, for God was good, and God
was all and in all; as truly and as much in the sinner
sinning as in the righteous man doing righteous acts;
as much honoured in and by the one as the other, for
He had equally willed, so far as a will could be predi-
cated of Him, the sin and the righteousness; with all
else which follows when pantheism is pushed to its
legitimate and logical consequences. They reappear
as Men of Understanding (*Homines Intelligentiæ*) in
the fifteenth century; and we recognize in their teaching the exact counterpart to that of the Libertines
who made war with Calvin at Geneva. The relations
of the heresiarch Amalrich of Bena, pantheist and
mystic, to these Brethren is very interesting, but I
cannot attempt to trace it here.

It was long, as would appear, before Rome woke to
a full sense of the greatness and urgency of the danger which from these various sects threatened her on
every side; of the need, if she would still sit as a
Queen, that she should address herself in earnest to
the meeting and overcoming it. There was no time
to lose. The North of Spain, the South of France,
Lombardy, Western Germany along the whole course
of the Rhine, the Low Countries, all these regions were
very hotbeds of the sects; while the cities which they
haunted most were these—Lyons, Toulouse or Tolosa
(that is *tota dolosa*, as a monkish chronicler interprets

the name), Milan, Basle, Strasburg, Cologne, Brussels, with others which might be named. It was a strange spectacle. While the master-builders were rearing to ever giddier heights the stupendous edifice of Papal power, raising story upon story, an ever-increasing multitude of obscure workers, bound together, if by nothing else, yet by a common hatred, and with a common resolution not to leave one stone of that edifice on another, were undermining its very foundations. During the latter half of the twelfth century canons which were never enforced, missions of which nothing came, abortive Crusades, these all, following hard on one another, were devised against an insurrection which was indeed formidable, for it was an insurrection of the spirits of men; but all of them proved ineffectual alike. And now a long-continued impunity had so emboldened the sectaries in Southern France that they openly held at Toulouse a Council of their own (1167); elected a Pope (he was indeed kept out of sight, residing somewhere in remote Bulgaria); and transacted other ecclesiastical affairs. With this Pope, with missions, with a zealous propaganda, with a freemasonry of mutual recognition, they may be said to have challenged the Church to a conflict, certainly were by no means content merely to be suffered to exist.

There were inner reasons enough why the sects should about the twelfth century have pullulated with a freer and a wilder growth than in any preceding age. The vast and imposing fabric which the medieval Church had been rearing through so many centuries was now completed, or nearly completed. But outside that Church were innumerable souls whose spiritual needs it wholly failed to satisfy; for whom it did not provide any spiritual food. Thus take it in one of its nobler aspects, its Scholastic Philosophy. What satisfaction was there in this for multitudes of the poor and humble that were simply hungering after the bread of life? Or regard it again in one of its most shameful aspects, the insatiable greed, the covetousness out of all measure, which, scandalous anywhere, was most scandalous in those high places where now it haunted the most. What marvel that men should loathe the ministrations of those, and they were many, who, whatever sacred names they might pretend, yet plainly showed that they worshipped Mammon as the highest god of all! To make Rome responsible for all the wild extravagances, the crimes and madness of the sects, would be palpably unjust. There is madness enough in the hearts of men, only waiting to show itself; there is wickedness too much, only seeking excuses for its manifestation; while yet it is impossible to acquit her of having largely contributed to provoke evils against which she afterwards waged war.

The first decisive token that the policy of leaving things to drift, or of applying weak palliatives, had come to an end was the letting loose against the Cathari by Pope Innocent III. of a crusading army under Simon de Montfort. We know, at least in outline, what followed. It is the darkest blot on Innocent's fame; and he who was not without his compunctious visitings, who could scarcely forget the words which St. Bernard had addressed to a predecessor of his own, "Assail them, but with the word, not with the sword" (*Aggredere eos, sed verbo, non ferro*), was himself doomed to discover how much easier it is to let loose human tigers, than to recall and cage them again.

The political results of this which, looked at from another point of view, was a struggle between Northern and Southern France, and the complete triumph of the former, do not come directly within our sphere; but they were so vast, and have proved so enduring, that I cannot wholly pass them by. This Crusade of Simon de Montfort—if we may degrade so noble a name by applying it to so execrable an enterprise, —changed, and changed forever, the whole aspect of the lands south of the Loire, regions which until this time could hardly be regarded as France at all. This country, under princes of its own, had developed, and was in the early part of the thirteenth century developing still further, a language, a literature, a civilization of its own. All perished; or where it did not perish, was thrust back into a position of abiding inferiority. Northern France had won, perhaps deserved to win, the day; while Languedoc,—I take the name in its largest meaning,—Provençal before, but now defeated and with its proper national life for ever broken, must itself become Frankish henceforward.

Notwithstanding the multitudes who, during the twenty years over which the horrors of the Albigensian War extended (1209-1229), had perished by the sword, at the stake, by almost every form of death, it was found, when all seemed done, that there remained not a scanty gleaning of heretics only, but an ample harvest which might be gathered in, if not for the garner, for the fire. Soon, however, it was plain that, if the work was to be consummated, a stronger and a sterner hand was required than that of the Bishops, each in his own diocese, for this. The work in their hands was carried on in a manner too desultory, too intermittent, it may have been with too many touches of remorse; and Pope Gregory IX., on the plea that they were overtasked already, transferred this matter of inquisition into cases of heretical pravity to officials specially thereto named and delegated by himself (1232). We must not suppose that nothing of the kind had found place already, for the rudiments of the future Inquisition must for some time have been forming; but here we have the first regular beginnings of this, as an organized and permanent institution of the Church. In the rules by which these Inquisitors were to be guided every principle of natural equity was outraged. The accused were not to be confronted with the accusers, were not even to know who their accusers, were; persons of infamous character might be received as witnesses against them; elaborate schemes for the treacherous entrapping of the accused were part of the instructions with which an Inquisitor was provided; a large share of the goods of the condemned were to go to the judges who condemned them; the remainder, if sometimes to the Papal exchequer, very often to the temporal princes who should carry out the Church's sentence; whose cupidity it was sought in this way to stimulate, and whose co-operation to reward. The guiltless children of the condemned were beggared: there cleaved to them the lifelong note of dishonour It was war, too, with the dead no less than with the living; for the digging up and scattering the bones of Wiclif was but one example out of many in like kind.

The machinery, so wonderful in its wickedness and

its craft, did not fail in its object. Persecution was successful:—as generally in the end it is, where, with sufficient power to back it, and knowing exactly what it intends, it carries this through with a ruthless and relentless persistency. By the middle of the fourteenth century there were probably few Albigenses more; or if single scattered heretics were still not uncommon, the more important of the organized schismatical communities had been effectually broken up. Their chiefs had perished. Of the rank and file some had conformed; others had found refuge and concealment in societies not so directly under the Church's ban; whole troops had shared in a common doom with their leaders; and thus in one way or another the peril of such a vast and successful revolt as at one time seemed imminent had passed away.

So scanty henceforth, scanty at least by comparison, the harvest of heretics in these quarters seemed likely to prove, that the Inquisitors must for a while have feared lest their occupation was gone. But this was not so. They were able before long to develop a new activity in Spain, and one perhaps bloodier than any which had gone before. In the latter half of the fifteenth century the Inquisition found its main occupation in the burning of Jews; Torquemada alone sending to the stake some eight or nine thousand. These, the descendants of such as had been baptized by force (1391), were accused of still retaining and practising in secret the rites of their Jewish faith. By aid of such executions the Holy Office was able to keep its machinery in order and its hand in practice; and thus neither was wanting to its work, when in the sixteenth century the Reformation in Spain yielded to it, if not as numerous, yet a far nobler band of victims than any which, with perfidious words of mercy on its lips, it had in earlier times delivered to the secular arm, and to a death the cruellest which could be devised.

Of all the bodies which thus in the Middle Ages joined hands in a revolt against the authority of Rome, and shared in a common hostility to her, the Waldenses, weak in numbers as compared with so many of the others, alone survived to greet the dawn of a better day. One would not willingly utter a single word which even malice could pervert into an apology for the persecutors ; yet allegiance to the truth compels to say that the Waldenses alone survived, because, resting on a Scriptural foundation, they alone were worthy to survive. That motley group of sects whereof you have just been hearing carried one and all in their own bosom the seeds of their own destruction. Under no conceivable circumstances could they have wrought any true deliverance for the suffering Church of God ; for it is only the truth, and this truth they had not, which can make men free indeed. What the triumphs of Islâm were in the East, such would have been the triumph of any one of these sects in the West. No strength of indignation against the means and the weapons with which the battle against them was fought and won, should prevent us from acknowledging this.

LECTURE XVI.

THE MENDICANT ORDERS.

AN age, in so many ways creative as was the thirteenth century, could scarcely remain barren in new associations for meeting the more urgent spiritual necessities of the time. It is true that during the last two centuries the number of religious Orders had increased so immensely that in the Fourth Lateran Council a further multiplication of such Orders was prohibited. Any one who would fain, as it was then called, enter a religion, must make his choice among the Orders already existing. Circumstances, however, are stronger than men and the resolves of men; and Innocent III., himself the author of this decree, sanctioned two new Orders which, almost simultaneously founded, were destined before long to cast into the shade all the earlier, and to exercise an influence far greater than they in their palmiest days had ever known.

It might have seemed that no new religious excitement was possible, that every combination of the existing elements of monasticism had been tried and exhausted, that all which the most ingenious asceticism could imagine had been pushed to the furthest possible limits. But it is the privilege of genius to evoke a new creation, where to common eyes all appears barren and worn out. A new idea found its utterance in the Mendicant Orders. Hitherto the monk, in his ideal perfection, had been one who, withdrawing from the world, had sought in prayer, penitence, and self-mortification, to set forward the salvation of his own soul ; now he should be one who in labours of self-denying love, in dispensing the Word of life, should seek the salvation of others. Hitherto he had fled from the world, as one who, in conflict with it, must inevitably be worsted; now he should make war upon the world and overcome it ;—nothing doubting that in seeking the salvation of others he should best work out his own.

Dominic Guzman (b. 1170, d. 1221) was a Spanish priest, of a noble Castilian name. Having accompanied his Bishop on a preaching mission in the South of France for the conversion of the anti-Catholic sects which were swarming there, he became aware of the imminent danger which threatened the Papacy from the widespread revolt of men's spirits. Nor was he less impressed by the unfitness of the secular or parochial Clergy to contend with spiritual weapons against the sectaries ; by the ignorance and sloth of the lower Clergy, the worldly splendour of the higher ;—this all contrasting most unfavourably with the simplicity in life of their adversaries, their diligence and zeal. He saw, too, how little help was to be gotten from the older monastic Orders. It was an aggressive Order, one that should boldly take up the challenge which the sectaries had thrown down, that the crisis demanded. Such an Order he was resolved his Preaching Brothers—the name expresses the central idea for the carrying out of which they existed,—should be ; devoting themselves to the preaching of the Word, to the spiritual oversight of the sheep everywhere scattered abroad, and, with this, to the repression and extirpation of all heresies.   This proposed extirpation of all *heresies*, in itself a most commendable work, was before long exchanged, by a change only too easy, for the extirpation of all *heretics*, truly or falsely so called; a task in which the Dominicans—*Domini canes*, or the Lord's watch-dogs, as they loved to be called,— obtained a bad eminence; for whether they were or were not the original founders of the Inquisition, there cannot be a doubt that in after years the principal working of it was in their hands.

We must here make a distinction between Dominic and the Dominicans.   When Dominic is charged with having followed in the wake of Simon de Montfort's crusading armies, which succeeded the more peaceful mission in which he himself had borne a part, when he is accused of approving, at least by his presence, the hideous cruelties and still more hideous perfidies which marked that war, or, worse than this, with having gleaned for the Inquisitor's fire what had been spared (where anything *was* spared), by the crusader's sword, it is mere justice to say that there is no contemporary evidence whatever to bear out these accusations.   Dean Milman does not scruple to say, "his title of founder of the Inquisition belongs to legend not to history."

The Albigensian Horror began in 1209.   It was not till its first fury had spent itself that he could hope to effect much in that line which he had already marked out as his own: but in 1215 he found his way to Rome. His projected Order did not find much favour at the beginning with Innocent III., who had no mind so soon

to go back from his own decree, and who thought that
this new earnestness might very well fit itself into one
of the already existing moulds. But after a while
other counsels prevailed. The Pope, who had seen in
a vision (for so runs the legend) the tottering wall of
the Lateran Basilica sustained by a Spaniard and an
Italian, and who now beheld in Dominic one who
might make one-half of that vision good, overcame his
hesitation and gave the Papal allowance to the new
Order. Honorius III. in the year following more formally ratified what Innocent had done ; and bestowed
on it the title of the *Fratres Prædicatores*, which it had
not hitherto in any authoritative instrument obtained.
The new Society did not mightily take hold of men's
hearts and imaginations at the first. For this it was
necessary that it should adopt the rule of absolute
poverty, which there cannot be a doubt that it borrowed from the Franciscans. It was this adoption,
some five years after the foundation of the Order
(1220), which first secured for it the wondrous future
that was in store for it, and enabled it to run a not
unequal race with that other Order, at once its rival
and its peer. At this same time this rule of absolute
poverty, which was of the essence of the Franciscan
Order, was only the accident of the Dominican. The
extinction of heresy was the end which Dominic proposed to himself; the renunciation of all worldly
wealth was only a means for the better attaining of
this end.

A man of a will which, itself indomitable, was mighty
to subdue the wills of others, of a strong practical turn,
of wonderful sagacity to read the signs of the times,
with absolute singleness of aim devoted to the interests

of that Church beside which he could not conceive any other, Dominic was yet wanting in many of those traits which so much attract us in the character of St. Francis. Even those who exalt him the most, and those who knew him the nearest, suffer this to be seen. "Austere" is the epithet which in a Papal Bull is applied to him ; while a line of Dante's about him, "Good to his friends, and dreadful to his foes," may be taken for praise or blame, or for something made up of both, as we will.

Francis Bernardone (b. 1182, d. 1226), called of Assisi, was the son of a prosperous merchant in that little Umbrian town, which the traveller, journeying to Rome and having just left Perugia behind him, may see from the railway a few miles distant to the left, nestled upon the lower slopes of the Apennines. Whatever may have been the vanities of his gay and brilliant youth,—and by vanities I imply no more than I say,—he was early taken hold of by the power of God's Word. He had already broken with the world, though he had not yet discovered what his wider mission should be ; when one day hearing the Gospel read which told of the sending forth of the Twelve Apostles without scrip or staff or shoes or purse, he exclaimed, "Here is what I wanted ;" and, without prolonging the time, he at once proceeded to fashion his life after this Apostolic pattern. Poverty, as Dante tells us, which had now been a widow for eleven hundred years, was the bride to whom he was espoused, and from whom he was resolved that nothing should divorce him. There were indeed Orders already existing of which poverty was the rule ; but their poverty was more or less illusory. The Order, as such, might be rich, and in its corporate capacity might possess houses and lands and money; it was only "peculiarity," as it was called, separate possession by individual members, which was renounced. But Francis aimed higher. He and his should be mendicants, beggars, that is, of their daily bread, having nothing in this world which they could call their own, however they might possess all things in God.

The men of his city had been already perplexed whether to admire or to mock, to count him a saint or a fool ; and certainly there did not want eccentric elements in his character, a fine madness, which might for a season suggest these doubts. They were now still more perplexed. But it was not long before the might of self-denying and self-offering love put all mockers and gainsayers to silence. And then there gathered to him one and another, and so a little company, whom he bade go forth, east, and west, and north, and south, to preach the Gospel to the poor. For, indeed, intense sympathy with the poor, a seeing and a serving of Christ in his suffering members, a craving to be himself poorest of the poor, not stooping to their aid as from a superior height, but himself tasting the very worst of their lot,—this was the master-passion of his soul. Had not his Lord said, "I am come to send fire on the earth ? " even the fire, as he rightly understood it, of divine love ; and this love, judge what we may of the idea on which his Order rested, has perhaps never burned brighter in human heart than in his. In the circle of that love the whole creation, animate and inanimate, was included. The sun was his brother, the moon his sister ; doves ate out of his hand; lay in his bosom. A poet, "a Minne-singer of the divine love," he has bequeathed to us a hymn in the vulgar tongue, which, with all its imper-fection of form (for indeed Italian poetry and, we may add, Italian language were hardly yet born), is worthy of all admiration. Nor is it without its significance that to two of his early scholars we are probably in-debted for two world-famous hymns,—one the most solemn, the other the most pathetic, in the whole circle of Latin hymnology,—the *Dies Iræ* and the *Stabat Mater.*

What remains of his life must be very briefly told. He too found his way to Rome in 1215, the year of the Fourth Lateran Council. Whether he and Domi-nic there met is doubtful. The account of the friendly counsel which at Rome they took together, the grace-ful story of St. Dominic celebrating, with St. Francis as serving Deacon, all this has no contemporary evi-dence to support it ; and may very possibly have been all invented with a view to allaying the jealousy between the Orders, by making it plain that no jeal-ousy existed between their founders. Other points are more certain,—as that Innocent III. was at first little disposed to extend any countenance to the beg-garly suppliant; that in his case as in Dominic there was something very like a repulse at the outset. On second thoughts, however, he gave allowance to Francis and to his rule ; being too sagacious a ruler to commit the fault which the heads of our English Church committed when they repelled and refused to enlist in the Church's service the zeal of Wesley and of his followers. The allowance was, indeed, only verbal ; for the Pope, no doubt, preferred to wait and see what would come of this new enthusiasm before further committing himself to it. Formal approbation Francis did not obtain till after Innocent's death. With such allowance as he had gotten he returned in triumph to Assisi. And now the little mustard seed which he had planted grew and grew, though he was not to see it as the great tree overshadowing the whole of Western Christendom, for, worn out with toil and travail and austerities, he expired at the early age of forty-four (1226).

The rapidity with which the two Orders spread was marvellous ; the Franciscan, which was the more democratic, and recruited itself from the ranks of the people, spreading still faster than the Dominican, which had always a certain aristocratic element about it, so that almost from the outset the direction of the upper classes fell into its hands. Thus not more than two and twenty years after the death of Francis his Order numbered 8,000 religious houses. Many causes wrought together for this. The Mendicants embodied the idea of the Evangelical life, as in those ages conceived, more completely than any of the preceding Orders had done. Living upon alms, and finding a table everywhere spread for them, they did not require, as the others did, permanent landed endowments before they could found their houses. They basked moreover in the peculiar favour not of the people only, but of the Popes, who soon recognized in them their most faithful militia. An extent, a number of members, an influence which it had taken older Orders two or three hundred years to acquire, they acquired and surpassed in twenty or thirty. Nor, however swift their subsequent declension may have been, is it to be

denied that in their earliest and best days a mighty
work of revival was wrought by them throughout
western Christendom. One might compare it in many
respects to the Methodist revival in England during
the last century, only that it was on a vaster scale and
over a far wider area. It is true that it was not always
" the sincere milk of the word" with which souls were
fed ; but whatever admixture of error and superstition
there may have been, it was much for multitudes, forgotten so long, that there should be any who cared for
their souls.   Bishop Grostête, intolerant of monks as
he was, could greet the first coming of the friars into
England with words like these, "The people that
walked in darkness have seen a great light."

What marvel if the Church, and the world which in
those ages was inextricably mixed up with the Church,
were persuaded that in Holy Scripture itself there
must be types and prophecies of the workers of these
wonders ; that some saw in them " the two anointed
ones, that stand by the Lord of the whole earth "
(Zech. iv. 11–14) ; that they were hailed as the two
forerunners of Christ's Second Coming, who should go
before Him in the spirit and power of Enoch and
Elijah ; each, indeed, having his own peculiar glory ;
the one to find his place in the Order of the Seraphim,
who love most ; the other in that of the Cherubim,
who know most ; Francis, so Dante describes him, an
Ardour, inflaming the world with the fire of divine
love ; Dominic a Splendour, causing the light of the
glory of God to shine over all the earth ? Such was the
language which was presently spoken about them ;
already in their lifetime there had gathered round them
a whole world of legend and of wonder.

But this immense success which waited on the Orders in their early days aroused other feelings besides those of admiration. It is easy to imagine the intense jealousy with which the Mendicants, their rapid growth, the special favour in so many quarters vouchsafed them, were regarded; and the many by whom this jealousy was entertained. There was first the jealousy of the older monastic foundations, beaten on their own ground and now hopelessly distanced by their younger competitors. There was the jealousy of the Universities; above all of the University of Paris, which saw with indignation one and presently more of its principal chairs of instruction invaded and occupied by these upstart intruders. There was the jealousy of the Bishops, who beheld their authority set at nought; the Mendicants, among other privileges bestowed upon them, being permitted to hold directly from the Pope, they and their houses owning but a shadow of allegiance to the Bishop in whose diocese they were. But above all, there was the jealousy of the parochial Clergy. Whatever their faults may have been, the parochial system itself was as all-important to the Church then as at the present day. It was now threatened with dissolution. The monks had not been permitted to celebrate, except within their own walls, the divine offices. But this with other privileges, as to baptize, to hear confessions, to administer extreme unction, to bury in their own churches,—this last permission a very mine of wealth —were all accorded to these favoured friars, who everywhere exercised their intrusive ministrations with no license obtained from the Bishop, no leave granted by the parish priest. They are accused of every-

where seeking to undermine the respect of the people
for their appointed guides ; bidding them to come
to those who knew the secrets of spiritual direction, who were not dumb dogs, blind guides, as others
were.   And multitudes came ; being only too glad
to confess their sins to the wandering friar whom
they never had seen before, whom perhaps they never
should see again; so sparing themselves the shame of
a confession to their own Clergy ; not to say that as a
rule, if we may believe Chaucer's word about him,
"He was an easy man to give penance." The mischief
reached such a height that Pope Innocent IV., in 1254,
made some feeble efforts to revoke or limit these
special privileges which his predecessors had lavished
on their new favourites with so prodigal a hand.   The
Orders, however, had grown too strong, and succeeded in retaining all or nearly all which had been
once conceded to them.

Praised, exalted, glorified at the beginning, it was
not long before an almost universal chorus of indignant complaint rose up against them.   They were
meant to be patterns of Evangelical humility,—this
stamping itself on their dress, their discipline, on the
very names which they bore.   But it very soon was
evident that the secret of humility does not lie in calling ourselves by humble names.   One may call himself "Servant of the servants of God," and yet lord it
over his fellow-servants with an arrogance unparalleled.   So these might name themselves Minors, even
as some, counting this too little, claimed to be Minims,
and some Postremists, without for all this being a whit
the humbler ; nay, rather, being only the prouder on
the strength of this ostentatious humility. Upon every

side were heard complaints of their intolerable pride, of their arrogant contempt for all but themselves.

Nor did it fare better with the schemes of compulsory poverty, which were to bring those who adopted them into a closer imitation of Him who made Himself so poor for us. None of those schemes will ever of themselves give us detachment from the creature, that poverty of spirit to which alone a blessedness is linked : not to say that, while Francis was still alive, evasions of the strictness of his rule forbidding even a corporate possession of worldly goods, began to find favour with many, and much more after his death. Poverty was the bride to which he remained faithful to the end; but it was a bride from whom his followers, or a large part of them, were only anxious to be divorced. They might not—so it was sought to interpret his rule—possess anything in fee ; but they might enjoy the usufruct of whatever lands, houses, and other worldly goods the piety of the faithful bestowed upon them, the absolute ownership being vested in the Pope. The property thus formally made over to the Pope, but of which he was only the trustee, grew to such a vast amount, that ere long these Orders united the boast of being the poorest, with the reality of being the richest, Orders in Christendom. Conscious as they must have been of this evasion of their vow,—an evasion so unworthy that at last John XXII. refused to be any longer a part to it, — it is strange to find this vaunt of their being the only genuine followers of Apostolic poverty continually in their mouths. The monks of the older foundations might be "possessioners"—for this was the invidious term which they applied to them—but not they, who had no possessions of their own. How soon the savour had departed, how swift the degeneration had been, we may gather from Chaucer, who is nowhere wittier, but alas! nowhere coarser, than in his unsavoury tale, of which a mendicant friar is the hero. This story, it is true, is put into the mouth of a summoner, an officer of the Bishop's court, to whom a begging friar must have been poison; yet, making every allowance, it reveals an abyss of contempt into which the unworthier members of these Orders had fallen, such as left almost no accusation too mean or too hateful to be brought against them.

And other matter of scandal and offence more than enough they afforded. Having triumphed over the older Orders, and thrust Benedictine and Clugnian and Cistercian, all whom men hitherto had honored the most, into the shade, they presently turned their arms against one another, each Society seeking to glorify itself in the surpassing glory of its founder. Already in the lifetime of these this unseemly rivalry between their several followers had begun, a rivalry which Dante covertly rebukes, when he puts the praises of St. Francis in the mouth of the greatest Dominican, and those of St. Dominic in that of a scarcely less illustrious Franciscan. But in such a pitting of founders one against the other, the Franciscans had manifestly the advantage. The first idea of a Mendicant Order belonged to their chief; all others, Dominicans, Carmelites, Augustinian-Eremites, did but follow his lead. Then, too, divine favours were his, so his followers averred, which were unique. Who but he could say with St. Paul, "I bear in my body the marks of the Lord Jesus?"

Let a word or two here find place on these marks or wounds, these *stigmata* in his hands, his feet, his side, to which they thus appealed. Assuming their existence as sufficiently proved by contemporary evidence, I can only reject the explanation which sees in them special marks of divine favour, imprinted on his body to bring him into closer conformity with his crucified Lord; while on the other hand I dismiss with scorn the suggestion that they were marks artificially and fraudfully brought about by the Saint himself, for his own greater glorification, with or without the assistance or connivance of others. There is no *a priori* ground for refusing credit to the statements of those who testified that they had seen these wound-prints and handled them. A like phenomenon has since repeated itself so often, there have been so many analogous cases verified beyond all doubt, some eighty at the least, by no means all in the Roman Catholic Church, that it is idle to urge a physical impossibility. The matter after all is not so unintelligible. We know something now of the reactive power of the spirit, which is the stronger, in moulding and fashioning the flesh, which is the weaker,—enough to bring all which here looks so inexplicable within the sphere of things natural. Figure to yourselves a man with a temperament so impressible, of an organization so delicate, penetrated through and through with the anguish of his Lord's sufferings, passionately and continually dwelling on the circumstances of his crucifixion, yearning, so to speak, to be crucified with Him. For myself when I so do, I can quite understand how all this uttered itself in these visible tokens; and I am as sure that there was no miracle as I am that there was no fraud. But if this "prerogative of the wounds" (for so it was called) was his and his only, St. Dominic had his prerogatives as well. This theme, however, I shall willingly quit; and you too will gladly learn that these rivalries, since such they were to be, after a while were transferred to nobler fields; and, in times when the Orders retained but faint traces of that which was originally their distinctive feature, the ablest sons of the one and of the other,—such as a Thomas Aquinas and a Duns Scotus,—contended in rival chairs of theology and philosophy which of them should rule the thought, and guide the intellect of Christendom. But of this long, and in many aspects honourable rivalry I hope to speak bye and bye. Here I must be content to express the astonishment with which I read in Lacordaire's *Life of St. Dominic*, that "no breath of jealousy has ever sullied the pure crystal of the friendship which has existed between the Orders for now six hundred years."

A few words in conclusion. What shall we say to these things? That whole work of the founders of these two Orders, shall we count it a fantastic tissue, shot through with threads of superstition and error, a piece of medieval extravagance, absurd from the beginning, and only meeting the failure which it deserved? Shall we say of St. Francis, with an historian of the last century, that the kindest thing to think about him is that he was crazy? This would not be a profitable attitude of mind and heart in which to regard that story of high self-sacrifice which you just have heard. Shall we say on the other hand that here was a wondrous outcome of the spirit of Christ, and that, if love had not grown cold, we should behold similar manifestations at this day? As little can I contemplate this as a just and wholesome conclusion to draw from this history.

But to answer that question aright, I would claim first to distinguish between the man and his work. The work, however marvellous the success which attended it at the first, I believe to have had seeds of failure sown in it from the beginning. The disciples of St. Francis,—for he was in fact the father of both Orders so far as they were Mendicant,—were to live upon the alms of the faithful. This sounds very well; but look at it a little closer, and what does it mean? Seeing that he did not invite his followers to a deliberate suicide, what was this but saying that they should live not upon their own labour, but upon the labour of other people; that instead of working for themselves, others should work for them? Now, doubtless, there are those who may lawfully leave to others the supply of their bodily necessities, in a just confidence that they give back to the world in another shape many times more in return; nay further, that they may not merely accept, but may claim this supply, with no injury thereby done to their spiritual life. St. Paul was such a one, though he very sparingly made use of this liberty; and Francis himself, and many with gifts far inferior to his, might do the same. But think of men gathered by thousands and tens of thousands, and after the first fine enthusiasm had passed away, often with no inward vocation, not a few seeking to escape the primeval law—"In the sweat of thy face shalt thou eat bread"—and how was this scheme of sustentation likely to work? We know how it did work, what a byword the begging friar ere long be-

came for all his ignoble arts, his shameless asking, his
importunity which would take no refusal, his creeping
into houses, "Sir Penetransdomos" as he was early
called (with allusion, no doubt, to 2 Tim. iii. 6, Vulg.),
his wheedling of silly women, his having of rich men's
persons in admiration because of advantage, his
watchings by wealthy death-beds, so to secure a legacy
to his house, his promising of spiritual benefits which
often he must have known were not his to grant, in
exchange for temporal gifts. Bonaventura, himself
the head of the order, and writing not fifty years after
Francis' death, does not scruple to say that already in
his time the sight of a begging friar in the distance was
more dreaded than that of a robber.

But this consecration of "able beggary," as Wiclif
indignantly calls it, besides working in this way for the
moral vulgarizing of those who practised it, made itself
injuriously felt in circles wider still, helped to cast a
general slight upon honourable labour. How could it
do otherwise, when they who were counted to have
chosen the highest life, not merely withdrew themselves from toil, but gloried in this withdrawal as being
a part of that perfection, or a means to that perfection,
which they aimed at? Nothing strikes one in South
Italy more painfully than the utter want of self-respect
evinced in this matter by the whole poorer population.
Man, woman, and child, whatever other occupation
they may follow, have superadded that of beggar,
which they exercise with no sort of shame, and as the
most natural thing in the world. Little as the sublime
Mendicant of Assisi foresaw or intended this, he did
much to bequeath to Italy the eating sore of an almost
universal mendicancy; made it for multitudes impos-

sible to understand the blessed links which link together the two utterances of the Psalmist: "Thou
shalt eat the labours of thine hands;" and, "O well is
thee, and happy shalt thou be!" And after all he
struck no mortal blow at the sin of covetousness.
Not money, but "the love of money," St. Paul tells
us, "is the root of all evil." That he struck no mortal blow at this even among his own followers, we
saw just now. Already during his life, still more
after his death, one pitiful evasion of the strictness
of his rule was devised and then another; while such
as were resolved to abide by the rigour of it despite of Papal decisions in favour of laxity (see p.
219), were dealt with as heretics, not a few of
them expiating their fidelity to their master's rule at
the stake.

On the idea by aid of which he hoped to regenerate
the Church I need not say more. So far as he did
effect anything considerable here, it was the man and
not the rule that wrought the mighty works. For him,
let him have fallen into what mistakes he may, he must
always remain one of the most wonderful figures which
the wonderful story of the life of Christ in his members presents. For him, who can doubt that he did
well, when, bidden by an inward voice to leave all for
the sake of Christ and Christ's poor, he was not disobedient to that voice, but chose what presented itself
to him as the closest possible conformity to the life
of his crucified Lord? It is these, these elect souls,
to whatever age and communion they may have belonged, let there have cleaved to them what extrav-
agancies there may,—who startle the world and
the Church from those dreams of careless ease and

indulgence into which the one is quite as ready to fall as the other; it is these, of whom but to read or hear, upbraids our selfish lives and rebukes our lukewarm sympathies for the suffering members of Christ.

LECTURE XVII.

THE WALDENSES.

WHEN God has a special work for any people to do, He often makes their outward conditions such as shall be the most favourable for their doing it. There is a real correspondence between them, on the one side, and their appointed home, the bounds of their local habitation, on the other. It was thus with the Jews. Till the fulness of time came, they were to be "a people dwelling alone and not reckoned among the nations;" and Palestine, as it would be easy to show, was exactly the land to keep them thus apart. But while thus the Jewish points of contact with the rest of the world were few, Greece, with quite another mission, had points of contact innumerable. All shore and harbour, Greece was everywhere accessible, everywhere invited and facilitated approach. Not otherwise the principal seats of the Waldenses had their fitness too. It is in mountainous districts, in remote valleys, such as those where they dwelt, that men cling the longest to old traditions, customs, faiths,—are least affected by the revolutions which are altering the general face of the world; while at the same time these mountains and valleys are not fastnesses which shut up their dwellers so strictly that they can neither influence others nor be influenced by them.

Certainly they were not so in this case. We must

not think of the Waldenses as rigidly confined to their narrow Alpine haunts. Geographically divided into two groups, according as they dwelt on the Italian or the French slopes of the Alps, their earliest home was on the French side, in Dauphiny and Provence, as their oldest name " Poor Men of Lyons," sufficiently attests. But they were numerous in North Italy as well; and far more widely scattered over the whole of central Europe than their present dwelling place and numbers would at all suggest. They had congregations in Florence, in Genoa, in Venice, above all in Milan; there were Waldensian communities as far south as Calabria; they were not unknown in Arragon; still less in Switzerland; at a later day they found their way to Bohemia, and joined hands with the Hussites there.

From the language which many at this day hold, one might be tempted to suppose that for several centuries, during a large portion of the Middle Ages, the true Church of Christ had retreated out of the open sight of men, and was nowhere to be traced except in the little communities which I speak of. Milton himself has not hesitated to claim for them the honour which belongs to those

> " who kept the truth so pure of old,
> When all our fathers worshipped stocks and stones."

With the fullest admission of the many grievous corruptions which during a long period deformed the Catholic Church, with a hearty acknowledgment no less of what we owe to these Alpine witnesses, we may still decline to accept this statement concerning the objects of our fathers' worship, or to read the past of the Church as in such statements it is implicitly proposed to read it.

For myself let me at the outset express my conviction that the whole attempt to ascribe to the Waldenses an earlier date than the latter half of the twelfth century, to throw back their origin some two hundred years, or sometimes much more than this, even to the times of Claudius of Turin (d. 839), is one which will not stand the test of historical criticism ; while the endeavour to vindicate for them this remote antiquity has introduced infinite confusion into their whole history. The date of Waldo, who, as I cannot doubt, is rightly recognized as their founder, we certainly know. When it is sought to get rid of their relation to him as embodied in the very name which they bear, and to change this name into Vallenses, the Men of the Valleys or the Dalesmen, it is a transformation which has no likelihood, philological or historic to recommend it. It was urged for long that a most important document of their own, *The Noble Lesson* (of which more anon), claimed a date for itself which would compel us to recognize the existence of Waldenses before Waldo, and thus earlier than the latter half of the twelfth century ; but no one sufficiently acquainted with the facts concerning this document, as they are now known, would affirm as much any longer.

Yet, with all this, our refusal to admit the remoter ancestry which is sometimes claimed for the Waldenses, must not be construed as a denial of all connexion between them and the remonstrants of an earlier date. The medieval Church System, so far as it was a departure from Apostolical simplicity, fashioned

2G

itself under continual protests; some of these utterly
insane, and encountering departures from Scripture
in one direction by far wilder departures in another;
but others having Scripture and the unbroken tradition of the Church from the times of the Apostles for
their warrant.   Now, if any choose to call some early
protesters of this better kind the ancestors of the
Waldenses, there is no reason why they should not
use this language.   Agobard (d. 841) was an ancestor; his contemporary, Claudius of Turin, was an ancestor; but they were ancestors only in as much as
they wrought in the same direction and were animated
by the same spirit.   When more is claimed for them,
we have no choice but to say that no historic connexion between these and those can be traced; that a
vast gulf of centuries, not historically bridged over,
separates them from one another.

Peter Waldo,—for we will not withhold from him
this Christian name, although there is no authority for
it anterior to the beginning of the fifteenth century,—
was a rich citizen and merchant of Lyons.   Not satisfied with those scanty portions of Scripture doled out
to the laity in divine services, and yearning above all
for a larger knowledge of the Gospels, he obtained
from two friends among the priesthood a copy of these
last and of some other portions of Scripture translated
into the Romance language, a collection also of say-
ings from the Fathers.   The whole movement remained to the end true to this its first motive—the
desire namely for a fuller acquaintance with the Word
of God.   That Word he now resolved to make the
rule of his life.   But how should conformity to this
rule be best attained?   Some may be slow to receive

it, but there can, I think, be no manner of doubt that
Waldo started very much from the same starting-point
as Francis of Assisi :—that the most Apostolic life, and
most nearly conformed to the pattern which the Saviour
left, was one of absolute renunciation of all worldly
possessions.   He too, as a first step, sells all that he
has, and bestows it upon the poor.   In the name which
he adopts for himself and for the companions whom he
presently associates with him, the same fact of a voluntary poverty, as that which above all they should em-
body in their lives, speaks out.   On this side of the
Alps they are Poor Men of Lyons ; on the Italian Poor
Men of Lombardy.

Before long it was brought home to him that this
Apostolic life was very incomplete, if it was not a life
of active service; that the knowledge of the Scriptures
which he and those associated with him had obtained,
they were bound also to impart.   And now he and his
began to preach in the streets of Lyons, to find their
way into houses, to itinerate the country round.   Waldo
had no intention herein of putting himself in opposition to the Church, of being a Reformer in any other
sense than St. Francis or St. Bernard was a Reformer,
a quickener, that is, and reviver of the Church's
spiritual life.   His protest was against practical mischiefs, against negligences and omissions on the part
of those who should have taught the people, and did
not.   Doctrinal protest at this time there was none.

But for Rome all forms of religious earnestness
were suspicious which did not spring directly from
herself.   A true instinct told her that such a community as was projected, growing out of the bosom
of the laity, drawing its spiritual life so directly from

Holy Scripture, could not in the long run work otherwise than unfavourably for her; and in 1178 the Archbishop of Lyons forbade their preaching or expound-
ing any more.   Such as did not submit had no choice
but to quit Lyons, and betake themselves elsewhere.
And thus it came to pass that not the city, already so
illustrious in ecclesiastical story, where Irenæus taught
aud Blandina suffered,—not the city of Agobard,—the
same which had already given to this company of later
dissidents their name,—but the Alpine mountains must
shelter these outcasts, and in turn be made famous by
their presence.

But even after this prohibition Waldo did not at
once renounce the hope that he might be permitted
to found a religious guild within the Church.   Depu-
ties of his with a copy of his translation of Scripture,
and with the rule of his proposed Order, found their
way to Rome, humbly seeking of Pope Alexander III.
his sanction and allowance.   An English Archdeacon,
Walter Mapes, who has left behind him some very
clever, but not always very edifying. poems in the
rhymed Latin of his age,—if indeed these are his,—was
present at the Papal Court at the time; and was one
of a Board who should make proof of what these men
taught, and report to the Pope.   The Archdeacon re-
lates with much glee how he prepared a theological
pitfall for them,—one, it must be owned, sufficiently
harmless in character,—into which, amid the laughter
of many present, these simple men, whose own theology was rather of the Bible than of the Schools, did
not fail at once to fall.   Whether this at all affected
the issue I know not; but the Pope, counting them ignorant and unlettered, as no doubt in one sense they

were, dismissed them with a refusal which would have condemned to absolute silence. Unable to obtain the Papal authorization they now went forward without it. Thus, running before they were sent, as Pope Lucius III. lays to their charge, they were at the Council of Verona (1183) by him put under the Church's ban. But they could cite Scripture; and urging words of St. James, "To him that knoweth to do good, and doeth it not, to him it is sin," they did not desist.

After a while Innocent III. saw the mistake which his predecessor had committed. Under his auspices a Society was founded (1209), embodying as much of Waldo's original intention as was consistent with due subordination to the interests of Rome. It was his hope to absorb into this "Order of Poor Catholics" those who were now in danger of being estranged from the Church for ever. But the new Order made no way, took no root. Even so potent a charmer as the great Pontiff himself was unable to entangle more than a very few in the yoke from which they had escaped. Failing this, he repeated a few years later, at the Fourth Lateran Council (1215), the Church's sentence against the Waldenses, including them under a common ban with the Cathari and the whole rabble rout of Manichæans and others with whom they have so often since been confounded; for, singularly enough, there has been from the beginning a temptation to mix up these and those; and that temptation has made itself felt not on one side only but on both, on the side alike of foes and friends. The motive in either case is not difficult to trace. Enemies have sought to confound, that so there might be imputed to the Waldenses any evil which had been brought home to the Albigenses; and, these last having been convicted of enormous errors in doctrine and practice, that the condemnation might embrace the Waldenses as well. Friends have sought to identify them out of the wish to recruit the scanty number of witnesses for Scriptural and Apostolical truth in the dark ages of the Church; as certainly it would prove no small numerical addition if the Albigenses might be counted among these.

And yet, neither then nor at any time before the Reformation was the attitude of the Waldenses to Rome, or the Roman Church to them, exactly the same as that which ruled between her and the other bodies which secretly conspired against her, or openly defied her. It is true that they were included in the same anathema as the others; that Rome, enduring no departure in great or small from her teaching, counted all dissidents worthy of death; but, for all this, the war between her and the Waldenses was not before the Reformation altogether the same which was waged between her and the Manichæan Cathari or the pantheistic Brethren of the Free Spirit. These latter were Irreconcilables, and never could be anything else. In their sight Rome was simply the Synagogue of Satan, and either she or they must perish: —the same moral universe could not hold them both. But neither in this nor in any other matter did the Waldenses own any solidarity or make common cause with the other sectaries of the time. For them the Church of Rome was a Church which had grievously fallen away from the purity of the faith,—which had overlaid the truth with numerous errors; but they did not deny that souls were saved in her, did not regard themselves so much a Church apart, as rather the sound kernel of the Church. Seeing that they attended divine offices in Catholic churches when they were permitted so to do, that their children were baptized by Catholic priests, that they received the Holy Communion at their hands,—of all which there is abundant proof,—it is plain that in their sight Rome as a Church had not absolutely forfeited her right to this name.

Then, too, however unfriendly Roman Catholic writers of that age may be, they bring no such charge against the Waldenses as they bring so abundantly against the other sects. Their enemies themselves being judges, their conversion was edifying ; they went not to law brother with brother ; they swore no profane oaths, indeed no oaths at all; a lie was in their sight a mortal sin. They shunned taverns, dances, and all occasions which might serve as provocatives to evil. They did not seek to grow rich, but lived, and were well content to live, by the labour of their hands,—the whole fashion of their lives a rebuke to the unholy living of too many calling themselves Catholics, nor least to the conversation of not a few who ministered in the holiest things. It would have been impossible, as a modern Roman Catholic Church-historian admits, to get up a Crusade against them.

Those who have the same enemies are not therefore friends ; but, admitting this, so long as the Cathari were a danger and a menace to the Roman Church, the intense aversion of the Waldenses to these " devils," —for so they called them,—must have constituted some sort of bond between the Church and them. Certainly it is not a little curious to read, and in a treatise written against them, that oftentimes a priest, being engaged in controversy with a Manichæan, invoked the aid of a Waldensian, as better versed in the Scripture than himself, by whose help to convince a gainsayer. The operation of all these causes could not fail to exert a certain influence on the relations between the Church and those whom she had put nominally under a common ban with the Manichæan and the libertine. It may be urged indeed that if she did not burn so many of these subalpine dissenters as she burned of the Albigenses, this is explicable from the fact that there were not so many, or nearly so many, to burn. This is true, and explains something, but not all. Even in proportion to their numbers they were much more rarely the victims of the Inquisition ; and in what has just been said an explanation of this may be found.

It is only too easy to place a stronger emphasis on the points of difference between the Waldenses in the earlier periods of their existence, and the dominant Church, than the actual facts would warrant. And doubtless the tendency of later times has been to put them forward as more distinctly protesting against the whole body of medieval accretions to the truth or departures from the truth, and thus more Protestant, than they actually were. Neither is it hard to perceive how this has come to pass. I do not urge here the temptation which lies so very near to us, when we write the story of some in whom we are deeply interested, to write it as we should like it to have been, not as it actually was. This may have done something ; but it is easy to perceive a more influential source of error. What the Waldenses learned to hold and teach after contact with the Hussites in the fifteenth century, and still more after communications held in the sixteenth with some chief continental Reformers, has been regarded as that which they held from the beginning. But it is altogether a reversing of the real order of things to make the Waldenses teachers of the Reformers: they were learners from them. Sufficient attention has not always been paid to the fact that, as a result of this intercourse, distinctive features of their own teaching had disappeared, distinctive features of the theology of the Reformation had been adopted. And the error of confounding what the Waldenses were and what they taught in the fifteenth and sixteenth centuries with what they had been and had taught in the twelfth and thirteenth was the more difficult to escape, seeing that, after this intercourse held with religious bodies stronger and often clearer views than their own, there was a not unnatural desire to bring earlier confessions of faith, hymns, liturgies, and the like, into perfect agreement with later convictions. Where this was done, if anywhere it was done, with intent to claim for the past of their history merits which did not rightly belong to it, such a falsification of facts deserves the most earnest reprobation. But such reactive dealing with their documents is explicable on perfectly honourable grounds, and may have expressed no more than their desire to bring these into harmony with later convictions.

The Noble Lesson, to which I have referred already, though not nearly so old as for long it was supposed to be (see p. 249), is about the oldest and most authoritative document to which we can appeal. This tractate, written in verse, is an earnest summons to

repentance, to amendment of life, to the exercise of
Christian graces, to the doing of good works,—all
this in view of the shortness of this present life; the
greatness of the rewards, and the terribleness of the
penalties which after death severally await those who
have done good or evil; with a solemn warning
against that peace which is no peace, against all those
false means by which the Church of Rome quieted or
rather stupefied men's consciences in regard of the
judgment to come.   But what is most remarkable is
that, while Christ's sufferings and death are there set
forth as the proof that as many as live godly must suffer persecution, there is, in all the five hundred or
more lines which make up this poem, only a single line
which contains a reference, and that but historically,
to the death of Christ as a redemptive act; no word
at all of the duty and blessedness of making by faith
the benefits of that death our own.   Elsewhere I find
the same immense omission; and indeed everywhere
a certain thinness more or less the characteristic of
all the religious literature of the Waldenses;—with
the exception indeed of one prayer in verse, called
Lo Payre Eternel, which, whether as theology or
poetry, appears to me to stand on a far higher level
than the rest.   And then, too, doctrines are put into a
prominence which would not justly belong to them,—
touching as they do but the outer circumference of
the Christian life, even if they were true; but which
we are still less prepared to welcome, when we are
persuaded that they are not true, but mis-interpreta-
tions of the words of Christ and his Apostles,—mainly
of his own words in the Sermon on the Mount; or
statements such as in their entirely subjective view of

things would go far to render the existence of a Church as a corporate body impossible.

It will be seen from what has been said, that if any-one turns to these authoritative writings, expecting to find in them the fulness and freeness of the Pauline teaching on the redemptive work of Christ, on the for-giveness of sin, on our justification by faith in Him, he will be disappointed. He will find the supremacy of Holy Scripture asserted as against every teaching and tradition of men; but the prevailing type of doctrine is less that of St. Paul than of St. James. Nor is this very strange. That, as we have seen, which constituted the original heart and kernel of the Waldensian move-ment was not opposition to any doctrine taught in the Church of Rome, but a desire, first stirred up through the reading of the Holy Scriptures, after the highest form of Christian life and that nearest to the Apostolical pattern. Only gradually, and not until after they had been cast out, did the Waldenses dis-cover that doctrinally also much was amiss in that body which had so violently separated them from itself. But even then it was the corruptions standing in the way of a high and holy living which called out their strongest protest. Indulgences, Purgatory,—and this in the face, as they said, of God's own Word, "As the tree falleth so it must lie,"—it was these, and such as these, abating as they did the moral earnestness where-with men should work out their salvation, which aroused their most indignant remonstrance. But for the set-ting forth of what are called by pre-eminence the doc-trines of grace, there are Doctors of the medieval Church who very much surpass them. St. Anselm and St. Bernard may have built on the one Foundation some "wood, hay and stubble" which the dissidents of the Alps would not have been tempted to employ; but, taking these two at their best and highest, there utters itself in them a trust in Christ and in Christ's merits alone, a passionate cry of the sinner for grace and for nothing else but grace, which coming from the heart reaches to the heart, such as I cannot say that I have found in all the writings of those with whom we now have to do.

Marvellous indeed is the sustaining, quickening, binding power of the Word of God. With a complex of doctrine theologically incomplete; having only imperfectly extricated themselves from errors which had in the lapse of centuries overgrown the Church; and even where they got rid of Roman error not always having seized with firm hand the truth of which this was the caricature or the denial; they yet lived on from age to age, a light in a dark place: they lived on too, which from one point of view is the more to their honour, without having produced a single theological genius or other preeminent leader of their own. The Friends of God could boast their Nicolas of Basle, invisible Pope of an invisible Church; the pantheistic Mystics could claim an Amalrich of Bena, and one half of an Eckart; the apocalyptic enthusiasts their Joachim of Floris; other religious bodies too had their single spokesman and champion, who stood high above the crowd;—but no one stands out among these: they hold their championship in common; the honour of it is shared among them all.

Let me note, before we part company with the Waldenses, for I cannot follow their history further, that the Reformation brought no remission of their trials, but rather an aggravation of them. As the result of the assimilation of their teaching to that of the German and Swiss Reformers, their antagonism to the Church of Rome, and hers to them, became sharper and more defined than ever; while, planted as they were in the very heart of the countries which had put back the Reformation and still remained constant to the Roman Obedience, remote from brethren of their own faith, they were in their isolation as sheep among wolves; and were subject again and again to persecution and outrage, now from the Kings of France, oftener from the Dukes of Savoy, sometimes from other neighbouring princes, who would fain share in the privilege of dipping their hands in the blood of God's saints. There are cruelties which it is an unspeakable horror even to read of, and which none should read of unless compelled by necessity; and these are of them. It was one of the most devilish of such persecutions, in 1655, which called out the noble remonstrance of Cromwell, and the cry to heaven of Milton—

"Avenge, O Lord, thy slaughtered saints, whose bones
    Lie scattered on the Alpine mountains cold,"

to which I have referred already.

But they lived through all; downtrodden, yet not crushed; as the bush ever burning, and yet never consumed. And now a serener hour has succeeded, and the temptations which threaten them in the present are not those which threatened them in the times which are past. We will not renounce a hope that this *ecclesiola pressa*, this little Church in the wilderness, may have been kept for great things; may yet have a

part, and an important one, to play in the recovering
of Italy to a living faith in God and in the Gospel of
his Son.   Thrown as the missionary activity of its
members mainly is upon the Italian side of the Alps,
let us hope that these will not be content with detaching and drawing out one here and one there from the
communion of the national Church, and in that way
discrediting and disintegrating the only Church which
the great body of Italians will ever know or accept ;
but will at least make the experiment, whether that
whole Italian Church may not be led to move as one
body in the way of reformation : and this a reformation
not borrowed in the gross from the South German or
Swiss Reformers of the sixteenth century ; but such as
a closer study of Scripture, a nearer acquaintance with
antiquity as it really was, and a due consideration of
their own historic, moral, and religious evolution in
the past, shall commend to their consciences.   And this
may be, if only they will have learned how easy it is to
destroy, how hard to build up ; that an actual house to
shelter us, which may not be all that we desire, is yet
a blessing not lightly to be cast away, even though a
building much more to our mind may rise up before
our eyes ; but one existing at present, and likely to
exist for long, only in imagination and hope.

LECTURE XVIII.

THE SCHOOLMEN AND THE MENDICANTS.

THE first period of the Scholastic Theology may be said to have closed with the condemnation of Abelard. The second period has its own peculiar features. The works of Aristotle have become far better known in the West than they were in the century preceding. Many of these, hitherto inaccessible, have been rendered into Latin, some from the Greek, some at second hand from the Arabic translations. For these last we have mainly to thank the Crusades; but Spain also yielded some. The partial ban of the Church under which for a time Aristotle lay has been taken off. Men run indeed into an opposite extreme ; they refer to him as "the philosopher," without counting it necessary to name him, just as Homer is "the Poet" for Greek commentators and scholiasts. "Master of those who know," he is regarded in the light of a supplementary Apostle, whom the heathen world has contributed as a complement to the Twelve ; or as a forerunner of Christ in the kingdom of nature, in the same way as was afterwards John the Baptist in the kingdom of grace. A citation from him on some ethical question is not less effectual to close a debate and decide a question than one drawn from Holy Writ. But with all this his influence tells more on the form than on the spirit; which is not to be wondered at, when we keep in mind that it is not his ethical writings, but his logical, which mainly rule the Middle Ages.

Under the shaping power of these the dialectic method predominates more and more. Every statement which can assume a syllogistic form is compelled to assume one. The second manner of the Schoolmen, it is true, was involved in the first; but they had not hitherto claimed the whole region of theology as their own; nor insisted, as now they do, that not merely this question or that, as it emerges, but every question, actual or imaginable, should pass through their mill, and submit itself to the conditions of treatment by them imposed. The jealousy of the hierarchy, which at first had stood in their way, has now disappeared. Scholasticism on the one side, warned by the fate of Abelard, is itself more cautious than when it first tried its power; recognizes the limits which it must not seek to overpass. The Church upon the other, conscious that it cannot dispense with this, the master-passion and the master-science of the time, and reassured that it has here an ally and not a covert foe, has become more tolerant.

I mentioned to you in a former Lecture how the Mendicants, who were very far from inheriting St. Francis' contempt for books, had forced their way, despite the most strenuous resistance from those already in possession, into some of the most important chairs in the chief Universities of Europe. The University which they first took by storm was that which bore the highest name, the University of Paris (1230); Oxford, next to Paris in reputation, followed before long. Nor can it be denied that their appearance on the scene gave a new impulse to all the academical studies, to that of theology above all. From the first they so made the chief problems which were occupying the minds of men their own, that for nearly two centuries it would be impossible so much as to attempt to tell the story of the Friars without telling that of theology as well; or, conversely, that of theology without telling also theirs, so inextricably intertwined and bound up are they with one another.

The Franciscans and Dominicans, owning a certain solidarity of interest, so long as they were maintaining a common cause as against the older monastic and academical foundations, were not the less divided against each other; and, the battle against those older being won, the rivalry between themselves which had hitherto displayed itself in a narrower, more personal sphere, now expatiated in a larger and a theological. Of this rivalry I have spoken a little already, but not in its theological aspects. It was soon found that wherever, within such limits as the Church allowed, there was room for a difference, if the Dominicans took one side, the Franciscans ranged themselves on the other. In the active competition for public favour which existed between the Orders, the Dominicans for a long time could boast a Doctor, to whom the Franciscans, much to their annoyance, could produce no peer. This was St. Thomas (b. 1228, d. 1274), son of a Count of Aquino in the kingdom of Naples, thence known as Thomas Aquinas, the pupil of Albertus Magnus, and himself probably the most successful organizer of knowledge since Aristotle whom the world has known. His *Sum of Theology* and other works might fill us with amazement, had he lived and laboured man's

21

allotted threescore years and ten, much more do they excite our astonishment if we remember that he died when scarcely two-thirds of these years were accomplished. The Franciscans indeed, who could put forward an Alexander Hales (d. 1245), the first of theirs who won for himself a chair in the University of Paris, and a John of Fidanza, better known as Bonaventura (b. 1221, d. 1274), could not have been said to be poorly furnished with scholars and saints; but it was only in Duns Scotus (d. 1308) that they felt themselves to have found at last one for whom without exaggeration they might challenge an equal place to that of the illustrious Dominican.

From that time forward, Thomists or followers of Thomas, which all Dominicans were, and Scotists, of Scotus, which were all Franciscans, divide men's suffrages between them; those outside of the two Orders attaching themselves theologically to the one School of doctrine or the other. There were serious differences between them, but these nearly always to the advantage of the Thomists. Thus the teaching of these on the matter of the Atonement was not, it is true, all which St. Anselm's had been; but it did not consciously depart from it :—they too taught that the offering of the Son of God was a "satisfaction" in the strictest sense of the word, and the only satisfaction which could anywhere have been found; therefore absolutely indispensable, if sin was to be forgiven; and drawing after it not by arbitrary decree but by moral necessity the redemption of those on whose behalf the ransom was paid. Not so the Scotists. The relation of Christ's propitiatory death to the sin of men, they said, was an arbitrary and constituted one. God was pleased by a gratuitous arrangement on his part to accept this particular sacrifice as an equivalent for the sins of mankind. He might have accepted any other substitute, or He might have dispensed with demanding any substitute at all. How near to Socinianism pure and simple they were here it is not difficult to see. What the Son of God did, an Angel, even a holy man, might if God had so willed it, and He was free to will it, have accomplished the same. The omnipotence of God might be honoured by such teaching; but at the expense of what is infinitely more precious, his justice.

In the matter of sin and grace, and of the relation in which these stand to one another, the Thomists, professing herein to follow the teaching of St. Augustine, have again the advantage. It must be owned that their doctrine of grace and the freedom of grace lacks much of the fulness and freedom of his from whom they professed to have learned it. Still it is far nearer to this than the Semi-pelagianism of the Scotists.

Then too the Dominicans were content to forfeit no little popularity by their resistance to the doctrine of the Immaculate Conception of the Blessed Virgin Mary;—practically the taking of her out of the number of those for whom Christ died. Among the "glories of Mary" this, if only it had been true, would have been the chiefest,—to wit, that she, no less than her Divine Son, had been from the very beginning exempt from any share in that transmitted fault of our nature which is the portion of all other children of Adam. Up to the middle of the twelfth century no teacher of eminence had accepted this doctrine; many, as St. Anselm and St. Bernard, had expressly condemned it, as contrary to Scripture, to the Church's use, to tradition, to reason. But it was popular, and growing in popularity; and from the time that Duns Scotus, always willing to find himself in opposition to Aquinas, made it his own, it became a distinctive note of the Scotists; all those who opposed having the offensive nickname of "Maculists" fastened upon them, affixing, as that name implied they did, a spot or stain on her whom God had made spotless.

But besides the theological, there were philosophical antagonisms between the Schoolmen, dividing them into two opposite camps—that of the Nominalists and of the Realists. I feel how extremely difficult, nay how impossible is any popular treatment of the subject upon the threshold of which we now stand; the absolute necessity under which I shall lie, of carrying you into regions in which your senses will prove more or less unexercised. As you listen you will hardly fail to say within yourselves, What have speculations such as these, philosophical and not theological, to do with Church history? I feel all this; yet I could not avoid the subject if I would. The controversy between Nominalists and Realists, philosophical at the beginning, and inherited from the old Schools of Greece, mixed itself up before long with all the theological controversies of the Middle Ages; it found its way into discussions, where at first sight it must have seemed merely a stranger and an intruder, but in which it presently vindicated its right to take a part and to count itself at home. Nominalism and Realism are severally the banners under one or other of which all the illustrious thinkers of those Ages rallied; and there could be no idler attempt than the attempt to trace the course of the Scholastic Theology, or indeed to trace the thought of the Middle Ages at all, without reference to them. Add to this that the controversy is not a dead thing, belonging to a dead past. Rather is it one of those imperishable controversies which seem to renew themselves with every new change which passes over the world of thought. Whether we may be aware of the fact or not, we have not escaped, as neither will those who come after us escape, from it. We are every one of us continually taking, whether we know it or not, one side or the other, implicitly avouching ourselves Nominalists or Realists, as the case may be.

What then was this grand dispute, which, seeming so remote from the practical life of men, yet, strangely enough, was able for centuries to fill the Schools with its tumult? It concerned itself, I may say generally, with names and with things; with things, that is, as they are gathered and grouped under common names on the ground of qualities common to them all. To these "universals," for such in technical language these comprehensive generic names were called, the Nominalist refused to attribute any substantial existence. He regarded them as mere abstractions, fictions, the breath of men's mouths, and no more. Only the individual had any proper existence for him. Generic terms might be useful mental implements, enabling the mind to grasp in some sort of unity the multiplicity of things; but this was their whole worth. All true knowledge was in his esteem the result of experience. Universals for him were names and nothing more; Nominalist therefore he was fitly called.

Not so the Realist. For him these universals corresponded very nearly to the ideas of Plato. They were not merely an imaginative framework which each man fills up with the results of his own experience ; but, so to speak, archetypal patterns, according to which the individual things, which are only weak "shadows of the true," are subsequently fashioned. Man is before men, not men before Man. Universals for him are realities, and the only realities ; and Realist is therefore the name which he bears. Take the following as the summing up of what just has been said : *Universalia post rem* was the position of the Nominalist ; *Universalia ante rem* was that of the Realist ; the last sometimes advancing so far to meet his opponent as to admit this statement, *Universalia in re*, which was the reconciling *via media* of the Aristotelians.

An example will often help us to understand what would have been nearly unintelligible without it. Here is the word "righteousness," with the notion corresponding to this which I have framed for myself. Do the various acts which have come within my ken give my notion of righteousness ;—a notion which I have abstracted from all these, combining them anew in my own mind ; and one which would have been inconceivable except by their aid ? Or, on the contrary, is the idea of righteousness, for men and for every man, anterior to these several righteous acts,—not borrowed or derived from them, but only recognized as finding a partial embodiment in each of them ; an idea which would equally have been, having its own independent subsistence, whether these acts, or any other like these, had ever been wrought or not? If I say the first, I am a Nominalist, and for me universals are subsequent to particulars,—have in fact no real existence whatever, however they may help me to sum up isolated phenomena under general heads. If I say the second, I am a Realist, and affirm that universals are anterior to particulars, are the abiding moulds in which these are cast.

You will, I am confident, by this time have perceived that the strife is not altogether one about words, that very important issues may here come into debate. A Nominalist need not be a materialist; though this and other charges, as tritheist, atheist, were freely laid against him, as necessary consequences of what he held; but a Realist cannot be a materialist, seeing that, if there be an anterior independent world of thoughts or archetypal ideas, there must be a Thinker, who can be no other than God. The Church could scarcely condemn a man for being a Nominalist, but it long regarded such with a suspicion not very much to be wondered at. Starting from the Nominalist's position, did it not inevitably follow that all invisible things, all which had not some sensible counterparts, were mere creations or forms of the intellect, modes of thinking? The disfavour with which the Church regarded them, not to speak of the shattering defeat which Anselm inflicted on Roscelin, one of their earlier champions (1092), so told against them that for a long time they hardly gave signs of life. But they were not dead. Before the coming of the end a man of rare genius arose, our English Occam, in many ways a forerunner of Locke; who, taking advantage of the excesses into which the Realists, so long undisputed masters of the field, had run, found in a Nominalism by him revived, and with its weak points strengthened. engines for the assaulting of the Church's dogma, such as needed only to be advanced a little further, and not the out-works merely of the heavenly Temple, but the very Sanctuary itself, would have come within the range of his assaults (see p. 202).

One of the most serious mischiefs attending the prevalence of the scholastic method was the extent to which it threw into the background the devotional study of Holy Scripture, and indeed this study alto-gether. Those texts by which a position of the Church might be defended, or a position of gainsayers and opposers assailed, were familiar enough; they were to be found in the manuals which were in all hands; but the complaint rose early on the part of the Biblicists,— for there were some who now obtained this honourable title,—that even those who made theology their study, less and less betook themselves to the divine fountains of knowledge; that Scripture itself was more and more neglected. And the charge, though often greatly exaggerated, had its truth. Manuals of theology, some of them first-rate in their kind, did yet by their method, and even by the very merits which they pos-sessed, abate men's study of that one Book for which all others in the world are no substitute and no com-pensation. Such was that famous Manual which had Peter Lombard (d. 1164) for its author;—his "widow's mite," as he called it, cast into the treasury of the Church; and which for nearly three centuries authori-tatively dominated the Schools, almost every Doctor adopting it as the text-book on which he lectured. This unpretending volume is a selection of proofs of the Church's doctrine drawn from the Fathers, mainly from St. Augustine, and from Holy Scripture; the citations, which for the most part are very brief, being pieced together by this "Master of Sentences" with admirable skill, and with an endeavour every where manifest not to restrict freedom more than a due sub-mission to the Church's scheme of doctrine absolutely required. Students of theology, who found, or be-lieved that they found, here or in other similar hand-books, all which was necessary for the establishing of the faith, came less and less to search the Scripture for themselves. It was possible, and not uncommon, to be a very famous Doctor, and at the same time a very sorry Scripturist indeed.

The Scholastic Philosophy had rendered in its day essential service to the Church. None who are capa-ble of judging will deny this. For minds which had lain torpid during a long and dreary night, it had ap-proved itself a healthy gymnastic, an intellectual ex-ercise which they could not without serious loss have gone without. One important province of Christian Apology it had occupied and made its own, as none before or since have done. And yet, despite of all this, whatsoever was soundest and best in the mind and heart of Western Christendom desired, in the fourteenth and fifteenth centuries, nothing so much as to be rid of it wholly. Nor is it hard to understand this mingled hatred and contempt,—for we can employ no softer words,—wherewith they regarded this the darling study of the ages preceding.

The true-hearted in every Christian land were yearn-ing more and more after a Reformation of the Church in its head and in its members. But the Schoolmen were not Reformers; they were, and always had been,

2 K

defenders of that which was. Every attempt to revive the higher life of the Church, to abate mischiefs which were impending, which indeed had gone very far to strangle that life, found the most determined opposition from them. I ventured to call them in a former Lecture the Knight Errants of the Medieval Theology, holding the lists against all comers. This, which once and contemplated from one point of view was their glory, was what now discredited, and justly discredited them the most. There was nothing which, if it formed part of the Church's accepted system, they had not at all times shown themselves ready to defend;—the most baseless pretensions, the grossest superstition, the abuse which was the mushroom growth of yesterday equally with the truth which had been once delivered to the saints. The withdrawal of the cup from the laity : transubstantiation, simony if practised by a Pope ; purgatory ; indulgences ; the burning of heretics ; and what not besides,—abusing their dialectic dexterity, they found reasons, and, in some sort of fashion, Scripture for all. With all their questioning, with all their affectation of independence, they never questioned any point, small or great, which the Church had determined ; or only questioned with a foregone purpose of setting it on a securer basis than ever, rearing some new buttress with which to strengthen it; for their fortunes, and the fortunes of the Church as it was, they felt to be bound up together, and that the overthrow of either would be the overthrow of both.

Scholasticism, very living once, was little better now than a mummy. Let us follow it to its grave. In the latter half of the fourteenth century the life had well-nigh gone out of it, but it lingered on through the larger part of the century following; Gabriel Biel, who died in 1495, being the last Schoolman of any name or reputation. It was now almost wholly occupied with questions generally idle and unprofitable, often absurd and profane; the green pastures of Scripture being more and more deserted for arid and dreary wastes, where there was nothing to refresh, nothing to feed the soul. The old controversy about " universals " had long been picked to the bone; but the wrangle over the skeleton went forward still. It was in vain that men like Gerson sought to recal it to nobler functions; to ally it, if this were possible, with the Mystic Theology, and thus to put some life and warmth into it. But it would take no new impressions; and all attempts to correct it served only to lay barer its faults, to augment its discredit, and to hasten its fall.

Meanwhile the progress of the Renaissance, the renewed acquaintance with those forms and models of perfect art which classical literature so freely furnished, brought into ever stronger contrast all of harsh, rugged, and repulsive which was in the form of these scholastic speculations: while beyond the form there was now next to nothing; or if something, that something utterly estranged from the actual life of men, and of no practical use or worth whatsoever. The New Learning which offered itself as a rival candidate for the homage and affections of men was in due time to reveal dangers of its own, and dangers the most serious. Of these I propose hereafter to speak; but it is easy to perceive how fair and attractive this New Learning must have showed, with all its human interests, and holding as it did the keys which opened into a wonder-world of grace and harmony and beauty, as set beside the formless, effete and old which was all that the Schoolmen had to offer.

If you wish to measure the depth of the contempt into which these sophists of our modern world had fallen, and what was the feeling of learned Germany about them, the *Life of Ulrich von Hutten* (b. 1488, d. 1523) and the story of the so-called *Letters of Obscure Men* (1516) would tell you something about this; while Luther, a little later, can hardly name Aristotle, —whom, not unjustly, he regarded as the father and prince of the Schoolmen,—otherwise than as "that arch-scoundrel Aristotle" (*sceleratissimus ille nebulo Aristoteles*). Would we understand in what esteem they were held in England, we may obtain a glimpse of this from a little fact,—namely that about this same time Duns Scotus, of whom you heard just now, the *Doctor Subtilis* of the later Schools, "the wittiest of the school-divines," as Hooker calls him, contributed the word "dunce" to the English language. To avouch oneself a follower of Duns, "a Duns-man," was equivalent to being oneself numbered among the dunces. There is a strange irony in such a close to an intellectual movement like that which we have been describing.

LECTURE XIX.

THE BABYLONISH CAPTIVITY.

THE Papacy for the better part of a century continued at those proud heights to which Innocent III., developing to the full all which was logically included in the Hildebrandine idea, had raised it. To this period belongs, as we have seen, the triumphant close of the conflict with the Emperors of the Hohenstaufen line: nor did there want during this time occupants of the Papal Chair, who, accepting the legacy of greatness bequeathed to them, showed themselves not incompetent to hold what others had won. But for all this, forces even then were too surely undermining that wondrous fabric which had been reared to such perilous heights. There happened here what is wont in nearly all such cases to happen, namely that hidden forces work for long, unnoticed save by a very few; and only some sudden catastrophe at the last reveals how effectual their operation had been. It is not "with observation" that kingdoms either of this world or of the other, rise or fall, come or go.

Let me name some elements of weakness cleaving to that which showed to the common eye as strong as it had ever been. And first, the edifice which those daring architects had planned paid the penalty which in this world is found sooner or later to be the lot of all over-greatness. It is not material buildings alone which may be reared too high for safety, in their very height containing the pledge of their own downfall. The vastness of this spiritual dominion, the absence from it of law and limitation, in which, after all, true and abiding strength resides, threatened its duration and were as a prophecy of its doom. There is perhaps no writing of the Middle Ages which at all brings us to the understanding of what this over-greatness was, to be matched with a treatise, very moderate in bulk,—*On Self-Consideration* is the name it bears,— which has St. Bernard for its author. It is by him addressed to Pope Eugenius III. This Pope had been his scholar at Clairvaux, and to his influence mainly owed his elevation to the Papal throne; so that St. Bernard felt little difficulty in warning him with all plainness of speech, and certainly he does not spare to use this, against the dangers and temptations which beset that perilous and giddy eminence to which he had been exalted. It is a picture full of terror, though drawn by a friend, of what it was to be Pope; a tracing by the hand of a master in the heavenly life, of the subtle influences, not from one side only but from many, which were evermore insidiously at work for the moral secularization,—we have no word in English corresponding to the German " Verweltlichung,"—of the man who, as standing at the centre of the spiritual life of Christendom, ought himself to be found the most spiritual of all.

Neither may we leave out of sight the growth of nationalities, the waking up, as from a long winter sleep, of one nation after another to a consciousness that it was not a mere limb of the Papacy, but a nation, with the possibilities of an independent national life of its own,—bound to follow after and unfold this, if it would attain the measure of its appointed greatness, and fulfil the part allotted to it, in the grand scheme of God's providence. The policy of Rome tended to the repressing and crushing of all which was individual and distinctive in the life of the separate nations of the European family, to a bringing of all to one uniformity of level. Where they had a use of their own in the service of God, she was not content till she had wrested it from them ; or, if under strong pressure she grudgingly allowed it, this was only for a time, the allowance being presently narrowed, and at the first favourable opportunity withdrawn. So fared it, for example, with the Gothic Liturgy in Spain, the Slavonic in the East of Europe. There was never upon her part any hearty and loving acceptance of the differences which individualized the nations of Europe, and made them as many members, each was its own office, of one and the same body. It was this awakened national feeling in France which enabled Philip the Fair to fight a winning battle with Boniface VIII., of which presently. It was the growth of the same national feeling in England which animated Edward III. and his Parliament and people in their resistance to Papal aggressions and exactions, and which dictated all that bold legislation which made his reign so memorable an epoch in the constitutional history of our land. Of this too hereafter I hope to speak something more.

With this quickening of national life, and indeed as a part of it, there went the discovery, that not the Latin only, but also the newly-formed languages of Europe were vessels capable of containing the precious wine of God's truth, and all other thoughts which were worth the thinking and preserving. Dante, in his *Divine Comedy*, the swan-like dirge of the dying and departing Middle Ages,—for such in one aspect it is, if in another the joyous greeting of a new and a better time,—Dante had most gloriously attested this. No one henceforward could affect to despise the tongue, vulgar or popular as it might be called, in which thoughts and imaginations such as his had been enshrined. Assuredly it was not a trivial gain that the reign of Latin, as the exclusive language of the Church, of literature, of learning, should thus be drawing to an end. It was a sure token that much else was drawing to a close as well.

And then too, important moral supports were slipping away from the Papacy; and not the less surely, that there was nothing to proclaim that they were thus disappearing. The enthusiasm for the Crusades, and for the Pope as the leader and manager of these conquests of the Cross over the Crescent,—for conquests they were long regarded as destined to be,—was waning, or indeed had wholly waned. He could no longer send some Prince whose absence he desired, upon a distant and dangerous enterprize, from which it was at least not impossible that he should never return; nor could he use an absence thus brought about for purposes of his own. As little could a Pope now make acceptance and fulfilment of the crusader's vow the condition of reconciliation with the Church, as Innocent III. had done in the case of Raymond of Toulouse; or deal with one who, having assumed the Cross, should afterwards evade or repudiate the obligation, as having drawn back to perdition,—as Gregory IX. dealt with the Emperor Frederick II.

Then again the vast sums of money raised to defray the expenses of these costly expeditions, but with the employment of which men were very ill satisfied, did not pass through his hands or accumulate in his treasury any longer. More serious default even than this, the Pope had no longer armies at his disposal, which, got together for one purpose, namely for the winning back of the Holy Sepulchre, he could launch in any quarter he would; qualifying as 'a Crusade, and there-fore as the fulfilment of the crusader's vow, a war waged at his bidding against any whom he was pleased to denounce as enemies of the Church.

It is in the Pontificate of Boniface VIII. (1294–1303) that we recognize the first unmistakable signs that the high tides which had upborne the Papacy so triumph-antly thus far, had reached their highest, and were be-ginning to ebb. He was exactly the man to bring about such a crisis. With the same unbounded pre-tensions as his most famous predecessors, but with none of their deep moral convictions, he put forward claims which even a Gregory VII. or an Innocent III. would, in the altered temper of the times, have found it hard to make good. For indeed the times *were* altered; proofs and arguments which passed muster once would not pass muster any more. Claiming for himself a divine authority to disinherit kings, to trans-fer their kingdoms to others, it was no longer sufficient to appeal to the words of Jeremiah, "See, I have this day set thee over the nations and over the kingdoms, to root out, and to pull down, and to destroy, and to throw down, to build, and to plant" (i. 10). As little did the words of St. Paul, "He that is spiritual judgeth all things, but he himself is judged of no man" (1 Cor.

2L

ii. 15), put beyond question that the Pope was supreme and final arbiter of all disputes in Christendom. Christ might have admonished Peter, "When thou art converted, strengthen thy brethren" (Luke xxii. 32); yet this was not any longer accepted as a decisive proof of Papal infallibility. He might have said to his disciples concerning the two swords, "It is enough" (Luke xxii. 38), whereas, it was argued, if He had disapproved, He would have said, "It is too many;" but when it was concluded from this that there were two jurisdictions in the world, the one spiritual and the other temporal, both to be wielded, the one *by* the Church, and the other *for* the Church, there were many whom this argument failed to convince. Nay, even an appeal to the fact that God had set at the beginning two lights in the firmament, a greater and a lesser (Gen. i. 16), the greater being a symbol of the priesthood, and the lesser of the kingdom,—this, which had done such excellent service in times past, to which Pope Innocent III. was never weary of appealing, was found now to have lost much of its convincing power.

It was not long before Pope Boniface found himself, in an evil hour, committed to a mortal quarrel with one as crafty, as proud, as rapacious as himself,—Philip the Fair (1285–1314), King of France; who now at the head of a strongly compacted monarchy took up the quarrel which the Emperors had dropt. Many differences between the two had been patched up, but this proceeded to extremities. Presently letters are exchanged in which all ordinary restraints and decencies of language are on both sides cast away; and in the end (Nov. 18, 1302) the famous Bull, called *Unam Sanctam* from the first two words, was published. In this the ever memorable statement occurs, " We declare, define, and pronounce that subjection to the Roman Pontiff is for every human being altogether of necessity for salvation." Philip was not terrified. Supported now as he would scarcely have been half a century earlier, by his States and by the public opinion of France, and very dexterously contriving to make the quarrel not a personal but a national one, he defied the Papal excommunication, and appealed against it to a future Council and a true Pope—ominous appeal, now for the first time heard. Had the battle been fairly fought out to the end, the King would in all likelihood have proved the victor. As it was, it reached an abrupt and violent termination. Boniface, surprised in his country palace at Anagni by a band of lawless soldiery led by a partisan of Philip (Sept. 7, 1303), did not survive for many weeks the shameful indignities, reaching, it is said, to personal ill-treatment, which from these he endured. Even Dante, who has the worst opinion of Boniface, speaks with a pitying indignation of the outrages to which the aged Pontiff was submitted.

A few words upon this Pope :—not so much for his own sake as on account of the part which in the Church's history he played; and having in view the manner in which all the subsequent humiliations of the Papacy are connected with this first humiliation, and links in the same chain. With it, as we shall presently see, is immediately connected the transfer of the seat of the Papacy to Avignon ; from this ill-omened transfer springs the Great Schism of the West; from the Schism, and with a view to the healing of this, the Three Councils ; while all these events effectually work together for the bringing about of the Reformation.   That Boniface was a proud, passionate man, ambitious of power, greedy of the world's wealth and honour, was the verdict of his own age, which few in after times have been disposed to reverse.   The current rumour of the time, that he hastened the death of his predecessor, the pious hermit Cœlestin, having first by fraudful devices induced him to resign, or in Dante's words,—if indeed the words have reference to Cœlestin,—"to make the grand refusal," rests on no sufficient grounds ; and is only worth repeating as an evidence of the esteem in which his contemporaries held him.   Of other charges against him, as that he was an Epicurean infidel, utterly without shame in the avowal and the practice of his vices, we hear nothing until the struggle between him and the King became a mortal one.   This charge at any rate Dante could not have believed ; who reserves a place in the "Dolorous City" for Boniface, but not in the circle to which he has assigned unbelievers and heretics.

Benedict XI., the immediate successor of Boniface, passed away in a few months,—his passage also, as some said, having been "assisted" by Philip.   And now the French King contrived that the choice should fall on one who had so sold himself to carry out the wishes and policy of France, that he did not feel anywhere safe from popular indignation except on the northern side of the Alps, and under the protection of him whom he had engaged to serve.   After a brief residence at Bourdeaux, and then at Poitiers, Clement V. fixed his seat at Avignon, which, though not French territory, was an enclave on every side surrounded by this territory.   There from 1309 to 1377 he and six

following Popes resided. " The Babylonish Captivity "
is the name by which this voluntary exile in a foreign
land, with the servile dependence on a foreign power
which this exile entailed, is often designated by earnest
Roman Catholic historians, and not by them alone :—
the name having been suggested, as I need hardly observe, by the seventy years or thereabouts for which
this Exile endured.

It is not hard to perceive the manifold ways in which
such a self-chosen estrangement from its Italian home
must have wrought injuriously for the Papacy. It was
no light matter that this should be thus torn away from
those roots which during the course of long ages it
had stricken in the Italian soil,—dissociated from the
reminiscences and traditions, always potent, of the imperial City. Then too the Popes could no longer make
plausible claim to be regarded as independent um-
pires and arbiters in the affairs of Christendom ; for
it was manifest that they had no choice but to work in
the interests and to fulfil the behests of the Monarch
who sheltered them. At the same time, feeling comparatively safe in that ignoble shelter, they allowed
themselves in insolences and aggressions on the
rights of other princes of Christendom, upon which
they would not else have ventured ; they advanced
claims to a universal monarchy which stood in ridicu-
lous contrast with their own absolute dependence on
the Court of France, a dependence so abject that there
were times when a Pope dared not give away the
smallest preferment without permission first obtained
of the French King.

Perhaps the worst instance of the subservience was
in the matter of the Knight-Templars. How far these

or any number of these, were guilty of the dreadful crimes by Philip the Fair laid to their charge is a question on which impartial historians have arrived at very different conclusions. It is only too likely that some among these Knights had not escaped the contagion of Eastern vices and Eastern infidelity ; but there can be no doubt that their enormous wealth was their real crime in the eyes of Philip ; that their trial was in most instances a frightful mockery ; and, if the Pope was indeed the upholder of righteousness on the earth, that here, if ever, was a case for his interference. Clement V. however, after just enough of hesitation and resistance to show that he was perfectly aware of the unrighteous judgments which he was invited to connive at, or rather bidden to approve, threw the mantle of the Papal sanction over the worst atrocities of the French King (1307–1314).

It was altogether an unlovely time ;—as unlovely morally as is materially that ugly fortress-prison called a palace, which the Popes have left behind them on the banks of the Rhone. The morals of the Court of Rome may not have always been very edifying ; but those of the Court of Avignon were immeasurably worse. Petrarch, who formed one of a deputation from the city of Rome beseeching Clement VI to return (1342), and who had other excellent opportunities of knowing, gives in his *Letters* a revolting picture of the place and of the things which were there done. It was a time also sadly wanting in traits of redeeming nobleness ; a time as ignoble as it was unlovely. The struggle between the Emperor Lewis of Bavaria and John XXII., which stands out as the prominent event, or series of events, during this period (1322–1347), is but a poor reproduction of the conflict between the Hohenstaufens and the Popes of their times, which had convulsed Western Christendom a century and a half before. All the grander aspects of the earlier struggle have disappeared; the aims are meaner, the actors less heroic, or not heroic at all. For the two Fredericks we have the weak and wavering Lewis; for Innocent III. and Gregory IX. we have John XXII.,—than whom there may have been worse and wickeder men in the Papal Chair, but scarcely one that more repels every sympathy; with others better than John, but certainly having no title to greatness.

The deputation in which Petrarch bore a part, and of which I spoke just now, was by no means the only one of its kind; for the Roman people or populace,—whichever we may please to call them,—fierce and fickle, ever on the brink of a revolt against a Pope when among them, could ill brook his persistent absence, threatening as did this, permanently to divert into other channels all the rich gains which in one shape or another, through the presence of the Papal Curia, had been wont to fall into their laps. It was indeed high time that the Exile should cease, if Rome, and indeed all Italy, which was daily becoming more Ghibelline and falling into a more hopeless anarchy, was not to slip away from the Papal grasp altogether; if the brief reign of a Rienzi (1347, May 20–Dec. 15) was not to be succeeded by that of some demagogue, who should hold the reins of power with a stronger hand than the so-called Tribune of the people had done. At length Gregory XI., after more than one baffled attempt on the part of his predecessors to find their way back to their Italian centre and again to root themselves there, succeeded in bringing the long Captivity—self-chosen banishment we might rather call it —to a close (1377).

As may be easily supposed words bolder than had ever been uttered before, words striking at the very root of the Papal system, and leaving none of its prerogatives unassailed, had found utterance during this time; and, more ominous than all the rest, these had not come from such as stood avowedly without the Church's pale, but from those within. Foremost among the threatening births of the first half of the fourteenth century is a book, the *Defensio Pacis*, written by a physician of Padua, Marsilio by name (d. 1328), in the immediate service of Lewis of Bavaria. No later hand has traced with a finer historic tact the mundane conditions which first made possible, and then favoured, the upgrowth of the Papal power; none has searched out with a more pitiless logic the weak places of the Papal armour. An epoch-making book Neander calls it; and certainly, for good or for evil, it was far in advance of its age: so far, that it is difficult to understand how it could very strongly have influenced its age. Purely Erastian in its manner of contemplating the relations between the Church and the State, presbyterian in its views of Church government, subjecting to a criticism often the most damaging much that hitherto had been assumed as historically certain,—it has been an arsenal which in after times has supplied weapons to many, who have little guessed from whence those weapons were drawn; who perhaps have fancied that they have found or forged them for themselves.

Nor was it only from the mouth of this Paduan physician that there issued words such as these, sharper than a two-edged sword. On the same side was ranged another greater than he. It is, indeed, nothing strange that in a Church wherein the corporate feeling was fast dying out, there should have been a revival of Nominalism under slightly altered forms ; a reassertion, that is, of the individual of his rights ; nor yet that this revival should instinctively have assumed an attitude hostile to the Church. But of this revival, and of William of Occam, the soul of it, I have spoken already (p. 271). Against these, and as bearing the word for Rome, there were only the later Schoolmen, who had quite lost their hold on the heart and intellect of Europe, with here and there a Papal canonist, who must have done her more harm than good by the insolent extravagance of the claims which he advanced, as though, under cover of words bigger than ever, he would conceal from himself and from others that the realities of power were vanishing away. There had been a time when if Rome fought her battle with carnal weapons, with the stake, the fagot and the dungeon, she yet was not wanting in trained champions, prepared to enter the lists and to maintain her cause with the weapons of the intellect as well ; and these, weapons of a temper as fine as any which heresiarch or reformer could wield. There was a time when she was not content with merely silencing an Abelard, but sought also to confute him. This was not so any more.

LECTURE XX.

THE GREAT COUNCILS OF THE WEST.

WE have seen the end of the so-called Babylonish
Captivity. But there was a dishonour worse even
than this behind; a mischief which, directly growing
out of the Captivity, was to work more potently even
than it had done for the stripping from the Papacy of
any ideal glory with which it might still be clothed.
There was the Great Schism of the West to follow,
which, beginning where the other ended, was not to
be healed for some forty miserable years. It is not
difficult to trace the connexion between the two.
During the long residence of the Popes at Avignon a
party had grown up in the Sacred College entirely
devoted to the interests of France, nominees of the
French King, eager to entangle the Church again in
that disgraceful bondage from which with so much
painful effort it had escaped. Over against these was
a smaller Italian party; with which naturally sided all
who desired to see the chief ruler of the Church
restored to some sort of dignity and independence,
and not any longer the creature of a foreign Monarch.
Gregory XI. dying in 1378, the struggle at once began between two nations, France and Italy, for the
possession of the Papacy and all the gains, moral and
material, annexed to this possession; France seeking
to retain, and Italy to recover them. The French Car-

dinals, though far outnumbering the Italian, did not venture to resist at Rome the election of an Italian Pope. This was Urban VI.; and unhappily it would have been difficult anywhere to find a man more fitted by harshness, violence, and cruelty to make a small breach into a great one. It was not long before the French Cardinals, withdrawing to a place of safety, declared his election void. Their lives, they said,— and this was not far from the truth,—would not have been safe from the fury of the Roman populace had they attempted to exercise any freedom of choice. They proceeded further to elect a Pope of their own, Clement VII. (1378), who at once returned to the old haunts at Avignon, and established himself there.

Such were the beginnings of the Great Schism which endured for eight and thirty years, and which in its effects has endured to the present day. Never again could the power of Rome be what before it had been. The nimbus of glory with which the early Middle Ages had encircled it, if any faint reflection of this lingered about it still, was hereby dissipated for ever. The great moral strength of the Papacy had lain in its seeming to secure unity for the Church, the Pope being at once the symbol of this unity and the pledge. It is true that there had been antipopes before. Alexander III., in the twenty-two years of his Pontificate, had triumphed over three of these. Nay, the monstrous spectacle of three Popes at the same moment had not been altogether unknown (1033). But the false had hitherto quickly succumbed before the true; there had been no continuous schism. It was otherwise now. Both held their ground, and now this very institution which was to secure the Church's unity was the prime source and spring of its discords and divisions. For little short of half a century all Latin Christendom was divided into hostile camps, and presented the ignominious spectacle of Pope and antipope, each of these anathematizing the other and all the adherents of the other. While salvation was believed to depend on being in communion with the rightful successor of St. Peter, no one during all this time could feel perfectly sure that he was in communion with the true Pope and not with an antipope and an antichrist. It was quite certain that one large moiety of Christendom was in this miserable condition; for if on the side of the Pope whom Rome in after times has acknowledged to be the true, were England and Germany and of course Italy, with Denmark and Sweden, Poland and Prussia, there were ranged on the side of the Avignonese, France and Scotland, Spain and Portugal, Savoy and Lorraine.

More sublunary, but not less real sources of angry discontent were found in the double burdens which were now imposed upon all who could be compelled to bear them. To raise sums adequate for the maintenance of one Court, with all its immense outgoings, had taxed the inventive genius of men skilled to the utmost in all devices for the drawing of money to the Papal Exchequer. But now, while the area from which supplies must be drawn had not been enlarged, there were two Courts, two Colleges of Cardinals,—occasionally three,—with all their costly machinery, to be maintained. To meet these needs there was almost nothing in heaven or on earth or under the earth, which was not set to sale; but on this matter I shall need to speak more at large hereafter. When to all the directly spiritual distresses of the time this intolerable burden was added, it is nothing wonderful that men sighed and cried, and asked what the end would be; or, losing all patience and all hope, demanded whether indeed an end would ever come.

Certainly it would have never arrived through the self-denying action of those from whom the mischief immediately proceeded. All appeals to the rival claimant's of St. Peter's throne, that they should take pity on a suffering Church, and bring the Schism to an end by a common resignation, were thrown away. It was in vain they were reminded that the Good Shepherd gives not his office only, but his life for the sheep. If one was willing, the other was not; or if both professed their willingness, some difficulty always arose at the last, each suspecting or feigning to suspect a fraud or treachery on the part of the other, and refusing to proceed any farther. And so through mire and dirt the tiara was dragged for long and shameful years, until at last the very Cardinals, with a College of whom the true Pope, whichever this might be, and the pretender were alike provided, became ashamed of their principals, of their falsehood and fraud and greed, and, uniting together, consented in the calling of a Council.

There was indeed but this one escape from the fatal labyrinth in which all were entangled;—namely that the Church, in General Council assembled, should declare herself, under Christ, the true source and centre of power; greater than any Pope; competent to act without him, to judge between rival claimants of the office, to remove therefrom, either for heresy or for any other notorious sin by which the Church was offended, an unworthy occupant, and to elect another in his room; and more than this, able to take such measures for her own reformation and for the excluding of scandals in the future as the necessities of the time demanded.   To the University of Paris, then at the height of its reputation, to John Gerson (b. 1363, d. 1429) its illustrious Chancellor, and to Cardinal d'Ailly (b. 1350, d. 1425) who had preceded him in the same office, belongs the honour of having laboured the most zealously and the most effectually for the healing in this way of the Church's hurt.   By their writings and discourses they familiarized the minds of many with proposals, which must have seemed, when first put forward, of an unparalleled audacity, falling only a little short of a questioning or denying the omnipotence of God.

We enter now on the story of the three Great Councils of the West, which constitute so remarkable a close to the pre-reformation period:—assemblies so stately in appearance, so impotent in fact; so large in their promise, so small in their performance; and which yet, while seeming to have done nothing, exercised in the times which followed an influence so penetrating and so vast.   The first of these is the Council of Pisa (March 25–Aug. 7, 1409).   The objects which it proposed to itself were two, but these most closely intertwined with one another:—the first the restoration of the peace, by a restoration of the unity, of the Church; the second the reformation of it in head and in members;—for this formula was now upon everybody's lips as the most adequate expression of all which all good men most desired.   It was an august assembly, though falling short of the more august gathering at Constance which was so soon to follow. There came together to Pisa of the two Obediences, twenty-three Cardinals, and either in person or by proxy some two hundred Bishops, nearly three hundred Abbots, with Doctors of theology and of the Canon and the Civil Law little short of five hundred; the representatives also of temporal princes and potentates were not wanting. The great Parisian Doctors whom I just have named, as they had contributed the most to the assembling of the Council, so were they now its inspiring soul. In the fact of thus coming together of its own authority, it had virtually declared that it was itself the legitimate seat of power in the Church; but this did not prevent it from proclaiming the same, and its own authoritative and œcumenical character, in a yet more formal manner.

And now, this first step taken, the rival claimants, Gregory XII. and Benedict XIII., were summoned to appear in person or by proxy before it. There was no reply, for both alike repudiated its authority. Hereupon their processes at once began: both, as notorious schismatics, heretics, perjurers, were set with all ignominy aside; and the Chair of St. Peter, to which by their crimes they had alike forfeited any claim, was declared to be vacant. But this done, the Council committed the capital mistake of electing at once another Pope, Alexander V., instead of proceeding first in the task of reformation, and only crowning the edifice when that task had been completed. At once a rallying point and a nucleus was given, around which might gather all the hostilities which were covertly at work in the Council; and these were many; for whom would a genuine reform so cut to the quick,

whose wings would it so effectually clip as the Popes ?
Unless he had been a man of rare magnanimity—
which Alexander, who to weakness of character added
the weakness of age, for he already bore the burden
of seventy years, was not,—his one object, as the most
far-seeing urged, would be to get rid of the Council at
the earliest possible day. And exactly this which they
had foreseen arrived. Having announced his intention
to redress a few of the worst and most crying abuses
of his own Court, he presently declared that it was impossible to proceed further with business, so thinned
had the Council been by the departure of many among
its principal members ; that he therefore adjourned it
for three years, when it should meet again, and complete the work so happily begun. The Council had
lasted in the whole a little more than four months.

Such was the lame and futile conclusion of this first
attempt to assert some other liberties in the Church
besides the liberty of the Pope to do therein what he
pleased. In some respects it left matters worse than
it found them ; for as neither of the deposed Popes
acquiesced in his sentence of deposition, and as each
had a certain following still, the immediate result was
that instead of two Popes there now were three ; and
that which should have been the Church of God, a
three headed monster, a Cerberus, as men did not fail
to call it. And now all went back again into its old
tracks, into these or worse. And thus, when Alexander, the chosen of Pisa, died in less than a year
after his election (1410), the College of Cardinals,
bribed or terrified, or both, chose a man for his successor than whom it would have been difficult in all
Christendom to select an abler or a worse. This was

Balthazar Cossa, better known as John XXIII., and among the Popes the last of this name; none, I suppose, after him caring to assume a name which he had associated with such infamies.

That a man steeped in these as he was,—"incarnate Devil," as men called him,—should of his own accord summon a Council, or in any way come to the light that his deeds might be made manifest whether they were of the light or of the darkness, was most unlikely. And yet to this he was driven; for having stirred up his enemies so mighty and so bent on his harm that he had no choice but to seek protection from Sigismund, the Emperor Elect, this protection was duly accorded to him on one condition—namely that he should proceed to fulfil the pledge and promise, now some years overdue, of his predecessors. With many misgivings, which the issue abundantly justified, John consented; these misgivings deepening into serious alarms when it was further insisted that not in Italy, with its crowd of servile Bishops outnumbering those of all the rest of Latin Christendom put together, but somewhere beyond the Alps, this Council should be held.

The Council of Pisa had been a remarkable gathering, but this of Constance (1414–1418) very far exceeded it, as it was destined to surpass any which should follow in the number and dignity of those who assisted at it. Need I remind you of the principal events by which it was signalized? They are so much better known than the incidents either of Pisa or of Basle that I shall be content, here at least, with their briefest recapitulation. The objects which the Council proposed to itself were three :—the first, to bring the

2N

Schism to an end ; the second, to pass a judgment on the doctrines of Wiclif and Hus ; and the third, to carry out that same reform, a reform of the Church in head and in members, which for all that were true of heart had been long the dearest object of their desire.

For the first, so far as that wicked man was concerned who desecrated the highest place in the Church by his occupation of it, the difficulty in getting rid of him was overcome more easily than could have been hoped.   Accused of crimes strange for their multitude and enormity, and not daring to face an investigation, he resigns.   For the second, the Wiclifite doctrines were condemned ; Hus and Jerome of Prague and the bones of Wiclif were burnt : but the Church affairs of Bohemia will demand to be treated of by themselves, and to them I propose to devote a separate Lecture. For the third, despite of past experience and warnings the most solemn, the former blunder is again repeated.   To many a Church without a Pope is as a hive without a queen-bee,—even a Gerson's courage failing him here ; and thus, before the Council addresses itself to the task of reformation, a Pope is again elected.   Martin V., who was thus chosen, was of character irreproachable, and indeed an angel of light as compared with his predecessor.   But the old story does not the less surely repeat itself again. The glory of the Council pales before the superior glory of a Pope, the first unchallenged one for more than half a century.   But he too hates to be reformed ; shows himself so fully resolved not to be reformed, that, even before the Council has broken up, there is already a revival, and under his direct authority, of some of the wrongs and abuses against which the Church had the most indignantly protested.

He has indeed only one aim, namely how to bear the Council in hand till a decent opportunity for dismissing it shall arrive. He very skilfully breaks up the ranks of the reformers, treating separately with the several nations, and entering into separate Concordats with each. With fair words and promises which even if kept would have profited little or nothing, he dissolves the assembly. When on May 16, 1418, he left the city which this Council has made famous for ever,—his bridle held on one side by the Emperor, on the other by the Elector of Brandenburg, a train of forty thousand persons, as we are told, accompanying him on horseback upon the first stage of his journey home,—it may well have seemed to him and to many that the Papacy had triumphantly extricated itself from the dangers which at one time threatened to reduce it almost to a shadow; that the wounds of the Babylonish Captivity and the Great Schism at length were healed. It was indeed wonderful that there should be any future for an institution which had gone through all the degradation which this had gone through. But the future could never be as the past had been. There are wounds, wounds above all in the reputation, which, without being deadly, yet never heal; or, if they superficially heal, leave a lasting weakness behind them.

I must hasten to the last of the Councils. The Papacy had come forth so little scathed from the perils with which at one time these assemblies menaced it, that a Council was no longer that word of terror which a little before it had been. There was more than one motive for summoning another, if indeed any help was to be found in them. Bohemia, wrapt in the flames of the Hussite War, was scorching her neighbours with fiercer fires than those by which she herself was consumed. The healing of the Greek Schism was not yet confessed to be hopeless, and the time seemed to offer its favourable opportunities. No one could affirm that the restoration of sound discipline, the reformation of the Church in head and in members, had as yet more than begun. And thus, in compliance with the rule laid down at the Council of Constance,—for even at Rome they did not dare as yet openly to set at nought its authority,—Pope Eugenius IV. called a third Council together, that namely of Basle (1431–1449). Of those who sincerely mourned over the Church's ills, the most part, after the unhappy experience of the two preceding Councils, had so completely lost all faith in these assemblies that slight regard was at first yielded to the summons; and this Council seemed likely to expire in its cradle as so many had done before, as not a few should do after.

The number of Bishops and high Church dignitaries who attended it was never great. A democratic element made itself felt throughout all its deliberations; a certain readiness to resort to measures of a revolutionary violence, such as leaves it impossible to say that it had not itself to blame for much of its ill-success. At the first indeed it displayed unlooked-for capacities for work, entering into important negotiations with the Hussites for their return to the bosom of the Church; till the Pope, alarmed at these tokens of independent activity, did not conceal his ill-will, making all means in his power to dissolve the Council. This, meanwhile, growing in strength and in self-confidence, re-affirmed all of strongest which had been affirmed already at Pisa and Constance, concerning the superiority of Councils over Popes; declared of itself that, as a lawfully assembled Council, it could neither be dissolved, nor the place of its meeting changed, unless by its own consent; and, having summoned Eugenius and his Cardinals to take their share in its labours, began the work of reformation in earnest. Eugenius yielded for the time; recalled the Bull which had hardly stopped short of anathematizing the Council; and sent his legates to Basle. Before long, however, he and the Council were again at strife; Eugenius complaining, apparently with some reason, that in these reforms one source after another of the income which had hitherto sustained the Papal Court was being dried up, while no other provision was made for the maintenance of its due dignity, or even for the defraying of its necessary expenses. As the quarrel deepened the Pope removed the seat of the Council to Ferrara (Sept. 18, 1437), on the plea that negotiations with the envoys of the Greek Church would be more conveniently conducted in an Italian city; and afterwards to Florence. The Council refused to stir, first suspending (Jan. 24, 1438), then deposing the Pope (July 7, 1439), and electing another, Felix V., in his stead; this Felix being a retired Duke of Savoy, who for some time past had been playing the hermit in a villa on the shores of the lake of Geneva. The Council in this extreme step failed to carry public opinion with it. It was not merely that Eugenius denounced his competitor by the worst names he could think of, declaring him a hypocrite, a wolf in sheep's

clothing, a Moloch, a Cerberus, a Golden Calf, a second Mahomet, an antichrist; but the Church in general shrunk back in alarm at the prospect of another
Schism, to last, it might be, for well-nigh another half
century. And thus the Council lost ground daily; its
members fell away; its confidence in itself departed;
and, though it took long in dying, it did in the end die
a death of inanition (June 23, 1448). Again the Pope
remained master of the situation, the last reforming
Council,—for it was the last,—having failed in all
which it undertook as completely and as ingloriously
as had done the two which went before.

Shall we lament the defeat of so many well-intended
efforts for the Church's good? Have we reason to
suppose that there was any true help for a Church,
sick at heart, sick throughout all its limbs, in that
which these Councils sought to effect; supposing they
had been able to bring this about, instead of succumb-
ing, they and their handiwork, before the superior
craft and skill which were arrayed against them? I
cannot think so. The Gersons, the Clemangises, the
d'Aillys, with the other earnest *Doctrinaires* who
headed this movement,—let them have the full meed
of honour which is their due; but with all their seeing
they did not see what is now most plain to us; they
only most inadequately apprehended the sickness with
which the Church was sick. For them the urgent
necessity of the time was a canonically chosen Pope,
and one who, if inclined to go wrong, might find the
law of the Church too strong for him; when indeed
what the time needed was no Pope at all; what it
wanted was, that the profane usurpation by a man of
the offices of Christ should cease altogether; that the

standing obstacle to the Church's unity,—a local centre for a divine Society whose proper centre, being the risen and ascended Lord, was everywhere,—should be removed. They would admit no errors of doctrine in the Church, but only abuses in practice; wholly refused to see that these were rooted in those, drawing all their poisonous life from them, and that blows stricken at the roots were the only blows which would profit. So far from admitting this, the most notable feat which in all their course they had accomplished was the digging up the bones of a dead man and the burning of a living, who had invited them to acknowledge their errors and to amend them.

And yet, failure upon failure as these Councils had proved, wholly as every gain which they had made for the Church was again lost before many years had elapsed, total failures they were not. They played their part in preparing the Church for a truer deliverance than any which they themselves could have ever wrought. The Hildebrandine idea of a Church,—a Society, that is, in which only one person had any rights at all,—this idea, questioned, disputed, denied, authoritatively condemned, could never dominate the Church and world, as for nearly three centuries it had done. The decrees of the Councils might be abrogated, and their whole legislation abolished; but it was not possible to abolish from men's minds and memories that such once had been. There needed many blows, and from many quarters, to overthrow so huge and strong-built a fabric as that of the medieval Papacy. It is impossible to doubt that by the Councils one of these blows was stricken.

A word or two more upon these Councils before we

close. And first,—we are, I think, often greatly surprised at the general helplessness which they displayed
in their struggles with the Papacy. One or two considerations may diminish this surprise. Thus it is easy
to see at what an immense disadvantage upon their
side the battle was fought. In any case the interval
between one Council and another must have been
considerable—the Pope made these intervals much
greater, and during them he could do very much as
he pleased. Then, too, while the Councils had nothing
to give away, the Pope had almost any amount of
canonries, deaneries, bishoprics, cardinalates, and what
not, in his gift; with these he could be, and was, a rich
rewarder of those who diligently sought and served
him; and had thus nearly all the venal talent of the
age at his command.

Defeated as the Councils had been, they left behind
them questions for solution which gave not a little
trouble to the victors. Thus the question whether
they should be recognized as lawful, and thus authoritative, assemblies of the Church Catholic or not (*Con-
cilia* or *Conciliabula*), was one of an immense embarrassment, an embarrassment which naturally was felt
the most strongly in the period immediately succeeding. It is a question which more or less perplexes Roman Catholic legists to the present day. The dilemma
was a very real one. If they were Councils indeed,
and truly represented the Church, then Councils might
meet without the authority of Popes, might set limits
to their power, might depose and elect them; all which
being admitted, what became of the Papal Supremacy,
the Papal Infallibility; or who could gainsay the claim
of the Councils to be the tribunal of highest instance,

the ultimate seat of all authority in the Church? But
if, in terror of consequences such as these, the name of
Councils was denied them, by what right did the
Popes who owed their election to the Councils, and
others in succession to them, who owed theirs to the
votes of the Cardinals by these same Popes appointed,
sit in the Papal Chair? To question or deny the com-
petency of those was to question or deny the foundations on which their own position rested. The solution which was found of this difficulty was ingenious in
its simplicity. Whatever things were done in the
Councils *conciliariter*, that is, as things ought to be
done in Council, were to stand; whatever otherwise,
must disappear; the Pope in each case being the
judge of what was so done and what not. In this way
the legitimacy of Conciliar acts, so far as they affected
the election of Popes, was saved.

For the rest, it was left to the ever-watchful action
of the Roman Curia to defeat any legal liberties which
the Church had gained, and after a while to annul the
whole legislation of the Councils, so far as the Papal
autocracy was in any way restricted thereby. Æneas
Sylvius, who had been a leader of the reforming party
at Basle, showed, as Pius II., the zeal of a renegade in
the active undoing of all which he had helped to accomplish there. In an ominous year, in 1517, this was
finally and completely effected.

20

LECTURE XXI.

WICLIF AND THE LOLLARDS.

It is long since we have dwelt with any fulness on English Church affairs. They will claim our attention now. John Wiclif, born about the year 1324 at or near Old Richmond in Yorkshire, had already fulfilled a distinguished career at Oxford, and obtained such honourable recognition there as that famous University could give him, when it was his lot to exchange an academical for a national, and in the end for an European, reputation. A vigorous resistance upon his part to the encroachments of the Mendicant Friars, who were swarming here as everywhere, has been often adduced as the first notable achievement which drew on him the eyes of men (1360). But there is much relating to the earlier half of Wiclif's career that passes for historic, while it rests in fact on very doubtful authority; and it may very well be a question whether the whole story of his collision with the Begging Friars does not belong to quite another and later period of his life.

Be this as it may, he was first known to all England on occasion of the demand, on the part of Pope Urban V., that the tribute which King John had engaged to pay in acknowledgment of the Papal overlordship, with the arrears now due of three and thirty years, should not be withholden any longer (1365).

The amount, a thousand marks a year, was small; but the honour and independence of England, compromised by this payment, was much; and Wiclif, who had a strong English heart, in whom the patriot and the theologian mutually sustained and strengthened one another, stood forth among the foremost of those who urged, and by argument justified, resistance to this demand. His place indeed was so manifestly among the first and the ablest of these as to draw upon him the deepest resentment of the Roman Court, and of all whose interests and passions were bound up with it. Edward III., as is well known, referred the question of payment to Parliament; and doubtless was neither surprised nor displeased with the reply, namely that King John had no power to give away the independence of England, and that it was ready to sustain the King in any resistance to this demand. The Pope, perceiving with what temper he had to deal, did not press the claim, nor was it ever again revived.

The incident was a very insignificant one, and characteristic of a very memorable epoch,—for such the fourteenth century was,—in the constitutional history of England. As iron sharpens iron, so our wars with France were doing much for the making of both countries. The misfortunes of France were welding her provinces more strongly together; while the triumphs of England, shortlived as they were destined to prove, raised the temper and courage of Englishmen, proud of themselves and of the princes who had led them to victory. Growing more and more conscious of an independent national existence, there were humiliations which they would not accept from one who

dwelt under the ignoble shelter of a French King—for
this was the age of the Papal exile at Avignon—and
spoke at this King's dictation.　Add to this that intolerable exactions and extortions, which had existed long,
but were ever waxing worse,—for wealthy England
was regarded as the milch-cow of the Papacy, which
could never be drawn dry,—had very nearly wearied
out the patience of Englishmen, so that they were
riper for resistance than ever before they had been.

And yet, with all this, a quarrel with Rome, possess-
ing as she did a garrison in every land, and grand traditions, all whose strength had not yet gone out of
them, was a formidable affair for a nation to undertake ; and could only be brought to a successful end
by the enlisting of all the national and patriotic spirit
in the land.　And thus it was felt not to be a small
matter that the most learned doctor at Oxford, the
most accomplished Schoolman of his age, of a reputation in which the most keen-eyed foe could not detect
a flaw, should be ranged on the side of the liberties of
England.　His good deserts were not forgotten in the
highest quarters ; and when it was sought to bring
him into trouble for some free utterances, not as yet
on doctrinal, but on disciplinary matters, the influence
of the Court, above all of John of Gaunt,—this exercised, it must be owned, in a very tumultuary fashion,
—was sufficient to protect him against his ill-willers
(1376).　When too in the year following a still more
serious attempt was made to silence him, the Pope
himself interfering, and demanding that the offender
should be surrendered to him, the same favour, rein-
forced as it now was by the active goodwill of the
citizens of London, defeated this second attempt.

Presented by the Crown to the living of Lutterworth (1374), but still retaining his hold upon Oxford, neither the one sphere nor the other, nor yet both together, fully satisfied his longing to bring home to the great body of the people the words of eternal life. Out of this desire sprang his Poor Priests. These were itinerant evangelists who passed up and down through the land, preaching everywhere. The urgent spiritual necessities of the time, and the entire abdication by so many of the parochial Clergy of their duty as preachers of the Word, must be taken as his justification in the sending forth of these; which yet he could not do but at some manifest cost to the Church's discipline and order.

Out of the same zeal sprang a still more important effort upon his part. Men may challenge and call in question portions of his work; but as many as believe that the Bible should be accessible to all, must acknowledge the obligations under which Christian England lies to him for his translation of this into the vulgar tongue. Under a sense of the vastness of this debt, I dwell not upon another debt which yet is not a small one; the debt I mean which is owing to him by the whole English speaking race for a work whose influence is felt to the present hour through every fibre of the English language. It would detract little from the glory of this version, even if that which Sir Thomas More urged were true, namely that the Scriptures had been already rendered into English. This, however, was not the case. Portions indeed had been rendered, mainly the Psalter, for the convenience of unlettered clerics. But as these translations had not been made for the lay-people, so neither had they reached them.

Here first was a version of the whole of the Sacred Book, and framed with a design to be read of all. The New Testament was naturally the first attempted, and may very well have been altogether from Wiclif's own hand. The whole Bible will have been finished in or very nearly about the year 1381.

There was a loud outcry of course. Translations from one language to another, it was urged, in the very necessity of things were imperfect,—which is quite true, but not reason sufficient for excluding them; and, as was well replied, was not the Vulgate itself a translation? Pearls were not to be cast before swine; the unlearned would wrest Scripture itself to their own harm; which therefore it was safest to keep out of their hands. But Wiclif held on his way, and made the perfecting of what he had begun a main business of the little which remained of his life. It was inevitable that a translation in which many had borne a part,—not all with the same notions of what the duties of a translator were, neither all endowed with the same mastery of tongues,—whatever its merits might be, should offer inconsistencies, inequalities, imperfections manifold. Here literal accuracy had been sacrificed to the attaining of greater clearness; there a too close adherence to the letter had caused the spirit to escape; while many passages through an over-literalness were unintelligible. No one can have been better aware than Wiclif himself of the shortcomings of his work. But other hands than his were to accomplish its revision, and mainly those of his faithful curate and underworker, John Purvey. This later recension has cleared itself of many of the harshnesses, crudities, and other smaller faults which clung to the earlier. The two recensions, I may mention, stand side by side, in parallel columns, in the noble edition, published by the Clarendon Press at Oxford, of this first English Bible—that on the left being the earlier, and either Wiclif's own or made immediately under his eye; while on the right is the later revision, which was not published till several years after his death. I need hardly remind you that this work of Wiclif with all its merits is the translation of a translation; that its original is the Vulgate; the Hebrew Old Testament, and with rarest exceptions the Greek New, being alike sealed books even to the most accomplished scholars of that generation.

A few words on the latter years of Wiclif's life. Twice he had been drawn into question; he was destined to be so once more. On the death of Gregory XI. (1378) followed the double election to the Papal throne, and on that the Great Schism of the West. This exercised a profound influence on Wiclif,—less upon his outer fortunes than his inward convictions; though it is quite possible that this Schism, occupying men's thoughts as it must, weakening too as it did the central authority, may have prevented the searching out of heretics for due punishment with the same energy as before; and that thus a man, the object of so keen a hatred, should after all have been suffered to die in his bed.

But of the effects of the Schism on his inward convictions he has left no doubt. When he beheld two, who both called themselves by the holiest name on earth, hurling anathemas each at the other and at all the adherents of the other,—shrinking from the em-

ployment of no weapons by which they might harm
one another,—equally hateful and equally contempti-
ble,—he no longer beheld in them a true Pope and a
false one, between whom to choose; but rather two,
false alike, the two halves of Antichrist, making up the
perfect Man of Sin between them.   Henceforth the
abuse of all abuses for him was not this matter or that
which the Papacy allowed or enjoined, but the Papacy
itself.   But Wiclif about this time came to another
important conviction, namely that the Roman doctrine
of Transubstantiation was anti-scriptural; and with
straightforward boldness which marked all his career
he announced this conviction in the pulpits of Oxford.
Hereupon followed the latest organized attempt to
suppress him (1382).   This found him weaker in outward supports than when exposed to similar attacks
at an earlier day.   Many were terrified by the com-
munistic outbreak known as Wat Tyler's insurrection, which occurred at the beginning of the preceding
year; and, without accusing him, accused his teaching
of having helped to bring it about, just as at a later
day the atrocities of the Peasants' War were laid to
Luther's door.   Then too, in the new reign,—for we
have reached the reign of Richard II.,—the Duke of
Lancaster was not that power in the state which once
he had been; and now that the points at issue were
not of discipline but of doctrine, in which as a layman
he may have felt but a feeble interest, even he coun-
selled submission.   Many others too, who had stood
with Wiclif when he assailed open and flagrant abuses, shrunk from making common part with him when
he ventured to question the Church's faith in its holiest mystery of all.

And yet, though his adversaries were able to go far in the condemnation of his teaching upon this point, —none of the other charges appear to have been seriously pressed,—in some strange way they were hindered from proceeding to the last extremity against his person. From Oxford indeed he found it prudent to withdraw; but the two closing years of his life he spent unmolested at Lutterworth, in the discharge of those duties of a parish priest to which he attached so high an importance. I may add that some of his most vigorous onslaughts upon the abuses and errors of his time, his *Trialogus* for example, belong to this latest period of his life. It is plain that he did not retire to Lutterworth under a tacit understanding with his enemies, that they should leave him alone, and he should hold his peace.

It would be pleasant to think that Chaucer had Wiclif in his eye, when he drew his exquisite portrait of "the poor Parson of the town;" but almost every line of that portrait belongs, as it seems to me, to an obscurer man, and not to one with whose good report or whose evil report all England was ringing from side to side. It is the portrait of one who, satisfied with reforming himself and feeding the flock specially committed to his charge, did not count it his mission to attempt to reform the whole Church, save in the way of setting a noble example to all. Add to this that it is scarcely on a pilgrimage to the shrine of St. Thomas of Canterbury that we should look for Wiclif. He was, as is well known, struck with palsy while celebrating the divine offices in his church at Lutterworth on the day of the Holy Innocents (Dec. 28, 1384). His adversaries transferred the occurrence of the fatal stroke to the day following, being the day of St. Thomas, that so they might trace in that stroke the just vengeance of the saint and martyr upon one who had dared to find fault with the honours so prodigally bestowed on him and the riches heaped on his shrine.

What shall we say in parting from Wiclif and his work? And first, with all due thankfulness to Almighty God that He raised up this witness for so much of truth, we, members of the Anglican Church, may be thankful too that the Reformation was not in his time, nor of his doing. From a Church reformed under the auspices of one who was properly the spiritual ancestor of our Puritans, the Catholic element would in good part, perhaps altogether, have disappeared. Overthrowing much, he built up very little. In that knowledge of Holy Scripture which by his translation he diffused among the English people, there were good foundations laid; but in the main we must see in him rather a clearer of the ground than a builder thereupon. His axe was laid at the root of much, of pilgrimages, of Indulgences, of Crusades—which in his time had grown to be mischievous impostures—of Transubstantiation; though whether in this last matter he shunned one danger without falling into another it is not easy to determine.

And yet, crude and immature as were parts of his teaching, manifestly erroneous as other portions of it were,—when for example he denied the lawfulness of war, the right of the State to inflict capital punishment on evil doers, or when he affirmed that it was every man's duty to refuse tithe to a priest who, according to his notion, did not discharge his duty, thus investing fallible and interested men with this judgment about

their fellows,—it is only fair to remember that some
things are laid to his charge that he knew not. Thus
there is an old charge against him, one as old as the
Council of Constance, afterwards taken up by the
German Reformers with whom Wiclif—"der spitzige,"
as Luther calls him—was never a favourite; and constantly repeated since. According to this charge, he
made the efficacy of the Sacraments and of other
Church ordinances to depend on the holiness of the
priest who ministered them. I need not remind you
that the Church would so be founded on the shifting
sands of the goodness of man, instead of the eternal
rock of the faithfulness of God. There is, however, no
truth in the charge; but statements innumerable in
his writings which do not imply merely, but directly
assert the contrary.

Wiclif's influence was not so merely personal that it
should die with him. He left followers behind him
eager to carry on his work. Lollards they were called
before long—a name already loosely applied in the
Low Countries and elsewhere to heretics of various·
descriptions; but which now, with the usual contempt
for accuracy displayed in the giving of opprobrious
names, was fastened upon them. His Poor Priests
survived him. Barefoot, and clad in long russet garments of coarsest material, they passed two and two
through the land, denouncing everywhere the sins of
all sorts and conditions of men, but with an especial
emphasis the sins, the luxury, the sloth, the ignorance
of the Clergy. As the Mendicant Friars had sought
to take this weapon of popular preaching out of the
hands of the Poor Men of Lyons, so these Poor Priests

in turn sought to wrest the same out of theirs. And they found a ready hearing. Half of England, as a hostile witness not long after Wiclif's death laments, was infected with Lollardy. Nor was it the lower classes alone of whom it had taken hold. Many temporal lords were at least its abettors. Armed knights and nobles would stand round the Poor Priests, when any unfriendly interruption of their preaching was feared. At Court the Queen Mother, and Anne of Bohemia, Queen Consort of Richard II., were well disposed. Oxford too remained Wiclifite for many years after Wiclif's death.

The year 1395 marks the highest point of influence and power which the Lollards in England ever attained. Up to that date they had been continually gaining ground. The Bishops, who would willingly have done more for their effectual suppression, had been embarrassed by the multitude, and oftentimes by the boldness, of the dissidents;—not to say that, in the desultory efforts in this direction which they did make, they invoked in vain the assistance of the secular arm. Richard and his advisers, without absolutely refusing to do anything, were evidently resolved to do as little as they could in the matter of persecution. But by the overthrow in Richard's person of one dynasty, and the coming up in Henry IV. of another, everything was changed. To Thomas Arundel, who succeeded Courtenay as Archbishop of Canterbury, more than to any other, Henry owed the success of his daring usurpation ; and Arundel, a bold and determined man, had made the putting down of the Lollards the task of his life. The Lancastrian Monarch, with his questionable title to the throne, had no choice but to make sure of the support of the hierarchy, which could only be purchased at one price. He was prepared, and his son after him, to pay that price. Laws of extreme severity against the Lollards were rapidly passed through Convocation and Parliament (1399–1400) ; and now for the first time in England heresy was made punishable with death. Dr. Hook indeed assures us that the whole measure was far more a political act, prompted by the fears of Henry IV. and his lay supporters, than an ecclesiastical one; that from the beginning of the Wiclifite troubles the English Bishops were reluctant to persecute, and were only hounded on from without. One would be glad to think this was true.

This much is certain, that these laws against heretics did not remain a dead letter. Of the preachers some recanted. It is a grief to find John Purvey among these, though there may be fairly a question whether he did not afterwards recant his recantation. Others, more steadfast than he, were silenced,—some by a lifelong imprisonment, some by the infliction upon them of those extreme penalties which now the law allowed. It is idle to say that persecution, if remorselessly employed and under fairly favourable conditions, may not prove a very effectual means for repressing opinions. It has sometimes succeeded in extirpating them altogether. This last it was unable to do here ; but much in the way of repression it did. Then too, the solemn condemnation at Constance of forty articles drawn, or affirmed to be drawn, from the writings of Wiclif, made a deep impression in England. Many had been laid hold of by the practical side of Wiclif's teaching, with little concern about the more purely theological; and had no intention of putting themselves, as they found that, adhering to him, they must now do, in opposition to the general voice of Christendom.   Nor can we doubt that the ferocious wars, at once civil and religious, which desolated Bohemia and the regions of Germany bordering upon it, were regarded by not a few as the legitimate outcome of the teaching of Hus, and thus at second-hand of Wiclif.   Was England to become a theatre of the like?

In the year 1431 the persecution ceased, at least for a long time; why, it is not very easy to explain. Probably out of sheer weariness on the part of the persecutors, and despair of ever fully attaining their object; while yet the strength of Lollardy was so far broken as no longer to threaten the very existence of the dominant Church.   Some speak as though, through the pitiless application of measures of repression, it had quite died out from the land, or only so obscurely existed that its traces could no longer be followed up.   This, however, was far from the case. Doubtless its aggressive force was spent.   From being a power claiming recognition in Church and State, and in fact demanding that both should be fashioned and moulded according to its notions, it had been violently forced back into the condition of a sect.   With the loss of Oxford, which had now returned to her allegiance to Rome, it had lost its theological centre and stronghold.   With the execution of Lord Cobham—"the good Lord Cobham," as he was fondly called—its political significance had disappeared.   Of the nobility and gentry who once favoured it some were dead; others had detached themselves

from a body, to belong to which seemed to argue dis-
affection or worse.   But of its continued existence, not
seeking any more to transform England at once, but
to reach its ends by slower means, by the winning of
one soul after another, abundant evidence remains.
Pecock in his *Repressor* speaks of having often con-
versed with the chiefs and leaders of the party.   Nay,
after an intermission of more than fifty years, in the
first year of the Tudors, the burnings began again
(1485).   They were going vigorously forward in 1511,
in which year a correspondent of Erasmus informs
him that wood was dear in England, and no wonder,
when the heretics afforded a daily holocaust; Erasmus
replying with a heartless jest that he could now less
than ever forgive those who, with winter at hand were
thus raising the price of fagots.

It was probably the continued vitality and the renewed activity of the sect which again excited alarm.
Large and open gatherings for the preaching of the
Word were not any more attempted.   The itinerant
preacher had given place to the itinerant reader, who
was never more active than at the close of the
fifteenth and beginning of the sixteenth century.
There were little assemblies or conventicles everywhere; and it might put to a wholesome shame our
careless unthankful use of Holy Scripture, to read
how precious the Word in those days was, how men
came together by night, at peril of their lives, in barns,
in stables, in lonely houses, to hear some tract which
should expound it, as Wiclif's *Wicket* or his *Lantern
of Light;* or, oftener still, to listen to Scripture itself,
—a Gospel, or the Apocalypse, dear ever to those
that suffer tribulation, or a Pauline Epistle, or, which

noticeably enough was a still more favourite reading, the Epistle of St. James. And so the Lollards lived on: and when the Reformation came at last, these humble men, as we may well believe, did much to contribute to it that element of sincerity, truth, and uprightness, without which it could never have succeeded; which yet, as must be sorrowfully owned, was miserably lacking on the part of so many, who played foremost parts in the carrying of it through, but who sought in it not the things of God but their own.

LECTURE XXII.

HUS AND BOHEMIA.

THE Wiclifite movement had at the outset and for many years after its author's death been purely an English one. It was not always to remain such; but was destined to acquire an European significance. Some sparks of the fire which Wiclif had lighted, blown over half Europe, as far as remote Bohemia, quickened into stronger activity a flame which for long years burned and scorched and consumed, defying all efforts to extinguish it. But for all this, it was not Wiclif who kindled the Bohemian fires. His writing did much to fan and feed them; while the assumed, and in part erroneously assumed, identity of his teaching with that of Hus contributed not a little to shape the tragic issues of the Bohemian Reformer's life. But the Bohemian movement was an independent and eminently a national one. If we look for the proper forerunners of Hus, his true spiritual ancestors, we shall find them in his own land, in a succession of earnest and faithful preachers,—among these Militz (d. 1374) and Janow (d. 1394) stand out the most prominently,—who had sown seed which could hardly have failed to bear fruit sooner or later, though no line of Wiclif's writings had ever found its way to Bohemia. This land, not German, however it may have been early drawn into the circle of German interests,

with a population Slavonic in the main, had first received the faith, as it will be remembered, through the
preaching of Greek monks. The Bohemian Church
probably owed to this fact that, though incorporated
from the first with the Churches of the West, uses and
customs prevailed in it,—as the preaching in the
mother tongue, the marriage of the Clergy, Communion in both kinds,—which it only slowly and unwillingly relinquished. It was not till the fourteenth century that its lines were drawn throughout in exact conformity with those of Rome. All this deserves to be
kept in mind; for it helps to account for the kindly
reception which the seed sown by the later Bohemian
Reformers found, falling as this did in a soil to which
it was not altogether strange.

John Hus (b. 1369, d. 1415), the central figure of
the Bohemian Reformation, took in the year 1394 his
degree as Bachelor of Theology in that University of
Prague, upon the fortunes of which he was destined to
exercise so lasting an influence; and four years later,
in 1398, he began to deliver lectures there. Hus
had early taken his degree in a school higher than any
school of man's. He himself has told us how he was
once careless and disobedient, how the Word of the
Cross had taken hold of him with strength, and penetrated him through and through as with a mighty purifying fire. What he had learned in the school of
Christ he could not keep to himself. Holding, in addition to his academical position, a lectureship founded
by two pious laymen for the preaching of the Word
in the Bohemian tongue (1401), he soon signalized
himself by his diligence in breaking the bread of life
to hungering souls, and his boldness in rebuking vice

in high places as in low. So long as he confined himself to reproving the sins of the laity, leaving those of
the Clergy and monks unassailed, he found little opposition, nay, rather support and applause from these.
But when he brought them also within the circle of his
condemnation, and began to upbraid them for their
covetousness, their ambition, their luxury, their sloth,
and for other vices, they turned angrily upon him, and
sought to undermine his authority, everywhere spreading reports of the unsoundness of his teaching.

Let us see on what side he mainly exposed himself
to charges such as these. Many things had recently
wrought together to bring into nearness countries
geographically so remote from one another as Bohemia and England. Anne, wife of our second Richard,
was a sister of Wenzel, King of Bohemia. The two
flourishing Universities of Oxford and Prague were
bound together by their common zeal for Realism:—
this may seem to us but a slight and fantastic bond; it
was in those days a very strong one indeed. Young
English scholars studied at Prague, young Bohemian
at Oxford. Now, as has been already noted, Oxford
long after Wiclif's death was full of interest for his
doctrine; and among the many strangers sojourning
there, it could hardly fail that some should imbibe
opinions, and bring back with them books of one
whom they had there learned to know and to honour.
Thus Jerome, called of Prague, on his return from the
English University, gave a new impulse to the study
of Wiclif's writings, bearer as he was of several
among these which had not hitherto travelled so far.

This man, whose fortunes were so tragically bound
up with those of Hus, who should share with him in

the same fiery doom, was his junior by several years; his superior in eloquence, in talents, in gifts,—for certainly Hus was not a theologian of the first order; speculative theologian he was not at all,—but notably his inferior in moderation and practical good sense. Hus never shared in his friend's indiscriminate admiration of Wiclif. When in 1403 some forty-five theses, which either were or professed to be drawn from the writings of the English Reformer, were brought before the University that they might be condemned as heretical, Hus expressed himself with extreme caution and reserve. Many of these, he affirmed, were true when a man took them aright; but he could not say this of all. Not first at the Council of Constance, but long before, he had refused to undertake the responsibility of Wiclif's teaching on the Holy Eucharist. But he did not conceal what he had learned from Wiclif's writings. By these there had been opened to him a deeper glimpse into the corruptions of the Church, and its need of reformation in the head and in the members, than ever he had before obtained. His preaching, with the new accesses of insight which now were his, more than ever exasperated his foes.

While matters were in this strained condition, events took place at Prague which are too closely connected with the story that we are telling, exercised too great an influence in bringing about the issues that lie before us, to allow us to pass them by, even though they may prove somewhat long to relate. The University of Prague, though recently founded—it only dated back to the year 1348—was now, next after those of Paris and Oxford, the most illustrious in Europe. Saying this I say much; for we must not measure the

influence and authority of an University at that day by
the influence and authority, great as these are, which
it may now possess. This University, like that of
Paris, on the pattern of which it had been modelled,
was divided into four "nations"—four groups, that is,
or families of scholars—each of these having in academical affairs a single collective vote. These nations
were the Bavarian, the Saxon, the Polish, and the Bohemian. This does not appear at first an unfair
division—two German and two Slavonic; but in practical working the Polish was so largely recruited from
Silesia and other German or half-German lands, that
its vote was in fact German also. The Teutonic votes
were thus as three to one, and the Bohemians in their
own land and their own University on every important
matter hopelessly outvoted. When, by aid of this preponderance, the University was made to condemn the
teaching of Wiclif in those forty-five points, matters
came to a crisis. Urged by Hus, who as a stout
patriot, and an earnest lover of the Bohemian language and literature, had more than a theological
interest in the matter,—by Jerome,—by a large number of the Bohemian nobility,—King Wenzel published
an edict whereby the relations of natives and foreigners were completely reversed. There should be henceforth three votes for the Bohemian nation, and only
one for the three others. Such a shifting of the
weights certainly appears as a redressing of one in-
equality by creating another. At all events it was so
earnestly resented by the Germans, by professors and
students alike, that they quitted the University in a
body, some say of five, and some of thirty thousand,
and founded the rival University of Leipsic, leaving

no more than two thousand students at Prague. Full of indignation against Hus, whom they regarded as the prime author of this affront and wrong, they spread throughout all Germany the most unfavourable reports of him and of his teaching.

This exodus of the foreigners had left Hus, who was now Rector of the University, with a freer field than before. But Church matters at Prague did not mend; they became more confused and threatening every day; until presently the same shameful outrage against all Christian morality which a century later did a still more effectual work, served to put Hus into open opposition to the corrupt hierarchy of his time. Pope John XXIII., having a quarrel with the King of Naples, proclaimed a Crusade against him, with what had become a constant accompaniment of this,—Indulgences to match. But to denounce Indulgences, as Hus with fierce and righteous indignation did now, was to wound Rome in her most sensitive part. He was excommunicated at once, and every place which should harbour him stricken with an Interdict. While matters were in this frame the Council of Constance was opened, which should appease all the troubles of Christendom, and correct whatever was amiss. The Bohemian difficulty could not be omitted, and Hus was summoned to make answer at Constance for himself.

He had not been there four weeks when he was required to appear before the Pope and Cardinals (Nov. 18, 1414). After a brief informal hearing he was committed to harsh durance, from which he never issued as a free man again. Sigismund, the German King and Emperor Elect, who had furnished Hus with a safe-conduct which should protect him, "going to the

Council, tarrying at the Council, returning from the Council," was absent from Constance at the time, and heard with real displeasure how lightly regarded this promise and pledge of his had been. Some big words too he spoke, threatening to come himself and release the prisoner by force ; but, being waited on by a deputation from the Council, who represented to him that he, as a layman, in giving such a safe-conduct had exceeded his powers, and intruded into a region which was not his, Sigismund was convinced, or affected to be convinced. Doubtless the temptations to be convinced were strong. Had he insisted on the liberation of Hus, the danger was imminent that the Council, for which he had laboured so earnestly, should be broken up on the plea that its rightful freedom was denied it. He did not choose to run this risk, preferring to leave an everlasting blot upon his name.

Some modern sophists assure us that this safe-conduct, or free pass as they prefer to call it, engaged the Imperial word for Hus's safety in going to the Council, but for nothing more—a most perfidious document, if this is all which it undertook; for the words,—I quote the more important of them in the original Latin, —are as follows, *ut ei transire, stare, morari, redire permittatis.* But the treachery was not in the document; and no body at the time attempted to find it there. If this had not engaged the honour of the Emperor, what cause of complaint would he have had against the Cardinals as having entangled him in a breach of his word ? what need of their solemn ambassage to him ? Untrue also is the assertion that this was so little regarded by Hus himself as a safe-conduct covering the whole period during which he

should be exposed to the malice of his enemies, that
he never appealed to it, or claimed protection from it.
He did so appeal at his second formal hearing (June
7th), the first at which Sigismund was present.   "I am
here," he there said, "under the King's promise that I
should return to Bohemia in safety;" while at his last
by a look and by a few like words he brought the
royal word-breaker to a blush, evident to all present
(July 6th).

But to return a little.   More than seven months
elapsed before Hus could obtain a hearing before the
Council.   This was granted to him at last.   Thrice
heard (June 5, 7, 8, 1415),—if indeed such tumultuary
sittings, where the man speaking for his life, and for
much more than his life, was continually interrupted
and overborne by hostile voices, by loud cries of
"Recant," "Recant," may be reckoned as hearings at
all,—he bore himself, by the confession of all, with
courage, meekness, and dignity.   The charges brought
against him were various ; some so far-fetched as that
urged by a Nominalist from the University of Paris
(for Paris was Nominalist now), namely that as a Realist he *could not* be sound on the doctrine of the
Eucharist.   Others were vague enough, as that he
had sown discord between the Church and the State.
Nor were accusations wanting which touched a really
weak point in his teaching, namely the subjective aspect which undoubtedly some aspects of it wore ; as
when he taught that not the baptized, but the predesti-
nated to life, constituted the Church.   Beset as he was
by the most accomplished theologians of the age, the
best or the worst advantage was sure to be made of
any vulnerable side which he exposed.   But there

were charges against him with more in them of danger than these. The point which was really at issue between him and his adversaries concerned the relative authority of the Church and of Scripture. What they demanded of him was a retractation of all the articles brought against him, with an unconditional submission to the Council. Some of the articles, he replied, charged him with teaching things which he had never taught, and he could not by this formal act of retractation admit that he had taught them. Let any doctrine of his be shown to be contrary to God's holy Word, and he would retract it; but such unconditional submission he could not yield.

His fate was now sealed—that is, unless he could be induced to recant; in which event, though he did not know it, his sentence would have been degradation from the priesthood and a life-long imprisonment. Many efforts up to the last moment were made by friend and foe to persuade him to this, but in vain. And now once more (July 6) he is brought before the Council; but this time for sentence and for doom. The sentence passed, his passion, if we may venture to use the word, begins. The long list of his heresies, among which they are not ashamed to include many which he has distinctly repudiated, is read out in his hearing. He is clothed with priestly garments, that these, piece by piece, and each with an appropriate insult and malediction, may be stripped from him again. The sacred vessels are placed in his hands, that from him, "accursed Judas that he is," they may be taken again. There is some difficulty in erasing his tonsure; but this difficulty with a little violence and cruelty is overcome. A tall paper cap, painted over with flames

and devils, and inscribed "Heresiarch," is placed upon
his head. This done, and his soul having been duly
delivered to Satan, his body is surrendered to the secular arm. One last touch is not wanting. As men
bind him to the stake, attention is called to the fact
that his face is turned to the East. This honour must
not be his, upon whom no Sun of Righteousness shall
ever rise. He is unfastened and refastened anew.
All is borne with perfect meekness, in the thought and
in the strength of Him who had borne so much more
for sinners, the Just for the unjust ;—and so, in his fire-
chariot of a painful martyrdom, Hus passes from our
sight.

Some may wonder that he, a Reformer, should have
been so treated by a Council, itself also reforming, and
with a man like Gerson (*Doctor Christianissimus* was
the title he bore) virtually at its head. But a little
consideration will dispel this surprise, and lead us to
the conclusion that a Council less earnestly bent on
reforms of its own would probably have dealt more
mildly with him. His position and theirs, however,
we may ascribe alike to him and to them a desire to
reform the Church, were fundamentally different.
They, when they deposed a Pope, when they proclaimed the general superiority of Councils over
Popes, had no intention of diminishing one jot the
Church's authority in matters of faith, but only of
changing the seat of that authority, substituting an ecclesiastical aristocracy for an ecclesiastical monarchy,
—or depotism, as long since it had grown to be. And
thus the more earnest the Council was to carry out a
reformation in discipline, the more eager was it also
to make evident to all the world that it did not intend

to touch doctrine, but would uphold this as it had received it.   It is not then uncharitable to suspect that
the leading men of the Council,—like those Reformers
at Geneva who a century and a half later sent Serve-
tus to the stake (1553),— were not sorry to be able
to give so signal an evidence of their zeal for the
maintenance of the faith which they had received, as
thus, in the condemnation of Hus, they had the opportunity of doing.   Nor may we leave altogether out of
account that the German element must of necessity
have been strong in a Council held on the shores of
the Bodensee ; while in his vindication of Bohemian
nationality, perhaps an excessive vindication, Hus, as
we have seen, had offended and embittered the Germans to the uttermost.

If any had flattered themselves that with the death
of Hus the Reformation in Bohemia had also received
its death-blow, they had not long to wait for a painful
undeception.   Words fail to describe the tempest of
passionate indignation with which the tidings of his
execution, followed within the year by that of Jerome,
were received there.   Both were honoured as martyrs;
and already, in the fierce exasperation of men's spirits
against the authors of their doom, there was a prophecy of the unutterable woes which were even at the
door.   Some watchword by which his followers could
know and be known—this watchword, if possible a
spell of power like that which Luther had found in the
doctrine of Justification by faith—was still wanting.
One however was soon found ; which indeed had this
drawback, that it concerned a matter disciplinary rather
than doctrinal, yet having a real value as a visible wit-

ness for the rights of the laity in the Church of Christ.
So far as we know, Hus had not himself laid any
special stress on Communion under both kinds : but
in 1414—he was then already at Constance,—the subject had come to the forefront at Prague; and, being
consulted, Hus had entirely approved of such Communion, as most conformable to the original Institution and to the practice of the Primitive Church.   On
the other hand the Council, learning the agitation of
men's spirits in this direction, had declared what is
called the " Concomitance,"—that is, that wherever
one kind was present, there was also the other; which
being so nothing was indeed withholden from the com-
municant through the withholding of the Cup.   At the
same time the Council had solemnly condemned as a
heretic every one who refused to submit himself to the
decision of the Church in this matter (June 15, 1415).

But there was no temper of submission in Bohemia,
—least of all when the University of Prague gave its
voice in favour of this demand.   Wenzel, the well-
intentioned but poor-spirited King, was quite unable
to keep peace between the rival factions, and could
only slip out of his difficulties by dying (Aug. 16, 1419).
Sigismund, his brother, was also his successor; but of
one thing the Bohemians were at this time resolved,
namely that the royal betrayer of his word should not
reign over them.   And thus a condition of miserable
anarchy followed, and in the end, of open war; which,
lasting for eleven years, could be matched by few wars
in the cruelties and atrocities by which on both sides
it was disgraced.   In Ziska, their blind chief, the Hussites had a leader with a born genius for war.   It was
he who invented the movable waggon-fortress whereof

we hear so much,—against which the German chivalry
would break as idly as waves upon a rock. Three
times crusading armies,—for this name they bore,—
thinking with no serious opposition to enforce the decrees of the Council, invaded Bohemia; to be thrice
driven back with utter defeat, disgrace, and loss; the
Hussites, who for a long while were content with
merely repelling the invaders, after a while, and as the
only way of conquering a peace, turning the tables, and
wasting with fire and sword all neighbouring German
lands.

A conflict so hideous could not long be waged without a rapid deterioration of all who were engaged in
it. The spirit of Hus more and more departed from
those who called themselves by his name. Intestine
strifes devoured their strength. There were first the
Moderates—Calixtines, Utraquists, or "Those of
Prague," they were called,—who, weary of the long
struggle, were willing to return to the bosom of the
Church if only the Cup (*calix*), and thus Communion
under both kinds (*sub utraque*), were guaranteed to
them, with two or three secondary matters. Not so
the Taborites, who drew their name from a mountain
fastness which they fortified and called Mount Ta-
bor. These, the Ultras, the democratic radical party,
separating themselves off as early as 1419, had left
Hus and his teaching very far behind. Ignoring the
whole historic development of Christianity, they demanded that a clean sweep should be made of
everything in the Church's practice for which an express and literal warrant in Scripture could not be
found. When at the Council at Basle an agreement
was patched up with the Calixtines on the footing

which I have just named (1433), a few further promises being thrown in, which might mean anything,
and as the issue proved, did mean nothing, the Taborites would not listen to the compromise. Again they
appealed to arms : but now their old comrades and
allies had passed to the other side ; and, defeated in
battle (1434), their stronghold taken and destroyed
(1453), their political power for ever broken, they too,
as so many before and since, were doomed to learn
that violence is weakness in disguise, and that the
wrath of man worketh not the righteousness of God.

Whether the Church of Rome made the concessions
to the Calixtines which she did, with the intention of
retracting them at the first opportunity, it is impossible to say.   This, however, is certain, that half a dozen
years had scarcely elapsed before these concessions
were brought into question and dispute ; while, in less
than thirty, Pope Pius II. formally withdrew altogether
the Papal recognition of them (1462) ; though a struggle for their maintenance, not always unsuccessful,
lasted on into the century ensuing. .

It was in truth a melancholy close of a movement
so hopefully begun. And yet not altogether the close ;
for indeed nothing in which any elements of true
heroism are mingled, so disappears as to leave no
traces of itself behind. If it does no more, it serves
to feed the high tradition of the world,—that most
precious of all bequests to the present age from the
ages which are behind it. But there was more than
this. If much was consumed, yet not all. Something,
and that the best worth the saving, was saved from the
fires, having first been purified in them. The stormy

zealots, as many as had taken the sword, had for the most part perished by the sword. But there were some who made for themselves a better future than the sword could have ever made. A feeble remnant, extricating themselves from the wreck and ruin of their party, and having been taught of God in his severest school, pious Calixtines too that were little content with the *Compacts* of Basle, a few stray Waldensians mingling with them, all these, drawing together in an evil time, refashioned and reconstituted themselves in humblest guise; though not in guise so humble that they could escape the cruel attentions of Rome. Seeking to build on a true scriptural foundation, with a scheme of doctrine, it may be, dogmatically incomplete,—even as that of Hus himself had been,—with their Episcopate lost and never since recovered, the *Unitas Fratrum*, the Moravian Brethren, trampled and trodden down, but overcoming now, not by weapons of carnal warfare, but by the blood of the Cross, lived on to hail the breaking of a fairer dawn, and to be themselves greeted as witnesses for God, who in a dark and gloomy day, and having but a little strength, had kept his Word, and not denied his name.

LECTURE XXIII.

OFFENCES.

No Church historian at the present day, to whatever branch of the Church he may belong, denies that grave abuses, to employ no stronger term, had found their haunt and home in the later medieval Church. In the obstinacy with which these abuses were defended by such as were most bound to make earnest war against them, these historians may not, and all of them do not, find a sufficient justification for that movement which we call the Reformation. Inadequately provoked some count this movement to have been, and in the measure of this inadequacy more or less sinful. But largely provoked all allow that it was; and not less that a share, greater or smaller, of the tremendous responsibilities of this event rests with those who stood out so long against the application of effectual remedies for patent ills. Of some of these ills, of offences very grave indeed which the Church permitted,—too often herself placed in the path of her children,—I have spoken already, but only by the way. I must now speak of them more in detail. In many aspects the subject is an ungrateful one. If only we keep in mind that it is the Church of Christ of which we are speaking, how can we escape a sense of deepest humiliation as we record the strange transformation which this had undergone, until its whole organization seemed little better than a vast and elaborate machinery for the wringing, under every conceivable plea, of the greatest possible amount of money from the faithful? But ungrateful as the subject may be, it is one which cannot be avoided.

I touched in a former Lecture on the endeavour of Gregory VII. forcibly to withdraw from feudal lords and other lay patrons the opportunities for converting the Church's property into family heirlooms, or of making still more shameful traffic with holiest things. As the issue proved, he did no more than change the seat of these ill doings. Instead of lay, they were now priestly hands,—and not seldom the hands which should have been kept the cleanest of all,—that were defiled with bribes. The tables of the money-changers, violently driven from the outer court of the Temple, were not cast forth, but retreated inwardly, and were set up again in the Holy of Holies itself; so that the bitter epigram of our English Owen, to the effect that men might dispute whether Peter had been ever at Rome, but none could deny the presence of Simon there, was not bitterer than the truth would warrant. Conscious of the charge to which many of the Popes lay open, the later Canonists taught that what was simony in others was not simony in them, seeing that everything in the Church was theirs; so that it was not in the power of a Pope to commit this sin, any more than in the power of God to lie, or otherwise to deny Himself.

The depths of shame to which it was possible to descend in this quest of unhallowed gain had been only partially sounded in the times which preceded the Avignonese Popedom. "Our predecessors," exclaimed Clement VI. (1342–1352), himself one of the worst offenders in this line, "did not know how to play Pope." During the Great Schism, as may be supposed, things did not mend, nor yet in the times which intervened between this and the Reformation; perhaps they grew even worse, as is the nature of things evil to do,—not to say that there were many obvious reasons why this should have been the course which they travelled. You heard just now of the impeccability which in this particular matter was ascribed to the Pope. Hear very briefly how far this impossibility of sinning was pushed.

"Provisions" or "Expectancies" were pre-occupations on his part of ecclesiastical benefices which were not yet vacant; which, if vacant, would not be in his gift. Looking forward to a vacancy, the Pope would address to the patron Letters Commendatory (*preces*), which before long were exchanged for Letters Mandatory (*mandata*), at first requesting, but after a while desiring, that whenever a vacancy occurred, such or such a person might be appointed to fill it; or, in more general terms, that it might be kept open until his pleasure in the matter was known. In this way he obtained possession for nominees of his own of the choicest preferments throughout all Western Christendom. Some of these were bestowed on such as he would favour; more were sold, the merchandise of them being carried on in the open day, without cloke or concealment; and with incidents which made this ugly traffic more ugly still. Thus it would often happen that a multitude of expectants had paid down the price for one and the same piece of preferment—this, which could only be held by one, having been sold by anticipation to many. Cardinal d'Ailly expresses his confidence that if a hundred applied, they would all receive the promise, all would be invited to pay down whatever the appointed tariff might be. Hereupon it would follow that one or another, suspecting or know-ing how matters stood, would pay a second price, and so procure a second Mandate from the Pope, annul-ling all his own recommendations save only this last; —perhaps, indeed, not the last, but to be itself over-lapped and superseded by a third, which, with the significant *Anteferri* endorsed upon it, should evacuate in its own favour all that had preceded it. It is stated in one remonstrant memorial that the lives of actual incumbents, whose benefices in their lifetime had been thus sold, and, it may be, resold many times over their heads, were not always safe from the holders of such expectative graces. It gives us an instructive glimpse of what manner of men sought and obtained these, that this could be so much as imagined.

But what made the matter worse was this, namely that the Papacy, existing, as it was tacitly recognized that it did, mainly for the benefit of Italians,—and such graces, in far the larger number of cases, being be-stowed upon these or purchased by them,—the most important benefices throughout all Europe came to be filled by persons totally ignorant of the language of those to whom they should minister. Not indeed that they often did so much as affect to minister, for they very rarely crossed the Alps into the barbarous world beyond ; but, remaining at home, drew the revenue of their foreign deaneries, abbeys, or what else it might be, by means of those Italian factors who swarmed in every land. Perhaps, taking all things into account, and above all that many thus appointed were " persons detestable in life and morals" (so one writing in 1311 assures us), this was in most instances the least harmful course which they could pursue, and their absence the greatest favour which they could confer.

It is here only just to mention that, even in the worst times of the Avignonese degradation, there were Popes, as a Benedict XII., an Urban V., to whose hands these blots did not cleave, and who would fain have cleansed, if they might, the hands of others as well as their own. It may be worth while also to hear how all this, if not defended, was palliated and the worst guilt of it shifted off upon other shoulders, by one of the cleverest, but one also of the most worldly-minded among the Popes. To some Germans who complained that all things were venal at Rome, Pius II., defending as Pope all which as Æneas Sylvius he had been the foremost to denounce at Basle, makes this reply, so thoroughly characteristic of the man :—" Complain not of the Holy See; complain rather of the ambition and greed of your own countrymen; who, running to Rome in quest of bishoprics or other preferments, and finding others their competitors there, emulously strive to outdo those other in the offerings of gifts to such as are supposed to have access to us. Those who have the pontifical ear are not angels, but men; and men very much as you find men in other countries, in France and in Germany. They do not extort—they accept what is pressed upon them."

These " Provisions," resented everywhere, were nowhere more indignantly resented than in England; and no wonder. The scale on which foreign ecclesiastics were quartered on the land, the extent to which its longsuffering was tried, may be estimated by the fact that in the year 1240 Pope Gregory IX. sent to the Archbishop of Canterbury and Bishops of Lincoln and Salisbury, requiring them to provide for three hundred Romans in the earliest vacant benefices, and restraining them from presenting any others until these his nominees had first been provided for. To nearly the same time belongs the refusal of Grostête, Bishop of Lincoln (b. 1175, d. 1253), to admit as a prebendary of his cathedral an Italian youth, nephew of Pope Innocent IV., which made so deep an impression on the popular mind of England. The fact that Grostête was in the main a strong Ultramontane should enhance, not diminish, our admiration of the firmness which in this matter he displayed; while at the same time it may suggest that in later times conclusions have been drawn from this resistance on his part, in regard of his general attitude toward the Papacy, which the actual facts do not warrant.

Time would fail me were I to enumerate all, or nearly all, the devices by which it was sought to fill full the Papal exchequer. Marvellous indeed was the ingenuity which some of these displayed. For example, it was claimed—Clement IV. being the first who advanced this claim—that all dignities, benefices, and the like, which became vacant through the death of the beneficiary while at Rome, should for the next turn be in the Pope's gift. But the matter did not rest here. Again and again the net was stretched wider, and at the same time its meshes woven closer, that it might embrace more and more within its folds. Thus Boniface VIII. extended the claim, so as to in-

clude every ecclesiastical office held by persons dying
within two days' journey of the spot where at the
time of death the Curia might be. It was a fruitful
source of revenue. In the necessity of things there
was a constant influx of the higher ecclesiastics to
Rome; and these, detained there by interminable suits
or by other causes, were exposed, not to speak of the
ordinary chances of mortality, to the deadly Roman
fevers, which then probably even more than now were
ever watching for their prey.

These abuses, and I have dwelt but on a very few of
them, were bad enough ; for, though they affected the
Clergy first, yet not the Clergy only. They must have
told most disastrously on the spiritual interests of the
laity as well, whose pastors could not fail to be morally injured by the consciousness of unworthy methods
whereby they had obtained their right to minister in
holy things. There were other abuses behind, which
not indirectly but directly affected for their harm, not
the priesthood only, but the whole body of the faithful;
and of some of these I have now to speak. And
first of Indulgences.

This huge abuse, as often fares with the hugest, was
only of gradual growth, and sprang up almost unper-
ceived, by such steps as I shall now describe. In an
age in which Church censures were taken much more
to heart than they are in ours, it lay very near that
such as had come under these should be permitted,
even invited, to substitute for penances thus imposed
upon them some other which promised to set forward
in one way or another the general interests of the
Church. It is plain, however, that in any such com-
mutation the substitute must not be severer than that

in whose place it came ; indeed, not *so* severe ; for
else there would be no sufficient inducement to make
the exchange. It must be exactly what its name imports—an Indulgence—something easier, and virtually
remitting a part of the penalty incurred. So soon,
however, as it was discovered that these commuted
penalties might be turned to some advantage in the
way of setting forward objects which the Church had
at heart,—a new Crusade, for example, or the building
of some magnificent cathedral,—the temptation was
strong to make them *much* easier, and so to bring as
many as possible to the pardon-mart, which thus
almost unawares had been opened. It was, of course,
always affirmed or implied that such Indulgences
would only profit those who brought with them a right
disposition of heart and mind, who brought, that is,
faith and repentance. And it was taught, at least at
first, that they would avail only for the remission of ecclesiastical penalties, that they did not reach farther
than this ; it being only after a while that their efficacy
was extended to Purgatory. But while precautionary
statements of this character could, no doubt, be found
in the writings of theologians, the pardoners,—those,
that is, who had purchased the exclusive right to vend
these spiritual wares within a certain district, and who
naturally desired to make their wares attractive,—did
not, we may be quite sure, seriously burden them with
any conditions or limitations of the kind ; the purchase of the Indulgence being itself accepted as the
evidence of a contrite spirit, and men too often suffered to believe that there was no world for which
these pardons were not good. It is easy to understand the extent to which all zealous repentance for

sins past, all watchfulness against sins to come, were
relaxed by the ease with which Indulgences were
obtained and the privileges attached to them.   There
were many Tetzels, as we cannot doubt, before the
last, and quite as shameless as he ; what was bad
enough in itself becoming much worse in the hands
through which it passed.   Nor is it wonderful that
earnest preachers of repentance long before Luther
should have been filled with the deepest indignation
at this murder of souls,—for so they were wont to call
it,—and in plainest words should have warned the
poor deceived people that trusting in these they were
trusting in a lie.

There was, indeed, an evident misgiving for a while
about declaring that to the Church had been committed the keys of that Middle World which is neither
heaven nor hell ; that the Church could thus remit the
pains, not by herself imposed, of Purgatory.   Before
long, however, all scruples on this head were set
aside—the domain in which Indulgences availed being
thus immensely enlarged.   Nor did matters stop here.
In 1477 Sixtus IV. declared that Indulgences had a re-
troactive value, might be obtained by the faithful not
for themselves only, but for the relief of such as had
already departed and were now passing through, but
had not finished yet, the discipline of those cleansing
fires.   It is easy to understand what an appeal there
was here to some of the best and strongest affections
of the human heart.   Who could endure selfishly to
withhold for some private gratification that which, if
rightly laid out, might mitigate or abridge the anguish
of a parent, a child, a wife, a husband, and deliver from
pains which, as they were often now described, differed

little, save only in their temporary character, from the sufferings of the lost?

But, as it was inevitable, it would be sometimes asked, was it certain that there was any bank on which the Pope could thus draw without fear that his drafts might be dishonoured? Yes, it was answered, there was a treasure which was inexhaustible. Alexander Hales, an eminent Schoolman and a countryman of our own, was the first to discover this treasure hid in the field of the Church ;—*thesaurus meritorum* it was called. But what he set forth as a pious opinion, Clement VI. elevated into a dogma (1343), and one which was capable of yielding very excellent service ; for, indeed, the convenience was manifest of drawing bills upon the next world, and getting them honoured in this. The fact of the existence of such a treasure, and of the Church's right to dispose of this treasure as it thought best, was arrived at by the following steps. All must allow that one drop of his blood who was Himself God would have sufficed to redeem the world ; which being so, it was plain that He who shed not one drop only, but poured out all, actually did and suffered infinitely more than in strict justice was necessary for man's redemption. There was a treasure of Christ's merits which in that redemptive act had by no means been expended. Then to the merits of Christ, in themselves inexhaustible, must be added those of the Blessed Virgin Mary, and of as many saints and servants of God as had kept not merely the commandments, but also the " counsels of perfection," and had thus wrought more of good than their own salvation required. All these works of supererogation, as by language drawn from the parable of the Good

Samaritan (*quodcunque supererogaveris*, Luke x. 35)
they were called, went into the same common stock,
for the Church was one ; they were all at the Church's
disposal, in other words at the Pope's, who alone had
the key of this treasure; for him to make over to
whom he would, supplying the deficient merits of one
by the super-abundant merits of another, that so nothing might be lost.

Oftentimes in Roman errors we have the blurred
reflection of Christian truths, and nowhere more noticeably than here : for what is this but a broken and
distorted reflection of a very glorious truth,—of this
namely, that in Christ there are treasures of grace un-
exhausted and inexhaustible, that the Church of which
He is the Head is indeed one body, a communion of
saints, so that no member of it lives for himself alone,
but the good of one becomes in a most real though
mysterious way the common good and property of all?

A few words on the year of Jubilee, and then, little
as we shall have exhausted, we may bring an unwelcome theme to the end. The institution of a Jubilee
year belongs, as does the doctrine of Indulgences out
of which it grew, to a period when the Middle Ages
were already in their decline, and the institutions
which most properly belonged to them were verging to
their fall. The immense success which attended this
new appeal to the devotion of the faithful may have
done much to conceal this fact from the eyes of men.
The Roman Church, and Rome, the city of her solem-
nities, could yet awaken a religious enthusiasm; was
still a magnet mighty to draw hearts to itself. The
year 1300, and the Pontificate of Boniface VIII., which

was to prove in its close so disastrous, saw the first Jubilee. As that year drew nigh, it was proclaimed that as many as, being in the proper frame of mind, visited the shrines of the Apostles, the churches of St. Peter and St. Paul,—for fifteen days, being strangers ; for thirty days, being Romans,—might obtain thereby a plenary Indulgence, the remission, that is, of all Church censures, and of all pains and penalties which these involved, whether in this world or in the world to come.

It was originally intended as a solitary opportunity, or one at any rate which at the soonest should recur again after the lapse of a century. But the success which attended it was so marvellous, multitudes so great were attracted to the city, the sums in one way or another drawn into the Papal treasury or spent at Rome were so vast, that the temptation to repeat the experiment at an earlier date was irresistible. And thus Clement VI., taking into account that for so many of the faithful it must be hopeless to expect in their lifetime the occurrence of this secular day of grace, and willing to bring its benefits within the reach of more, did in 1343 pronounce that the Jubilee should be celebrated every fiftieth year ; justifying this by an appeal to the fact that the days of Pentecost were exactly so many. Urban VI. in 1389 further limited the intervening time to thirty-three years, which was the number of Christ's years upon earth ; and Paul II. in 1470 to twenty-five, and at this it has since remained. Many as made the journey to Rome, you must not suppose that an actual pilgrimage thither was a necessary condition for the securing of the spiritual benefits of the Jubilee. Whatever these might be, they were equally obtainable by paying to a Papal factor, such as might everywhere be found, something about the sum which a pilgrimage to the city would have cost. Multitudes actually went; but not a few were satisfied with this vicarious going.

A very significant commentary on these schemes of pardon,—stopping so very short of the Cross of Christ, and, instead of leading up to that Cross, very often leading away from it,—was the appearance about the middle of the fourteenth century, first in Italy and then in Germany, of the Flagellants. These were penitents, men and women, who, stript to the waist, wandered in long procession from city to city, chaunting hymns and litanies, and inflicting on themselves the severest discipline of the scourge, from whence they had their name of the Flagellants or the Scourgers. Wofully astray they may have been, and were. The blood without which is no remission was not their own, but Another's; the stripes wherewith they must be healed were Another's; while yet, amid all their confusions, it was for that precious blood, for a fellowship with the sufferings of Christ, that they were blindly feeling. It is nothing wonderful that the Church frowned on these demonstrations, did all in her power to put them down, significant as they were of the little worth which the sin-laden heart of man ascribed to the schemes of pardon in which she was inviting her children to trust.

Mischiefs and causes of offence of a different class are yet to speak of. I have spoken already of the claims which the Popes made to draw all greater causes for ultimate decision to their courts. Being in

their own sight what they were, they could scarcely
have done less. But the liberty of appeal which was
thus encouraged and invited threatened to subvert the
whole discipline, and indeed well-nigh to dissolve the
whole framework of the Church. After a while it was
not greater causes only which were drawn to Rome ;
but whosoever wished to elude or to defy the authority
of his immediate superior, did, under one pretext or
another, claim to bring his wrongs before the supreme
Ruler of the Church. Apart from the continual conflict in which Rome was thus engaged with temporal
princes and potentates, who could ill brook this giving
of the go-by to all national courts, she could not shut
her eyes to the other manifold mischiefs which attended
the abusive exercise of this privilege of appeal. We
may imagine, though feebly, what these must have
been, when we call to mind the slowness of communication in those ages, the long delays in courts already
choked with business, the temptation to the underlings
of the Curia to multiply delays so gainful to them, the
spirit of opposition to legitimate authority which was
everywhere fostered. But how renounce, or even
seriously abridge, a right which so flattered her pride ;
which was such a living testimony continually borne to
her supremacy ; which in manifold ways brought such
wealth into her exchequer ; and which, it is only fair to
add, did sometimes hinder or redress an injustice
which would not else have been set right ? Various
attempts to set limits to the right of appeal, to put
some obstacles in the way, profited but little. The
one remedy was not tried,—namely to restore to the
several national Churches and States those rights of
self-government, of which she had robbed them in

whole or in part; but Rome, making this restoration, would have ceased to be Rome.

The same determination to draw all to one centre showed itself in the multiplication of exemptions from every jurisdiction save that of the Pope himself. The first ambition of monastery or convent was to obtain exemption from the authority of the Bishop in whose diocese it stood, to hold directly from the Papal See. For this it was willing to pay, and did pay, a yearly tribute. The exemption which other monastic houses obtained one by one, and by special favour, was bestowed in mass on the two Mendicant Orders,—being included in the *Mare Magnum* (for so it was called) of the privileges heaped upon them. But to others also it was imparted with no niggard hand. It is easy to imagine the extent to which all efforts of Bishops to exercise wholesome discipline in these dioceses were crippled or wholly baffled hereby.

With this glance at abuses which had been rife for centuries; which, as years rolled on, were not decreasing but growing rather in malignity; which, if healed at all, were healed so slightly that they presently broke out afresh, showing themselves more inveterate than ever;—we have a claim to ask, when the right or the wrong of a Reformation is discussed, Was there not a cause? Let its excesses have been what they may, the rent in the seamless robe of Christ ever so lamentable, was there not intolerable evil to be abated, while yet this evil was obstinately resolved that it would not abate itself? When I say "would not abate itself," do not conclude that there were not from time to time those in high places, some in the highest place of all, who would fain have healed the hurt of the daughter of their people ; and who, if they did not see all,—for who could see this ?—yet saw something of the frightful bottomless slough into which the Church had sunken, and would fain have lifted it out from this. There were Popes who earnestly desired a reform, who honestly laboured for one. But the system had grown too strong for any single man, even though he should appear to have all power at his beck. There were too many to whom the evil thing, that which needed above all to be got rid of, was as the very breath of their life. In the time of Leo X. there might be counted some eight hundred officials in the Roman Chancery and Datary, not to speak of a multitude of other placemen, most of them having paid highly for their offices ; a serried phalanx in actual possession, and prepared to offer the most determined opposition to any and every reform by which their gains would be diminished. With the best intentions, how helpless, in the face of the resistance passive or active of these, must a Pope have proved, generally an old man and with few years to live,—the average duration of a Pontificate from first to last having been less than seven years;— a stranger altogether, it might be, to the intricacies of ecclesiastical affairs, or to the procedure of ecclesiastical courts. Who can wonder that honest attempts at reform were frequently defeated, or that, if a little seemed to have been won, all before long slipt back into the old ruts again ; things ever traveling from bad to worse, until at length for a violent disease a remedy as violent arrived ?

LECTURE XXIV.

THE GERMAN MYSTICS.

THE German Mystics will claim our attention to-day.
German I call them, so to mark the distinction between them and other mystics, of whom something
has been spoken already (p. 213). If those were
mainly French and Italian, or, to use a term which
would embrace both, Romanic, these are German
above all, and by their "innigkeit"—I look in vain for
a corresponding word in English—they declare as
much. Cologne too and Strasburg are their chief
centres, and after these, Basle and Constance, Brussels and Nüremberg. But the men whom we name by
this name not always employed as a title of honour,
how shall we describe them? I had rather that my Lecture taken as a whole should answer this question.
Meanwhile I will say generally and by way of prelude,
that the evidence of divine things which the Schoolman
found in the consonance between faith and reason
reasonably exercised, each sustaining and confirming
the other, the Mystic sought and claimed to find in a
more immediate fellowship and intercommunion with
God, an illumination from above which was light and
warmth in one. "Let Him kiss me with kisses of his
mouth,"—this, with the Bride of the Canticles, he
asked, with nothing short of this would be content;
claiming in his higher moments to lose himself in God

352

and in the ocean of his being, as the drop of water loses itself in the sea. This last comparison, one of very frequent recurrence, gives us a hint of spiritual dangers which were before him, and which he did not always escape; and of these we shall have presently to speak. In much which he longed for the most, he did but reach out after that which all souls, in which the true hunger has been awakened, must desire, namely immediate experience of the grace and goodness of God, an actual tasting and seeing that He is gracious.

We have watched the Scholastic and Mystic Theology in fruitful union with one another, each in a manner regulating, each completing the other, in St. Anselm and in St. Bernard, in Hugh and in Richard of St. Victor. As however the Scholastic lost itself more and more in barren strifes, the Mystic, detaching itself, assumed an independent development of its own, and, without intending this, a position of antagonism to that which had been once its fellow-worker and ally. The fourteenth and fifteenth centuries, which are those of a Scholasticism ever sinking lower, ever losing more and more its hold on the hearts and spirits of men, are the centuries in which the Mystic Theology is in its fairest bloom.

Never were the strong consolations which only a living faith could yield more needed than at that time. It was a time of great tribulation for Western Christendom, for Germany above all. The conflict between the Papacy and the Empire had revived again, and, though not the war of giants which it once had been, seemed as far from a settlement as ever. It had drawn after it what has been called the Long Interdict (in 1324 it began); the suspension, that is, for long years of all means of grace which the Church could withhold ;—means which most men still regarded as absolutely necessary to salvation. There was everywhere intestine war, city against city and kingdom against kingdom. There was a Church so corrupt that it seemed incapable of enduring either its ills or the remedies of those ills. And then upon all of this came the frightful Black Death (1347–1353), sweeping away in its course two-thirds of the population of Europe. God's judgments were in all the world, and many made worse by them;—only the elect being purified and made white in the fires.

There was much in the mystical Theology, this religion of the inner man, adapted to the needs of such a time as this; much to quicken and deepen the spiritual life of souls. The Church might be full of scandals without ; a mere mechanical devotion might for many have taken the place of all worship of God in spirit and in truth; but it was still possible for men to retire into the sanctuary of their own hearts, and to find Him and to worship Him there. The Councils, towards which men were already looking, might or might not reform and renew the outward face of the Church ; but the Mystics would reform and renew what was more within their power, and what they felt more nearly to concern them, namely their own hearts. If every external basis and support for government and religion had given way, they said, we have at least ourselves left us. Within the circle of our own thoughts we have enough to content us. There, if we seek it, we can find order and peace and holy quiet.

This, like all other genuine reforming movements

of the centuries which preceded the Reformation, lost itself therein; but only lost itself by finding there the fulfilment of what it had of true and good, with the rejection of what was otherwise. In this instance the disturbing elements were many; and we have no choice but to dwell on them a little, seeing that they are found not in those who hung on the outer skirts of the movement, but in largest measure in him who for genius and original power was the foremost figure in it; so that it only came to the fulness of its beneficent working when it had on many points released itself from him and from his influence.

Of Eckart's life we know very little; neither the time of his birth or of his death. For a date, by aid of which securely to anchor him to the period to which he belongs, we must be content with 1304, in which year he became Chief Provincial of the Order of St. Dominic in Saxony. He has attracted no little attention in recent years, has been put forward as one of three, the leaders in pantheistic speculation of the modern world;—Erigena, from whom he is divided by three hundred years, and Hegel, separated from him by a still longer interval, being the other two;—one might rather have expected to find Spinoza completing the triad. This much, indeed, is certain, namely that he was, and was felt to be, quite the leading spirit among the speculative Mystics of his own age. From his greater light the others borrowed their light, and their lesser urns were filled from his.

Not unacquainted with Aristotle, but holding more closely to Plato, nourished by the mystical element so largely to be found in Augustine, but without Augustine's wholesome doctrine of sin and of the Fall, work-

ing up into his system all which he could assimilate
from Erigena and from the writings ascribed to Dio-
nysius the Areopagite, but attaching himself still more
closely to Amalrich of Bena, and cultivating relations
full of danger with the Brethren of the Free Spirit,—
Eckart is not for all this a mere eclectic, picking out
portions from other men's schemes of philosophy, and
ingeniously piecing them together. All of most characteristic which we find in the later Mystics, we find
already in the bud, or often in the full flower, in him;
but in him pushed to extremes which frequently approach perilously near to the brink of the abyss of
pantheism, and sometimes do not stop short on the
brink. What has come down to us of Eckart's own
writings is little; while, little as it is, my own acquaintance is only with select portions of this: yet this
acquaintance is sufficient to convince me that he cannot be acquitted of the charges already in his own day
brought against him; for, indeed, in his latter years
Eckart was seriously compromised with the Church,
so seriously that, high Dominican as he was, the Inquisition hardly kept its hands off him;—perhaps
would not have done so much longer, if death had not
closed all his accounts on earth:—but much obscurity
rests on this part of his history.

Where God dwells in a man—this is a statement of
his,—He so dwells in him that He keeps nothing back
from him of life or being or godhead, which He does
not impart; the gift of Himself being absolute, complete, and without all reserve. We are here, as you
will at once perceive, on the threshold of that deifica-
tion of man, that breaking down of the everlasting distinction between the Son of God and the sons of God,

which is the characteristic danger of this theology; and which, when the high tides of ecstatic transport have ebbed away, will have left no Saviour at all for any man, or, which amounts to the same thing, will have left every man his own Saviour.

But there is more than this. Eckart in another place, says, "I will not thank God because He loves me; for He cannot leave off to love me; whether He will or no His nature compels Him thereto. I will thank Him because He cannot leave off this goodness of his." Now in judging of such language as this it is only fair to take note that he who employed it was plainly well pleased to put things in a startling way; and that the paradox is often in the putting rather than in the thing itself. But yet all these statements, with other to the effect that God imparts Himself to the creature because He cannot help it, that the creature does not need the Creator more than the Creator needs the creature, must be owned to play dangerously near to the edge of the precipice. No doubt there is a divine necessity in God. He cannot lie, He cannot deny Himself; but it is another thing when it is sought to bring the outcomings of God toward the creature under the same conditions of necessity. Nor can it be pleaded that Eckart is only playing on the edge of a precipice, when he utters such words as these: "A truly divine man has been so made one with God, that henceforth he does not think of God or look for God outside of himself."

Eckart, one has said, was a man drunk with God. God for him is not the Supreme Being, but rather Being. All other Being is swallowed up in his. It needs but a very slight acquaintance with the history of past speculation to know how inevitably and how swiftly such excesses avenge themselves; how soon extremes meet; and how near to "All is God" lies another statement, "All is Nothing," being as the obverse of the same medal. Eckart did not arrive at this; but others did, of whom and whose speculations when we read, we are compelled to own that modern Nihilism is a very old story indeed.

But to return. In the face of all which bears so dangerous a meaning, there are passages in Eckart's writings which assert with all clearness the distinction between God and the creature; which set forth the relation of man to God as a seeing of God, not as a becoming God; and which vindicate an unique dignity for Christ, as Son of God in a sense quite different from that in which others are sons as well. These passages are not, I think, always reconcilable with other in his writings; but, being set beside those other, testify that there met in him all the tendencies, scriptural and unscriptural, churchlike and unchurchlike, which were working in his time. And thus it came to pass that he shared the lot of more than one great teacher,—as, eminently, of Socrates in the old world, and of Hegel in the new; who, without intending this, saw in their lifetime, or left behind them at their death, two or even more schools of followers, these separating off to the right and to the left, and severally claiming to be the true guardians of the master's teaching. So fared it with Eckart, whom churchmen and speculative pantheists alike claimed as theirs; and in whom no doubt both could affirm with truth that they recognized much that was their own.

It will be seen from what has been said that Eckart's interests were speculative rather than practical; philosophical rather than theological. It was not so with his most distinguished followers. The three most eminent names among these are Tauler ("the Illuminated Doctor," as he was called, d. 1361); Ruysbroek ("the Ecstatic Doctor," d. 1381), and Amandus Suso (d. 1365). Each of these has a character of his own: Tauler is the more practical; Ruysbroek the more contemplative; Amandus Suso the more poetical. Of these the Scholars, all alike are clear of the pantheistic antinomian errors, which,—so far as his teaching went,—the Master hardly escaped, even if he did escape; they all indeed earnestly witness against those errors. But I have dwelt so long on the master-spirit as to forbid me to dwell, as I would willingly have done, on those who followed in his train.

In such time as remains to me I would rather consider in what relation to the Reformation the Mystics of the fourteenth century stood. It is a question of much interest; for as in the fourteenth and fifteenth centuries all things else were working together toward that great event, so doubtless was this which occupies us to-day. But it is a question which will be best answered by a brief consideration of the position which the Mystics occupied in relation to the Church of their own time. They took then, we may first observe, no position of conscious opposition to the Church. Still they were very far from being what the Schoolmen, at least for a time, had been, a support to it and a strength; nay, rather, without intending this, they did much to weaken its authority, and prepare

the way for its fall.　They did not make war on, nor
even seek to set aside, that vast and elaborate machinery of external helps for the furthering of the spiritual life which they found ready prepared by the Church
for her children.　But it was plain, not so much from
what they said and did, as from what they did not
say and do, that they ascribed to this machinery very
little value,—their estrangement from it being the
more significant that they seem themselves quite un-
conscious of its existence.　They do not resist, renounce, defy,—they simply pass by much which they
most counted necessary for salvation. I have read that
in all Thomas à Kempis' numerous writings there is
but one reference to the Pope.　Assuredly he would
have been himself surprised if any had told him this.

The German Mystics in another way, and again
without intending it, helped to prepare the way for
others who should succeed them.　Of the rise of the
modern languages of Europe into dignity and importance I have already spoken something; but what
others had begun in giving to these their place and
their rightful honour they carried further.　The dominion of Latin as the sole language in which men
could preach or pray, theologically think or debate,
had its advantages so long as the modern languages
of Europe were unformed barbarous dialects.　But
what is right at one time may under altered circumstances become a wrong.　It *had* become a wrong
that men could not hear the great things of God in
the tongues wherein they were born, now that in those
tongues the glad tidings could be told so well.　The
famous preachers among the German Mystics did
much to redress that wrong; to throw down such

barriers as still hindered a perfect recognition of this fact. Their sermons in the German of their age, some published, far more unpublished, survive in immense numbers to this day.

And yet with all this, and taking the Mystics at their best, and not at their worst, judging of them and of their teaching by their most favourable representatives, it is sufficiently plain, for all history attests the fact, that there dwelt in them no power to heal the worst ills of the Church. When we liken them, as I am disposed to do, to some river which, with many turbid elements at its head-waters, did yet, as it ran, more and more clear itself from these, I can imagine some who hear me asking in their hearts, How came it that more than two centuries were still to run before the Reformation, so grievously needed, arrived? What was wanting in these, that they did not bring that about? To this question we have no choice but to answer, Much every way. There was wanting in the first place a sufficiently deep apprehension of sin. Their apprehension of this—it is mainly, but by no means exclusively, of Eckart that I speak—was rather metaphysical than ethical. It was a sense of need and defect as clinging to and inherent in all finite creaturely life, —this rather than the consciousness of the transgression by every man of a divine law; which transgressions required to be made good, and could only be made good by such a work of sacrifice and propitiation as that which the Son of God accomplished once for all on his Cross. For them this objective historic fact, while they did not at all deny its doctrinal significance, was very far from being that central point of their theology which it must be in any theology which shall

permanently satisfy the deepest needs of men's hearts.
Not Christ *for* us, not the historic Christ who having
suffered once on earth now lives in heaven for evermore, but Christ *in* us, is for them the centre round
which everything revolves.   One might almost suppose from their teaching that the Lord of Glory lived
and died and rose again that He might be thus repro-
duced in those whom He had been pleased to call his
brethren.

Here again was a temptation to extenuate the sin-
fulness of sin, to diminish the significance and the consequences of the Fall; here an explanation of the
Pelagian leaven from which the Mystical Theology
cannot be adjudged to be free; for, seeing that this
"new creature" in us must be always an imperfect
one, every motive was at work to lead to the reducing
to a minimum men's estimate of the malignity of sin,
—to a regarding of it as not so sinful after all, as
rather deficient good than efficient evil.   There was
wanting to the Mystics exactly that which was *not*
wanting to the better among the Reformers.   The
glory of these last was the even poise with which they
gave their full rights at once to objective and subjective Christianity; to the religion of the written Word,
of Creeds and Sacraments, on the one side, and at the
same time upon the other to the religion of the inner
life, of the feelings; of the mystical union between the
faithful and their Lord : not allowing either to wrong,
or in any way to obscure and to cast into the background the other.

Luther was ever forward to acknowledge what he
owed to the Mystics, above all to Tauler, and to *The
German Theology*,—a little volume, one of the most

precious bequests which the later Middle Ages made to the times which should come after. But there was that in him which was not in them, and which yet there is need should be in us all, namely the profound sense of guilt and condemnation, and then of a release from these; and of this release by an act not of our own, but of Another, the benefits therefrom resulting being made ours by means of our faith.

In drawing this subject to a close, I am unwilling to leave without honourable mention the Brethren of the Common Life; and Ruysbroek is a point of historic contact between them and the Mystics properly so called. These Brethren, whose headquarters were Deventer in Holland, were honourably distinguished by the same freedom of spirit which characterized the Mystics in the stricter sense; but they were more practical, and wholly exempt from the dangerous excesses into which so many of those other ran. The "Common Life," from which they drew their name, had monastic features about it; but at the same time it was a freer life than that of the established Orders, and one without vows. In many ways these Brethren did excellent service during the fourteenth and fifteenth centuries, above all by the schools which they founded, and the education, at once scholarly and Christian, of the young which they promoted. Among them was trained the author of the book, which, after the Bible, we may be bold to say is dearer to more hearts than any other book in Christendom; which has been printed many thousands of times, and for which Orders and kingdoms have contended;—a book which, despite of all that is wanting to it, deserves the reputation which it has obtained. I need not say that I refer to Thomas à Kempis (b. 1380, d. 1471), and to his work, *On the Imitation of Christ ;*—for his work, and not that of any Gerson or Gersen, we may boldly affirm that it is. It was in a school of these Brethren that Erasmus obtained, at least in part, his early education, possibly from them his intelligent love for the great writers of the ancient classical world. Parallel to these associations of men were companies of pietist women, Beguines and others, who, in like manner retaining their freedom and not coming under direct vows, lived in communities, and gave themselves to works of mercy. Many attempts were made by the established Orders to disquiet these, whom they could not pardon for living a religious life without belonging to a "Religion" properly so called; while more than once a Pope, satisfied that they meant no mischief, without distinctly approving or sanctioning associations of the kind, discouraged and defeated attempts to bring them into trouble.

We have another token of a reaction against mechanical devotions and servile work-holiness in the spread at this time of some who called themselves the "Friends of God." The name, blessed to receive, seems somewhat presumptuous to take; but those who thus made it their own would no doubt have replied to such a charge, that they did receive it and that from the lips of their Lord; for did not his own words at John xv. 15 declare as much? They would have further urged that the name expressed a fact,—namely, that the service of Christ's true disciples was the free service of love, and that such a service was theirs. It is hard to define with accuracy the attitude of Rome to these; whom it sometimes tolerated, against whom it sometimes waged a desultory war. They for their part had not so broken away as to organize themselves into independent and hostile communities, though it was not long before many whom the Church regarded as heretics—some justly and some unjustly—sheltered themselves under this name. Among these Friends of God Nicholas of Basle, of whom one would willingly know more, stands out the most prominent. Neander and Milman and not a few others have assumed as certain,—though it has lately been shown to be not at all so certain as they assume, —that he was the anonymous layman from the Oberland who so greatly helped in bringing Tauler to a deeper heart-knowledge :—the profoundly instructive story is abundantly familiar to all who are interested in the spiritual development of one, the best known among the Mystics. This Nicolas, invisible Pope of an invisible Church, as one has called him, evermore hunted by the Inquisition, but long escaping its snares, passed up and down through Western Christendom, everywhere ministering to a hidden people who owned his spiritual sway; until at length his good fortune forsook him, and on a visit to France he fell into the hands of foes who had long watched for his life, and died the fiery death at Vienne. Here we must for the present conclude.

LECTURE XXV.

LATIN AND GREEK.

WHEN I have brought these Lectures to a close, and
their end is not now far off, the Latin Church will be
found, if I mistake not, to have occupied four-fifths at
least of our time and attention. The proportion thus
devoted to it may seem to some beyond the measure
of its claims, very much the stronger as these claims
must by all be admitted to be. But it is not so. We
are wont to speak of the "thread" of a stream;
meaning by this whatever in it has motion and progress, as distinguished from lagoons, back eddies, and
standing waters, where forward motion is none.
Church history also has its "thread;" and, if this is to
be followed, it must be followed in the West—at least
during the period which in these Lectures we claim
for our own. In the Latin Communion is movement;
in the Greek comparative immobility. There the flexi-
bility of youth, or of manhood which is youthful still;
here the stiffness and rigidity of age.

We may, it is true, urge too far the improgressive
character of the Greek Church,—the absence from it
during the times which immediately concern us of any
productive energy, of the power to adapt itself to new
conditions and new needs; and some have done so.
Much which distinguishes the Latin Church the most
has its analogies and correspondences, not seldom its

366

anticipations, in the Greek. This too has its Mystics. Maximus, that glorious Confessor (b. 580, d. 662), would, I suppose, take rank with the foremost Mystics of the West; a star of the first magnitude, in whatever part of the Church's firmament he might shine. It too boasts its Schoolmen, though they are not called by this name. In the co-ordinating and combining into one organic whole of all the theological materials at his command, and in the use which he made of the logical formulas of Aristotle for the better accomplishing of this, John of Damascus (d. after 754) first showed the way; nor was it till some centuries later that any organizing genius in the West followed in the path which he had marked out.

But it is points of difference rather than points of likeness between the two Communions, and the lamentable issues to which those differences led, that will mainly occupy us to-day. In the crowning of Charles the Great as Emperor,—really of the West and of that alone, though no such limitation was intended by those who professed to give, or by him who received this crown,—the separation of Italy, Rome included, from the secular denomination of the Eastern Emperor was involved, however some faint umbrages of allegiance may have survived for a while. But the Christians of East and West still constituted one Church; and it took a longer time to dissolve the bands which knit them together. Two centuries were needed of interminable wrangling, of quarrels which were made up only to break out anew, before that quarrel came which no reconciliation should follow.

The enormous rent in the mystical body of Christ

was a catastrophe of which the remoter causes reach very far back into earlier periods of the Church's life. Herein it resembles very closely the separation between Judah and Israel—a separation which we are sometimes tempted to regard as the result of the accidental clashing of one man's craft and ambition and the youthful insolence of another: while yet on closer scrutiny we may discover the seeds of the dissolution of the national unity to have been sown long before; and that falling away from one another of the northern and southern Tribes, which in the end actually arrived, to have been on the very point of arriving many times before. Still less can the Schism of which we are now speaking be said to have come by surprise, or to be traceable to causes fortuitous and unlooked for. The surprise for each thoughtful student of Church history must be rather that the fatal moment did not much sooner arrive,—that the external communion had survived so long. For indeed it is hardly too much to say that this disruption lay involved in the distinct and diverging characteristics of the Greek and the Roman. So soon as ever the love of many had waxed cold, and that grace which alone knits men into one, and reconciles national distinctions in a higher unity of the Spirit, had ceased effectually to work, it was almost inevitable that a breach— it might be a little sooner, or it might be a little later —should follow.

This divergence between the Greek and Latin mind had not failed to make itself felt even while East and West were still in unbroken communion. It had done so in manifold ways; perhaps in none more strikingly than in the different character of the disputes which

agitated the one branch of the Church and the other.
In the East the disputes turned all upon questions of
high speculative theology :—the relation of the Son to
the Father; whether there were in Christ two Persons,
or only two Natures, a human and a divine ; how far
and in what ways these Natures mutually acted upon
and modified one another; whether the recognition of
them did not draw after it an obligation to recognize
in Him two Wills, harmonious indeed, but still distinct ;
with other questions moving in the region of transcen-
dental theology—questions of profoundest importance,
but some of them apparently, though not in reality, remote from our practical Christian life; and nearly all
of them pushed by Greek controversialists into needless subtleties and refinements.   But while the Greek
Church was the principal sphere of these discussions,
often scarcely heard of beyond it, or, if heard of,
awaking no lively interest,—sometimes incapable of
being so much as stated in the Latin language ; the
West also had questions of its own, which were eagerly
debated by it, but from which the Greeks in their turn
stood aloof, as not seriously affected by them.   To the
Greek had in the main belonged the Arian and Nestorian, altogether the Monophysite and Monothelite—all
that had to do with God as He subsists in Himself, or
in hypostatic union with man ; while the Pelagian controversy, turning on the mighty antithesis between sin
and grace, on the question how far man is fallen, and
what helps he needs to set him upon his feet again, belonged exclusively to the West.   In the West too were
brought to a definite issue practical questions of
Church discipline, as for instance, the conditions under
which the baptism of heretics should be allowed to

stand good, with other questions of a like kind. Keeping all this in view, it is both interesting and instructive to note the different blazon and boast of the one Communion and of the other; the Greek taking for its highest honour that it is the " Holy *Orthodox* Church," the Latin that it is the "Holy *Catholic* Church;" in other words, the one that its speculation is right, the other that its dominion is universal. How much which from the first was nearest to the heart severally of Greek and Latin utters itself here.

In enumerating the preparations for dissension, and in the end for division, we must not omit the broad distinction of language. When indeed Constantine transferred the seat of empire to the city which he called by his own name, the majesty of Rome demanded that the language which Romans spoke should still be retained as the language of the Court, of the legal tribunals, and of the public edicts, however Greek translations might sometimes be appended to these; and it was doubtless Constantine's intention and expectation that Latin should continue the spoken language of the New Rome which he had founded. But this could not be. The barbarous dialects of Spain and Gaul might give way before the Latin; but Greek, which displaces other languages, is itself displaced by none. Constantinople before very long became a thoroughly Greek city,—the capital of a thoroughly Greek Empire,—with a Greek-speaking population, who indeed were willing to call themselves Romans and their language Romaic, but who would advance no further than this. The dream that New Rome might be the centre of the Latin no less than the Greek world, after some faint approaches to fulfilment in the days of Justinian (501–565), for ever passed away.

It is not easy to overrate the extent to which this difference in language wrought in preparing the way for a disruption, or in making it permanent when it had once arrived. Nothing perhaps so knits men's hearts together as having common objects of affection and honour. But it thus came to pass that the illustrious fathers and teachers of one half of the Church were almost or altogether strangers to men of the other. In a bitter writing of a Greek controversialist put forth just before the final breach, he complains that the famous Doctors of the East,—Athanasius and Basil and Chrysostom and the Gregories,—so far from being esteemed saints, were held in no reputation or reverence at all by the Westerns. These, it is true, though this would not have mended matters, might have retorted with perfect truth that the standard-bearers of their faith,—a Cyprian, an Ambrose, a Jerome, an Augustine, were as little honoured in the East, were as completely unknown even to their very names. And this was true, with only a partial exception in favour of Gregory the Great, whose work *On the Pastoral Care*, and his *Dialogues*, had been translated into Greek; his day also being held in honour in the East.

The Greek Church with its unbroken traditions; with the treasures of ancient learning which it held in its keeping; with a theological literature preceding by two centuries any that the Latin could boast; having determined in Councils where hardly a Latin Bishop was present all the leading theological questions that had risen up, and embodied these determinations in a

Creed to which no Latin had contributed a syllable ;—
this Greek Church, that *had done* so much, looked
down on the Latin as on a Church of barbarians. But
the Latin had what was far better for present service
than all that dead material, than all that consciousness
of having accomplished mighty things in times which
were gone by.   It had the stirrings of a new life within it.   The past might belong to others ; the present
and the future it felt to be its own.

The very different results of the Invasion by the
Northern tribes, as this invasion affected severally the
Greek and Latin Communions, did much to shape the
fortunes of the one and of the other.   That immense
flood of the nations which overwhelmed the West, but
overwhelmed it only as the Nile with its fertilizing
waters overwhelms Egypt, brought the Greek Church
also into imminent danger and distress ; but did not
swallow it up.   Overliving the peril, it travels on in
the same tracks as before.   There is for it no breach
of continuity, no new beginning ; only a prolongation
of the old ; it leaves ever farther behind the days of
youthful freshness and strength.   The rejuvenescence
which the West found, the East had missed.   Taking
" Middle Ages " not as a mere chronological term, but
as marking off certain centuries with distinguishing features of their own,—for the Greek Church, as I think
I have observed already, there were no Middle Ages ;
and when we are tempted to judge harshly of those
Ages, it may be sometimes well to ask ourselves
whether we would willingly be as that Eastern Church
is ; whether Modern Europe could advantageously
have done without the rough, but bracing discipline to
which in those Ages it was submitted.

I have traced some of the remoter, let me mention now some nearer and more patent causes of disunion. Quarrels as to the limits of jurisdiction there were, but these I pass by. Touching more closely the hearts of men were certain divergences in doctrine and in practice which had either existed from the beginning or grown up by degrees, and which served to draw more sharply still the line of unfriendly demarcation between East and West; some of these so slight and pitiful that, as causes to divide great Christian communities from one another, one is almost ashamed to name them; but of which a few require to be named. Thus the Greeks brought a whole list of charges against the Latins, as that they fasted on Saturdays, that they made the sign of the Cross amiss, that their priests shaved the beard, that they used unleavened bread in the Holy Eucharist, that they did not abstain from things strangled and from blood. Of these and other like differences in ritual one would willingly believe that, unless deeper grounds of estrangement had been behind, they would not have been pressed as they were, nor made to contribute their share to the breaking of the bond of peace between those whom Christ had bidden to be one.

Even that which showed, at first sight, as so immense a divergence between the doctrine of Latins and Greeks was not, after due explanations made, a difference so touching the foundations of the faith as to require that those who were divided upon it should refuse to hold communion with one another. This much all "sons of peace" acknowledge now; while not a few go much farther, and are sure that if only the contending parties would dispassionately consider

each other's mode of speech, they would find that *no*
difference existed between them,—that, while using different language, they intended the same thing. That
the Holy Ghost proceeds or issues from the Father
and the Son, had been always the prevailing faith of the
Western Church; even as it was the strongest conviction of all its best theologians that any statement
short of this, any which should leave the Son and the
Spirit with no other relation to one another except
that of their common relation to the Father, would
imperil the entire doctrine of the Holy Trinity, which
indeed only found its completion herein. To have
withheld this prerogative from the Son would have
called in question his equal Deity; and the long struggle with the Arians had brought this home to the
minds of men, above all in Spain, where the struggle
had been the most terrible. It was there, at the Council of Toledo (589), that in the Nicene Creed to the
words "I believe in the Holy Ghost, ... who pro-
ceedeth from the Father," were added the words "and
from the Son." Many who embraced this truth with
their whole hearts were yet offended at what was thus
done, above all at the manner of its doing. So early
as the time of Charles the Great and Alcuin there
were serious misgivings, not as to the doctrine expressed by the *Filioque*, but in regard of the introduction into the Creed, by one branch of the Church only,
of words so important, and the making of them thus
an article of faith; nor did there want earnest deliberations whether they should not be withdrawn. It
was felt, however, by many that it would be one thing
never to have introduced the words; but quite another,
after they had been introduced, to withdraw them;

while others more boldly defended the addition; and in the end nothing was done. Meanwhile the Greeks, who only after a time had their attention drawn to the interpolated clause, were deeply offended;—offended at any change made in the Church's symbols by one portion only of the Church; and, engaged as they were in the battle for the truth against the dualistic heresies of the Eastern Manichæans, still more offended at the allowance thus given, as they said, to two originating fountains of Deity, or, as they charged the statement with implying, to a duality of Godhead. Let it be taught—for with this as many as were not seeking occasions of strife declared themselves content,—that the Holy Ghost proceeds from the Father *by* the Son; but that the Father is the one Beginning, Cause, and Source of Deity.

And yet this question of the single or double Procession, giving while it did a doctrinal basis to the antagonism between East and West, was very far from being that which most effectually rent them asunder. There was one point of difference which did far more for this; one claim which Rome was resolved that Constantinople should admit, and which Constantinople was resolved never to admit—the claim, that is, of the Roman Pontiff to be recognized as supreme Arbiter, to whom every greater cause must be brought for final decision. The Churches of the West, among which that of Rome towered as the sole apostolic, might learn little by little to acquiesce in such pretensions; but not so the Eastern, and least of all that of Constantinople. If the Bishop of old Rome would endure no equal, the Patriarch of Constantinople, falling back on the Council of Chalcedon and its recognition of his equal dignity, would tolerate no superior; and the more the usurping Roman Bishop extended his rule over the Churches of the West, and revealed the autocratic character of that rule, the more resolved were those of the East, Constantinople leading the way, to resist every attempt to place a like yoke upon their necks. On other points a compromise was possible. An explanation might remove a theological difficulty; but it could do nothing here.

If the strain and stress of the approaching separation relaxed a little in the tenth century, it revived in strength in the eleventh; and in this the final catastrophe arrived. A violent writing on the part of the Greek Patriarch, Michael Cerularius (1053), was replied to by one as violent on the part of the Pope. The Papal Legates at Constantinople could procure no satisfaction from the Patriarch there; and on July 16, 1054, they laid an act of excommunication, well charged with anathemas against the Patriarch, on the high altar of St. Sophia. This was not, indeed, a state of things altogether novel, for already during the Monophysite controversy there had been a suspension of intercourse between East and West for thirty-five years—from 484 to 519. Nothing is so easy as cursing, and the Greek Patriarch retorted with anthemas against the Pope, the other Oriental Patriarchs making common cause with him; and thus the Schism was at length consummated, which now after more than eight centuries shows, at least as between Latin and Greek, no tokens of abatement; and which, more than all other causes combined, has delivered the fairest regions of the East, once the most favoured seats of the Church, to that bastard faith of Islâm, standing where it ought not, even there where, except for the sins of Christians, it never would have stood.

And yet within fifty years from the date of the Schism there began the first of a long series of events which, extending over nearly two hundred years, might have seemed to open in a wonderful manner a door of reconciliation and way of peace. How could the Crusades fail in working a happy work, and in drawing again to one another, by the bonds of such mighty benefits conferred and such mighty benefits received, the hearts which had been for a while by various unhappy chances estranged from one another? So it might have been hoped. The Crusades had in effect an altogether opposite result. There was too often insolent violence on the part of the strong; treacherous intrigue on the part of the weak; and these efforts for the deliverance of the East, even when made in good faith, only served to increase the exasperation, to separate from one another by mutual suspicions, and ere long by the sense of mutual injuries, the helpers and the holpen more widely than ever.

Most effectual of all for the defeating of any better hopes which such alliances between East and West might have encouraged was that disgraceful episode which the Crusades offered—namely the temporary setting up of a Latin Empire at Constantinople. This Empire, under sentence of death from the beginning, lasted little more than half a century (1204–1262); but what a legacy of burning hate it must have left behind it, as the Greeks treasured up in their memories and revolved in their hearts the wrongs and the rapine, the desecrated churches, the profanation of all ac-

counted by them the most sacred, the insults and outrages innumerable, which during this time their Latin
oppressors had with so prodigal a wantonness heaped
on them and on their faith. Innocent III. may have
flattered himself that by sanctioning and allowing, as
in the end he did sanction and allow, that perfidious
transaction, the seizure of Constantinople by the
armies of the West, he was helping forward the reunion of the Churches which was so near to his heart.
He was indeed making that reunion, which anyhow
was hard, many times harder; causing it for centuries
which have not yet run their full course, to be impossible.

It was long, however, before this impossibility was
recognized by those in the high places either of the
East or the West. There were from time to time
negotiations for the bringing of such a reunion to
pass, and on both sides motives which impelled to this.
Thus, doubtless, it would have proved most grateful to
the arrogance of Rome, if only she could add to the
number of her vassals the obstinate rival who had con-
tested her superiority so long. Nor is it less certain
that the Byzantine Court, every day more hardly
pressed by the Ottomans, was on various occasions
sincerely anxious to arrive at such terms of reconciliation as should place the armies of Western Christendom at its service. This, however, was never more
than a movement of the Court and, it might be, of a
few courtly prelates and an obsequious Patriarch, advanced very probably for this very end. Terms of
agreement might be come to ;—they were so more than
once, at the Council of Lyons (1274), and again at that
of Florence (1439): but no further advance was made.

On this last occasion the Greek Emperor, John VII. Palæologus, had himself accompanied his theologians on their mission to the West; and he and they, after draining deeply there the cup of humiliation, returned home bringing a settlement with them. Dictated by the stronger party, this was little else than a thinly veiled surrender by the Greeks of all which was in dispute. Its conditions were no sooner known than they were indignantly repudiated by the vast body of clergy and laity. All who had any hand in arranging them, all the "Latin-minded" as they were called,—and there could be no worse charge,—were denounced as traitors; Metrophanes the Patriarch, his name changed by popular hatred to Metrophonus, or The Matricide, being counted the worst traitor of all. And now the latest glimpse of hope that aid might be obtained from the West disappeared; and in less than fourteen years Constantinople, after the heroic defence of an Emperor who knew when and how to die, was taken (May 29, 1453); and the church of Justinian, desecrated to a mosque, has remained such to the present hour. Some two hundred years earlier the mosque of Cordova had been transformed into a Christian church; but here was now a very lamentable redressing of the balance.

A very few words more before we leave this part of our subject. As the Western Church secured to itself a magnificent future by taking moral and spiritual possession of those Teutonic races which in the Providence of God had been brought within the sphere of its influence, so the Eastern recognized as its mission the conversion of the Slavonic tribes; and found in them, and in the imparting of the Gospel to them, security for its own future,—a pledge that however the Empire of the East might perish, the Church of the East should not perish with it. Admitting, as we must admit, that this Church's missionary zeal fell below that of the Western, still it was very far from neglecting altogether the duty of imparting to others that precious truth of which it was itself the keeper. It thus came to pass that long before the overwhelming catastrophe of the fifteenth century, a nation destined to have an immense share in moulding the future history of the world had received from Constantinople the seeds of the Christian faith,—not indeed of that faith in all its primitive purity, for none can give better than they themselves possess; but what it had, the Greek Church had freely given. I need hardly say that I refer to Russia. Everywhere in the East there are ghosts of a greatness which has forever vanished away. But while so much there belongs to an unreturning past, here are a nation and a Church, fresh and young, and only now beginning to play their part in the world's story. With Russia, and with the fortunes of Russia, the future of Eastern Christianity is manifestly bound up. That this future is destined to be a remarkable one it is impossible to doubt.

You must learn from others the circumstances which led to the conversion of Vladimir, to whom the Russian Church looks back and looks up as its founder (980). I can do no more than call your attention to the far-reaching significance of that event; and this, whether we contemplate it as the drawing of Russia into Christendom, or more particularly as the drawing of it into Eastern Christendom. If in far-reaching

world-historic importance that conversion falls behind
the conversion of Clovis, it is very little wherein it
falls behind; and perhaps the future may declare that
in the remoter consequences which it entailed, it did
not fall a whit behind. Even without Russia and the
moral and material forces of Russia at its back, the
" Orthodox " Church would still be a power in the
ecclesiastical and theological world. With Russia it is
a power and a great one, in the political world as
well, and, if the signs of the times do not greatly de-
ceive, every day will show this the more plainly.

LECTURE XXVI.

THE REVIVAL OF LEARNING.

W<small>HEN</small> we brand a long period of history, sometimes the whole medieval time, with the title of the Dark Ages, there is a large amount of injustice in this language; just as, when we celebrate a Revival of Learning, the image which suggests the phrase may very easily be urged too far. A revival is a returning to life of that which was dead, or which seemed dead. But the activities of the human mind were by no means dead, nor yet in a state of suspended animation during those times; neither were the helps to learning so few and insufficient, least of all during the later Middle Ages, nor the number who had really profited by these so small, as is often taken for granted. Many classical authors of Greece and Rome, whose writings were then, as they will always remain, the most efficient instruments of intellectual culture, had never been lost sight of in the West; the Greek, it is true, being only accessible by means of imperfect translations. That ancient world of which these spoke was known, not indeed with the fulness and accuracy wherewith it is possible to know it now, but much better than is generally supposed. Already in the fourteenth century Dante (b. 1265, d. 1321) and Petrarch (b. 1304, d. 1374) had done much to extend a familiarity with the best Latin

poets; and Boccaccio (b. 1313, d. 1375) something for
awakening a wider interest in the masterpieces of
Greek literature; so that this Revival of which we are
wont to speak as the glory of the fourteenth and fifteenth centuries was by no means a resurrection of
classical learning from the grave, nor even as an
awakening of it from a trance.   This awakening had
already taken place.

But with all these qualifications made, the significance of what was then coming to pass, its bearing on
the fortunes of the Church, must by no means be
slighted or overlooked.   It was not as the first spring,
succeeding upon a long winter sleep; for that long
winter sleep had been broken long ago; but it was a
fuller outburst of the buds and blossoms in a more
genial time.   Many circumstances wrought together
to give exactly at this epoch a new impulse to learning, to the study above all of Greek and Latin antiquity.   Books, as I have said, were not so rare in the
later Middle Ages as we sometimes fancy; but, admitting this, the Invention of Printing (about 1440)—
a new gift of tongues we might be tempted to call it,
if only it had been always turned to worthy uses—lent
wings to knowledge, put within the reach of hundreds
and presently of thousands what had hitherto been
within the reach but of two or of three.

Nor were there wanting any longer the living teachers and interpreters of that language and literature of
Greece, which could least have endured the absence
of these.   It is true that in the cloisters of Calabria,
the old Magna Græcia, acquaintance with Greek had
never quite died out; but the monks there had done
little or nothing to spread the knowledge of it beyond

their own walls. Now, however, two events, these two indeed most closely connected with one another, brought about a large accession of efficient teachers. The first was the Council of Florence (1439). I have already called your attention from another point of view to this latest endeavour to bring about a reconciliation of East and West, and to the motives out of which that endeavour sprung. It failed, as all previous attempts of a like kind had done; but the negotiation had brought many of the most learned Greek theologians and scholars to Italy, of whom some conformed to the Latin Communion and remained. Bessarion, Archbishop of Nicæa, afterwards a Roman Cardinal, and twice very nearly Pope, was perhaps the most illustrious of those who thus sought shelter betimes from the coming storm. Others also there were who did the same; and when, a few years later, the catastrophe actually arrived which the healing of the Schism should have averted, and Constantinople fell at last before the arms of Mahomet II. (1453), the West,—and Italy above all,—was covered with the fugitives from the mighty ruin.

Some of these, escaping it might have appeared with no more than their lives, yet indeed brought with them treasures of price, and such as made their welcome secure. Besides a living familiarity with the Greek tongue they brought with them manuscripts of Greek authors hitherto unknown, or known only by bald and incorrect translations, in the West. Constantinople, it is true, had created little in the way of a literature of its own during the last eight hundred years of its existence; but, ever since the remarkable quickening of interest in classical studies which signalized the close of the ninth century, Byzantine scholars had been very careful guardians of such. treasures of Greek literature as had not already perished,—had been diligent in the preserving and multiplying of such knowledge as was needful for the right understanding of these. The day had now arrived which should show that this watchful care had not been exercised in vain.

The more distinguished among these refugees from the East were received with open arms, oftentimes with extravagant honours, by the princes of Italy:—as notably by Alfonso V., King of Naples (1442–1448) ; by Lorenzo the Magnificent (d. 1478) and other of the Medici at Florence ; and at Rome by Popes such as Nicolas V. (1447–1455), Pius II. (1458–1464), and, somewhat later, Leo X. These last, as they played the gracious host, little dreamt that they were entertaining such as, without meaning any treacherous return for this kindness, should yet work to the authors of it no little harm. Professorships, canonries, and not seldom posts higher still of academical honour or ecclesiastical dignity, were found for them. Not the famous cities of Italy alone, but almost every little town had its *Academia*, the centre of classical studies and of a stirring intellectual life. Petty tyrants of the Romagna, retired condottieri like Malatesta, counted their little Court incomplete if it did not include one Humanist at the least. I lighted lately on a passage in the *Essays* of Montaigne, which describes in a very instructive manner what at this time was going forward not in Italy alone, but over all Europe. "My father," he writes, "set on fire by that new kind of earnestness, wherewith King Francis I. embraced letters and raised them into credit, did with great diligence and much cost endeavour to purchase the acquaintance of learned men; receiving and entertaining them as holy persons, and who had some particular inspiration of divine wisdom; collecting their sentences and discourses, as if they had been oracles; and with so much more reverence and religious regard, by how much less authority he had to judge of them: for he had no knowledge of letters, no more than his predecessors before him."

A passage like this attests that it is not in Italy alone that this admiration for the New Learning and for the bearers of it was working. Still, as Italy was the cradle, so for a long time was it the principal seat of this newly awakened passion for the lore of the ancient world. It was no affected enthusiasm there. Affectations, insincerities enough may have clung to its skirts, as these ever cling to the skirts of a grand movement; but the enthusiasm itself was genuine; and Heeran has perfect right when he says, " Men would have brought the Greek Muses to Italy, if they had not themselves sought refuge there." Thus, when Ficinus burned a lamp continually before the bust of Plato, as others might have burnt one before the shrine of some saint, it was a fact, and a very significant one, which he expressed thereby. But the movement did not remain an Italian one merely. It was not long before the more promising of the youth of every part of Europe,—Colet and Linacre, for example, from England,—streaming over the Alps, sought to share such advantages as only the schools of Italy in fullest measure could offer. It is impossible without liveliest interest to plant oneself in those times, when almost every day had its own discovery, and this of something more precious than the gold-mine and the diamond-field which constitute our chief surprises now —some precious manuscript brought to light and shaking off the dust of centuries, some new region of knowledge unfolding itself before the eyes of men.

When indeed one marks the immense influence which the old Greek and Roman world, so soon as it began to be intimately known, and its literature above all, exercised on the thought and imagination of Europe, the intense homage which at once this commanded, one is compelled to own that it was well familiarity with it did not earlier begin. Such a familiarity would inevitably have killed the original thought and productive energy of the Middle Ages, which the modern world could have done very ill without. Awe-struck by the perfection of form to which the master-pieces of the ancient world had attained, failing to realize of how much grander truths they were themselves the guardians, the men of later times would have shrunk from entering into competition with that which showed so immeasurably above and beyond them; and in form did, no doubt, immeasurably transcend anything, to which, except after long efforts and many failures, they were likely to attain. It was permitted therefore to the Middle Ages to have their say, to utter all which was in their heart, before the veil was more than very partially withdrawn which hid from men's eyes the treasures of the old classical world.

"Humanists," as we have seen, was the title they bore who threw themselves without reserve into the study,—worship shall we call it?—of classical antiquity,

The name is a very instructive one. They claimed
by it, for the studies which they pursued, that these
contained the truest and highest culture of humanity,
that through these what was most truly human in man
would receive its highest development. It is worth
while to ponder this name, for it at once reveals them
to us in their strength and in their weakness; what in
them was worthy of praise, and also where they went
wrong, and where indeed they were sure to go wrong;
what the perils were which beset these new studies;
what the gains great and manifold which true religion
might derive from them.

The mischiefs which might attend them did not fail
soon to appear. A passionate and exclusive admiration for what was ancient, in other words for what was
heathen, soon displayed itself in a visible estrangement
on the part of most among the Italian Humanists, not
so much from the Church as from Christianity, from
the living Gospel of Christ. With the Church they
were willing enough to keep terms. Many of them
occupied its high places, enjoyed its emoluments;
indeed it is not too much to affirm that in Leo X. a
Humanist filled the Papal Chair. There were no deep
moral convictions which drove them into opposition to
the Church, no fire in their bones so that they could
not keep silence. Only let them be free to employ
the shafts of their wit on the barbarous Latin of the
Schoolmen, to hold up to ridicule the ignoble squabbles
of the Friars, and they left unassailed the capital abuses
of the time, and were themselves in turn unassailed.
Frivolous, profane, freethinking, having assimilated
themselves only too faithfully to that heathen world
which they admired, we never read that the Inquisition

with all its activity troubled itself about them. For indeed the Church of Rome seldom persecuted mere laughers and mockers. She knew too well that she had nothing to fear from these; they were rather wel-come to her than otherwise, as safety-valves for the escape of the indignation and scorn which, violently compressed, might have proved dangerous indeed. It was those who were in deep religious earnest whom she feared, and in whom, with a true instinct, she recognized her foes.

The Humanists of Italy before very long showed unmistakably of what spirit they were, out of what root they grew. Their insatiable vanity, their bitter envyings one of another, their shameless adulation of the great of the earth,—adulation which, if it failed to bring its due return, they could exchange in a moment for the foulest abuse,—their writings so often steeped in the worst heathen impurities, and their lives to match, their denial of the primary truths not of Chris-tianity alone, but of all religion,—as the freedom of the will, the immortality of the soul, the judgment after death,—told only too plainly of this.

The rise of a new heathenism within the bosom of the Church—for it was often nothing less than this,—belonged almost exclusively to Italy, the corruptest portion of Christendom, as nearest to the centre of corruption. Savonarola saw the danger, and earnestly witnessed against it; but among the famous names of Italy he stands almost alone. In other lands, in Ger-many and England, the study of classical antiquity assumed a much healthier direction. To more than one it was given to consecrate the gold and silver which he had brought out of Egypt to the service of

the tabernacle.   Our own most prominent Humanists
are Sir Thomas More, Chancellor of England, and John
Colet, Dean of St. Paul's.   Melanchthon stands out as
the German representative; Erasmus as the Dutch.
For these, and for others like-minded, this study took
its true place; not as the final goal of all studies, but
as a help and handmaid to that which is the queen of
all, namely to Theology, or the knowledge of the true
God.   Here these better Humanists did excellent service.   It, indeed, is hard to see how the Reformation
could have done without them.   Its strength lay in its
appeal to the Word of God as above every doctrine
and tradition of men : but, to make this appeal of any
worth, the interpretation of Scripture must be established on sure foundations of grammar, so that no
doubt may remain that its sense has been truly appre-
hended.

The Humanists were thus most useful in hastening
on the Reformation.   They did some excellent service
in the skirmishes which went before the battle ; and
even in the battle itself, at the first clashing of the opposing hosts.   And yet from them as such, even where
they had not degenerated into worshippers of the old
mythologies;—and as such utterly heartless and insin-
cere for the work of the true God,—a Reformation
could never have proceeded.   There were some abuses
which they could clearly see and indignantly denounce
and in so doing they may have often found themselves
in the same ranks with the true Reformers.   But for
the waging a successful conflict with a system so
mighty still as that of the Church of Rome, or indeed
for the challenging of it to a conflict at all, there
needed much more than an insight into the corruption

of that system. There needed the faith which over-comes the world; which counts God's truth dearer than the life itself; there needed an inward bleeding compassion for souls flattered and fed with deceitful hopes ; and the study of the illustrious writers of Greece and Rome gave none of these things; nay, when pursued to the exclusion of other studies, in-stead of kindling men's affections for the truth, cooled them rather. A Reformation carried out in their spirit, supposing that the motive power for effecting this could have been found, would have proved not a Re-formation, but a Revolution ; could have ended in nothing but in sheer unbelief.

Very instructive to us here, as showing that not from a Revival of Learning,—not from this alone, nor from this chiefly,—there should come effectual help for a suffering Church, is the history of Erasmus (b. 1467, d. 1536), himself the chief of the Humanists, a king in the world of letters, and quite the most remarkable figure in the age which immediately preceded the Re-formation. And the story of his life is the more full of teaching, seeing that he was by no means one of those semi-pagan scholars, of whom I spoke just now. On the contrary, while he displayed a ceaseless activity in the editing and elucidating of classical authors, this heathen learning had not all, nor the best of his affec-tions. The truth in Christ, so far as he had appre-hended it, was dear to him. He did much with his pen for preparing the way of the Reformation ; and this not negatively only,—assailing some of the worst abuses of the Church, and the favourers of these, with the shafts of his pitiless wit ; but in ways more posi-tive,—producing various works invaluable in their time, manuals of Christian faith and practice; and, above all, publishing the first edition of the New Testament in the original language which had ever appeared. Its appearance indeed one cannot regard otherwise than as providentially timed, falling in as it exactly did with the year which immediately preceded the Reformation (1516.)

So far most are agreed about him; but his after attitude, when he stood face to face with the Reformation, has been very variously judged. Those who judge him the most hardly state the grounds of their judgment and of their griefs against him very much in language such as follows:—The foremost man of his time so long as the movement was mainly a literary one,—so soon as ever it assumed a more earnest shape, he declined to take any active share in it. He gave, indeed, to Luther a few words of encouragement at the outset, but when he saw that the struggle would be for life and death, he disengaged himself from it, saying with ignoble self-scorn that others might affect a martyrdom, he did not feel himself called to this honour. He would very gladly have persuaded the heads of the Church to abate some of its most crying and flagrant abuses; but, finding them resolute to abide by these, he was not prepared to break with them altogether. And thus he lived far on into the Reformation period in an ambiguous position, like the bat in the fable, which was owned neither by the birds nor by the beasts. He had spoken too much about the corruptions of the Church not to be regarded with dislike and suspicion by all who clung to these,—for it was he, they said, who laid the egg which Luther hatched; but he was perhaps regarded with a

stronger dislike, one largely dashed with contempt, by
as many as beheld in him one who, for the retaining
of his worldly advantages, his favour with the great, his
literary ease, had been untrue, as they counted it, to
his deepest convictions; and who, after sounding a
trumpet which summoned others to the battle, was
not, when the battle joined, himself found in the ranks
of the combatants.

Such was very much the indictment drawn up
against Erasmus in his own time; and in language
not very different from this many speak about him in
ours. It is not without its truth; while yet considerations are here left out, whose omission is not
altogether just. Erasmus, let it be remembered, did
not begin his career as a Reformer,—and it was
only by the way and by accident that he was such,—
but as a Humanist; and in the main he was faithful
throughout to the duties which this name imposed.
One may wish that he had looked higher and seen
deeper. Yet when he refused to advance any farther,
and separated himself and his fortunes from those of
the more ardent Reformers, this was not a stopping
short upon his part at the prospect of danger on a
line whereupon he had hitherto been travelling, but a
refusal to allow himself to be violently transported
from his own line to quite another, to one upon which
he had never professed to travel; for he had always
declared that a Reformation in Luther's sense and
carried out in his spirit involved so much of danger,
might be attended with such frightful calamities, as
would far outweigh any problematical good which
was to be gotten from it. There may have been,
I am sure there was, a more excellent way than that

2Z

which he chose ; but I am sure also that it is easy
to say things about Erasmus, which shall be bitterer and more full of reproach than the actual facts
of the case, if duly weighed in the balance, would
warrant.

LECTURE XXVII.

CHRISTIAN ART IN THE MIDDLE AGES.

I HAVE written elsewhere as follows, and will venture to repeat myself here, the book from which I quote having been long out of print:—"How little could friend or foe of the new-born faith have foreseen, that out of it there should unfold itself a poetry infinitely greater, an art infinitely higher, than the old world had ever seen; that this Faith which looked so rigid, so austere, even so forbidding, should clothe itself in forms of grace and loveliness such as the world had never dreamt of before; that poetry should not be henceforward the play of the spirit, but its holiest earnest; that those artless paintings of the catacombs had the prophecy in them of more wondrous compositions than man's eyes had ever seen; or that a day should arrive when above many a dark vault and narrow crypt, where now the Christian worshippers gathered in secret, should arise domes and cathedrals embodying loftier ideas, because ideas relating to the Eternal and the Infinite, than all those Grecian temples which now stood so fair and so strong; but which aimed not to lift men's hearts and minds from the earth which they adorned."

Time, however, was needed for the bringing about of this. During the first three centuries the mere question of existence had taxed all the energies of the

Church, which had thus little thought or care to bestow on aught which was not vital to her. When a distinguished French statesman was asked what he did during the Reign of Terror, his reply was, "I lived;"—that was exploit enough in such an evil time. The Church in like manner, "lived" during those days of trial; and so far as art was concerned, more could not be demanded of her. With Constantine the condition of things was altogether changed. Emerging from the catecombs she sought to clothe herself in some outward beauty that should bear a faint correspondence to that spiritual beauty of which she was conscious within. As was natural, her earliest efforts were to appropriate and adopt forms which she found ready-made to her hands; to try whether she could not subdue these to her own uses, fill them with her own spirit. That she should make this attempt was inevitable, but inevitable too that a very partial success at the best should attend it. The outer form and the inner spirit of any true work of art are so closely bound up together, the one being not so much the vesture as the incarnation of the other, that the contradiction which here made itself felt between the heathen form and the Christian spirit effectually wrought for the injury, often for the marring, of both.

Thus nothing can be poorer than the Christian poetry written during the fourth and fifth centuries in the old classical metres. As we read the hexameters of Juvencus or Sedulius, there is a constant sense of unfitness, of incongruity between the form and the spirit, as of new wine poured into bottles stiff and old, to the spoiling of both; while with Christian alcaics and sapphics it fares, if possible, worse. Even Prudentius, who was a poet of true genius, and who was nearer success than any other, cannot be said to have more than very partially succeeded. It was not till the classical framework of Latin verse was wholly shattered, quantity absolutely ignored and accent substituted in its stead, the latent powers of rhyme being at the same time evoked, that Christian Latin poetry attained the perfection which fills with astonishment all who are capable of judging, as they contemplate this second birth of Latin song; this rejuvenescence of a language and a literature which had seemed to have run their course, and to have uttered all which was in their heart to utter.

The complete failure of all such attempts became ever plainer as the Church grew more and more conscious of her ideal dignity, of her superiority to the world around her and the world which she had left behind her. With the hopes and aspirations which now were hers she could less and less endure to be embarrassed by old traditions, to be shut in by laws and limitations, the justice or necessity of which she did not acknowledge. As time went on she more and more transgressed, broke through and defied these, even while as yet she had nothing better of her own to substitute in their stead. Detaching herself from the old Græco-Roman world, and entering on untrodden ways of her own, she ventured on a grand but hazardous experiment:—how far, that is, she could array herself in garments of grace and beauty which her own hands had wrought, for ever laying aside, however rich and gorgeous they might seem, such as had not been made for her, at the best became her ill, and often did not become her at all.

It was not till about the fifth century that the Church gave any clear intimations that she would thus develop an independent art of her own. The tokens of any such intention on her part displayed themselves first, as was inevitable, in the matter which was most immediately urgent, in the houses, that is, which she was now free to rear to Almighty God, and which she could not therefore leave any longer unbuilt. There were many reasons why the heathen temples should not be the models which she chose for imitation. That they were quite too small, being often little more than the shrine of the God or goddess to whom they were dedicated, would have been reason enough; but there was a deeper moral objection behind. The heathen temples were too closely linked with the service of false gods, in other words of devils, were haunted with too many impure associations and profane memories, to be tolerable to the earnest Christians of those days.

There was less in the basilicas to offend and to repel. These were courts or halls of justice, serving also in their ample room as places of general resort, where, as in a mart or exchange, the business of this world was transacted. We hear it often repeated that the early Christians obtained from the grace of favouring Emperors some of the existing basilicas, which by them were turned to uses higher than any which they hitherto had known. This, however, has never been proved. What is certain is that the churches which the faithful now proceeded to build were fashioned upon the pattern of the basilica, with such modifications as enabled them to satisfy the higher demands of that new service to which they were put,

and to be indeed, according to the prophecy wrapt up
in their name, houses of the Great King. A serious
and stately edifice the basilica at the outset was,—as
indeed, whatever changes it might undergo, it never
ceased to be; truly Roman in its character; primarily
designed for use, yet not rejecting beauty, so far as
beauty was content to wait upon utility. I should be
passing out of the region of history into that of archæ-
ology were I to attempt to trace the steps by which a
building, originally serving mundane purposes, was
transformed into one serving heavenly; the roof little
by little reared to loftier heights; arms thrown out to
the right hand and the left, so to make space for the
crowds of worshippers who thronged its courts; these
arms, or transepts as they came to be called, impressing, without intending anything of the kind, a cruci-
form shape upon the building, which was not the less
welcome because it came thus unsought; while what
had been the Prætor's seat in the couch or recess at
the eastern end suggested the spot where now should
be the Bishop's throne, with the presbyters, his as-
sessors, ranged in semicircle round him. Much more
there is well worthy to be noted in the readiness with
which the basilica lent itself to all the needs of Christian discipline and worship; so that even after houses
of God, grander and more original in conception, had
risen up at the bidding of mightier artists than the
builders of these, it still kept and keeps its place as an
abiding form of Christian architecture.

The basilica in its severe simplicity belonged, as we
have seen, to the West. The style which we call
Byzantine was born, as its name imports, in the East;
or, at any rate, was an Eastern modification of a

Western building. Everything leads us to the conclusion that, up to the time of Justinian, the ecclesiastical architecture of New Rome differed little, if at all,
from that of the Old. Justinian himself reared many
basilicas. But the edifice by which he gained a name
for himself as one of the foremost church-builders of
the world, excelling, as was his own boast, even Solomon himself,—is St. Sophia's at Constantinople (537).
It would be too much to say that this is the actual model upon which the whole church-building of the East
has since been modelled; but it has certainly made its
influence felt throughout all, has moulded and modified
all. At Ravenna, the Byzantium of the West, the glorious church of St. Vitalis (547) will give no unworthy
notion to as many of us as have never travelled farther
eastward, of what this style at its highest can effect.

With whom the idea originated of grafting an entirely novel feature on the basilica, and one which
should dominate every other, which indeed sometimes
should be the sole feature, that namely of a central
dome,—"the spreading cupola, the liveliest copy
which men's skill could frame of the vault of heaven"
(Freeman),—with whom, I say, the honour of this invention lay, it may be impossible to affirm; but New-
Roman or Byzantine, and not Old-Rome, it certainly
was. In Agrippa's Pantheon one element of the
grandeur of the dome had been anticipated, namely
its vastness,—but not its elevation; for the dome of
the Pantheon, springing from low walls, makes no
effort to lift itself from earth to heaven. The rearing
of the dome to those astonishing heights, till it stood
as a heaven within the heaven,—this was the novelty.
In this, and in the successful mastering of all the

structural difficulties which this presented, its main glory consisted.

At the same time, sublime as the church of Justinian is, this, and the other churches innumerable which are formed on its pattern, have weaknesses and drawbacks of their own. Thus, not to dwell on mere technical embarrassments,—on the enormous weight of the dome thus suspended high in air, needing as this did piers the most massive to sustain it,—there were other faults, and these more fundamental, which clung to it. As in the Byzantine State, so in the church of the true Byzantine type, everything is centralized. The dome, and the space immediately beneath the dome, is all ; or, at best, everything else is secondary and subordinated to this. There is no leading up of the heart and eye to the Eastern end, and to the chiefest mysteries which are celebrated there, to the Sun of Righteousness which might be looked for as rising there with healing on his wings : while all those arrangements for divine worship and for the distribution of the worshippers which grew so naturally out of the basilica, have been disturbed ; others, which only imperfectly fulfil their object, needing to be substituted in their room. The Byzantine church is but the basilica with one magnificent Oriental feature added to it, and that feature only imperfectly adapting itself to the purposes for which the building was designed. The Orient, for Ravenna must be regarded as an Oriental city, was the region in which it moved and reigned,—a much narrower region than that which the basilica claimed as its own.

With the eleventh century a new era of church-building begins. The apathy which possessed the minds of multitudes as they drew near to the conclusion of a Millennium, persuaded as they were that with the year 1000 the world would come to an end, and that therefore any labour, except for the supply of immediate necessities, would be labour in vain,—this apathy passed away, when it was perceived that the end was not yet. It was succeeded, so soon as the fatal term was left behind, by a ponderous burst of activity, displaying itself in a thousand ways. In no domain did it this more signally than in that of Christian architecture. "Arise, let us build," is everywhere the word. But what men built was not the old Roman basilica, and as little the domical structure of Byzantium; while yet in the new style—Romanesque it is called—borrowing, as it does, features from both, these styles were brought into fruitful association.

The life of Romanesque architecture, as compared to the life of other styles, was comparatively brief. It did not hold the foremost place for quite two centuries, from the eleventh to the end of the twelfth. During this time it has diverged into two branches, with sufficient features in common to justify our including of them under a common name, but at the same time of a marvellous diversity. There is a Northern Romanesque, of a grand and austere simplicity, well fitted to that rugged North which it adorns. Durham and Caen may be accepted as the crowning glories of this, as is the cathedral of Pisa of ornate Southern Romanesque. If we regard the Basilican as the first, and the Byzantine as in chronological succession the second order of Church architecture, the Romanesque will constitute the third. Lombard it is sometimes called, but by a misnomer; neither is

Secondary Roman, which some have styled it, to be praised. "I claim," Mr. Freeman has said, "for Romanesque to be looked on neither as debased Roman nor as imperfect Gothic; but as a genuine independent style, of which Italy and Norman England produced two varieties of coequal merit." Its chief characteristic is delight in the multiplication of the arch, not so much for the support as for the ornamentation of the building. Within and without there is the same prodigal employment of this form. But the arch is round, and chiefly used for decoration. There is no hint as yet of the immense structural effects, and effects more marvellous still, which, by the employment of the pointed arch might be secured.

Christian architecture had done many wonderful things; but it had not spoken its last word, nor shown all which it could accomplish, until the unfolding toward the close of the twelfth century of that which is as "the bright consummate flower," the crown and completion of all which had gone before,—the style which, satisfying at once the aspirations of the Christian spirit and the exigences of art, has adorned all middle Europe, and as far north as Drontheim, with those cathedrals which are at once the admiration and despair of the after world. The name of Gothic, by which we now call this style, is, as learners are often reminded, an absurd misnomer; having been originally a random term of contempt equivalent to barbarous, given to this birth of the genius of the North by the Italians of the Renaissance, who had no eye for the glory of it, and no faith in any styles but those which had been handed down from the ancient world. Vasari (d. 1564) is reported, I know not how truly, to

have been the first to make this application of the
word. It is not a misnomer only, but a misleader as
well,—saying at once too much and too little. It says
too much, for Goths had nothing to do with its invention ; any people called by this name having disappeared centuries before from the earth. It says too
little, seeing that it makes no attempt to seize and to
express the chief characteristics of this style. It is
not the less true that to find the appropriate name is
not so easy. Ogival, borrowed from the French use,
is quite too hard a word; and, though it does not suggest error, has the disadvantage of suggesting, to us
at least, nothing. Romantic, which has been sometimes proposed, may be dismissed at once ; defects
quite as serious cleave to it as to Gothic. Then too,
being as this style of architecture is, an explosion of
genius nearly simultaneous in Germany and in Northern France, to call it German would be unjust to
France, which, pointing to Chartres, to Rheims, to
Amiens,—that triology unique in grandeur of conception and perfection of detail,—to Notre Dame of
Paris, and to many more, might justly complain that
the whole question of the priority of invention was
thus, without so much of a hearing granted, given
against her. At the same time, calling it French, we
might be doing an equal wrong to Spires, to Cologne,
to Strasburg, and to other cathedrals not unworthy to
be named in the same breath with these.

I know not what better can be done than to give
this style its name from the pointed arch which is its
distinguishing feature and the key to its marvels; for
though this arch was not now employed for the first
time, it never played a foremost part till now. Like

almost everything which is destined to exercise a mighty and permanent influence, it entered unnoticed and at unawares into the world. Brought in all likelihood from the East, and domiciled first in Sicily, it was only after a while that the capabilities of decorative beauty and constructive power latent in it were revealed. Neither is there any exact moment or place to which pointing we can say that then and there the pointed arch was first employed. Existing side by side with the round arch, and suggested, as some have thought, by the intersection of two such arches, it was only by steps which cannot always be accurately traced, that, wrestling in conflict with this, it won the day, and was bold to claim a future of unparalleled magnificence for its own.

It had a right to claim it, for what difficulties now were solved, what possibilities of grandeur and beauty were now brought within reach! All fear of laying too heavy a weight on the arches might now be dismissed. The pressure, not so much lateral as perpendicular, was comparatively easy to deal with. Higher and ever higher rose the principal lines of the Gothic cathedral,—lines no longer horizontal, level that is with the earth, and never losing their nearness to it ; but vertical, climbing up into and piercing the heaven, themselves a *Sursum corda* uttering itself in stone. Words are weak to express the marvel and the glory of the buildings which in emulous rivalry covered in a little while the face of Germany, of Northern France, of England. For the building which now, obedient to the architect's wand, sprang up, was not merely a stupendous fabric of richest elaboration, of rarest audacity of conception. It was in all its parts, in great and in small, a symbolism,—the embodiment in material forms of an idea, and that idea the grandest which the world has known; a spiritual poem taking visible shape and fashion before the eyes of men; admitting the amplest variety in detail, but not the less under law; as much under a law ever present and ever active as the *Divine Comedy* of Dante, and like it a poetry and a theology in one.

But while it fared thus upon our side of the Alps, the Renaissance was more and more making itself felt in Italy, and not least in modifying the character of Italian Church architecture. There was a return to the old classical forms; not indeed to these pure and simple, for it was impossible to ignore altogether all that had been accomplished during the last thousand years, but to these forms in the main. Whatever the genius of a Bramante, a Brunelleschi, a Michael Angelo could bring about,—whatever the most lavish enjoyment of the costliest materials, of the richest marbles, of the most elaborate mosaics, of gold and of silver,—whatever the most amazing dimensions could effect, nothing of this was wanting. But the essential character of the Renaissance, that which was at once its strength and its weakness, namely that it owned this world as the sphere in which it was well satisfied to move and did not reach out after a higher, made itself felt here, as it did in every other province and domain of art. St. Peter's at Rome astonishes and imposes, but fails altogether to strike with religious awe. The same may be said, though not quite so strongly, of the cathedral of Milan, which may be regarded as the point where Northern or Gothic and Southern or Italian art meet and mingle.

I have dwelt so long on the Christian architecture of the Middle Ages, that little time is left me to speak of their other arts. And yet I have only assigned to it that larger portion of our time which it might fairly challenge ; for indeed Architecture is *the* fine art of the Middle Ages ; the queen to whom all other arts are but as handmaids. It was not, in fact, till the twelfth century that churches began to be decked with sculpture at all ; which for a long time after remained merely a subsidiary ornament. Statues may fill every niche within and without of a cathedral,—there are said to be four thousand in that of Bourges,—and certainly none can deny the magnificent decorative effects, and often the profound symbolism of the splendid series of sculptures which adorn the west fronts of so many of the French cathedrals ; but for all this, Sculpture is there in the service of a greater than itself ; and it is not till the Middle Ages are nearly spent that it claims (first I should say in Donatello, b. 1383, d. 1466) an independent existence of its own.

Painting too remains for a long while in the background, though not so completely as does Sculpture. Compared with this it shows itself capable of rendering service which, for reasons that lie very deep, Sculpture is incapable of yielding. This in all ages has been strongly felt. The Greek Church, indeed, for which pictures are favourite assistances to devotion, and which has passed through such terrible trials rather than suffer these to be wrested from her, absolutely disallows raised sculptural representations of things sacred either in the church or in the house. This superiority of Painting over Sculpture in the sphere of religious art is sufficiently intelligible. Of these sisters Sculpture is the more sensuous, Painting the more spiritual. Sculpture too is subject to various limitations from which Painting is free; colour is wanting to it, and atmosphere, the oppositions of darkness and light, the suggestion of vast distances, the grandeur of immense multitudes gathered to a single spot and under the influence of the same emotion. And then, if the beauty of the human form is that which more than all else Sculpture aims at reproducing, it can never in the Church be forgotten that there is a worm at the root of this beauty; that in all save One it is from the first bound over to decay and death and to all the dishonour of the grave. The heathen world did not feel this; or in its passionate worship of mere physical beauty contrived to forget it. Admiring too, but not reverencing, the body, it had no scruple about setting forth the beauty of the human form without covering or concealment; or, what scruple it had for a while, this before long had been dismissed: while in Christian art,—in art, that is, which stood under the immediate influence of religion,—such an absence of honourable shame was inconceivable. All this explains how it came to pass that Sculpture exercised a far more potent spell on the heathen world than it exercises upon us; while the modern or Christian world, yielding the palm of excellence in this domain of art, claims in Painting to have evoked forms of grace and beauty whereof the antique heathen times did not so much as dream.

Certainly it is a very narrow temper which finds fault with the employment by the Church of those ancillary helps, adorning and beautifying, which Art supplies. We may heartily welcome them; but, as a general rule, only upon one condition—namely, that no more is used of them than it may be fairly expected that the worshippers will be able to absorb and take up in such a reasonable service as He who is Spirit demands on the part of his worshippers. Some words of the Cambridge Platonist, Henry More, seem to me to express excellently well what are the due limits which the artistic element in worship should not over-pass :—" Such," he says, "is the truth and simplicity of the Christian religion, that if the authority of the Church think good to recommend any additional cir-cumstances of divine worship, they must not be for in-effectual pomp and show, but for real use and edifica-tion, affecting such a beauty and comeliness as Nature does in living creatures, whose pulchritude is the result of such a symmetry of parts and tenour of spirits as implies vigour and ability to all the functions of life. And truly there should be no more ceremony in the Church than the use thereof may be obvious to under-stand, and the life and power of holiness may throughly actuate ; that our minds may not be amused, lost, sunk in, or fixed upon, any outward things here, but be car-ried from all visible pomps to the love and admiration of our Blessed Saviour in Heaven, and of that heavenly and divine life that He came into the world to beget in the hearts of all true believers." It would be un-true, in my judgment, to aver that the limits here laid down were not often overpassed. The Church's ritual, with all its glorious surroundings, was often, so to speak, as some glass, opaque where it should have been translucent, and stopping for itself the light which it should have transmitted to others. The Puritan excess was a not unnatural reaction against the æsthetic in worship, developed as this last was to an extent that would have been only justifiable if the higher spiritual worship had advanced hand in hand with it, which assuredly was not always or nearly always the case.

LECTURE XXVIII.

ASPECTS OF CHRISTIAN LIFE AND WORK IN THE MIDDLE AGES.

WHEN we attempt to compare the Middle Ages in their religious aspect with the ages which have succeeded them, there is error and exaggeration on either side into which it is abundantly easy to fall. There is the error and exaggeration on one side of unduly depreciating those ages,—to which Protestants are most addicted; as on the other side there is that of magnifying them over much, extolling them as "ages of faith," with a tacit subaudition that all which came after have been ages of unbelief,—into which Roman Catholics more often run. There is much to explain and account for both excesses. Thus if some set these ages too high, this is not seldom the reaction of generous spirits, who feel that injustice has been done them, and who, instead of redressing the scales, disturb them in the opposite direction. Nor is this the only explanation. Doubtless in those ages religion claimed to mingle as a present influence, penetrating and pervading the every day life of men, far more than now it does. Reminders in one shape or another of a higher world-order, behind that world of shows and phantoms in the midst of which we move, were far more numerous then; nor can it be denied that the world is now left in the exclusive possession of domains of human existence which Faith once claimed, in part or wholly, as her own.

Yet in measuring age against age it is often forgotten, and nowhere so often as here, that the outward manifestations of religion may be, and have been before now, not the effluence and utterance of its inner spirit, but a substitute for it. Thus in lands where the medieval tradition is the strongest we see not seldom an entire divorce between religion or outward devoutness and morality, and this without any conscious hypocrisy on their parts who are religious without being moral. The Italian brigand wears little leaden saints in his hat; he has his favourite shrine at which his devotions are duly paid: and all this with no sense of the tragic contradictions between one half of his life and the other. Gasperone, who closed his career in a Roman prison, had committed murders out of number; but boasted, and no doubt counted it a fair matter of boasting, that he had never committed one on a Friday. We may then freely accept the fact that life was more thronged and crowded with religious observances in the Middle Ages than it is now, without accepting this as a convincing proof that a larger proportion of those who professed the faith of Christ owned the obligations of God's moral law, and ordered their lives in conformity with it, then than now.

But it is not the admirers of medieval Christianity only who thus exceed. There is, as I have said, another extreme; that namely of so dwelling on what was amiss and out of joint in those times,—the scandals, the offences, the disorders, the superstitions,—that we lose sight altogether of the work of grace and power which the great Head of the Church was then, as at all times, carrying forward in the hearts of his people. Those tempted to lose sight of this would do well to study a little more closely some centuries in which, as men are wont to tell us, the light was the least, and the love had grown the coldest. Without changing their mind about the presence of evil in them, and this in amounts terrible to think of, they will perhaps change their mind about the absence of good. The tenth century has a very bad name in Church history, as among the Dark Ages the darkest, —an age, as Baronius describes it, in which Christ was indeed still in the Ship, and therefore it was not submerged; but in which He was sleeping there. I have no desire to question this verdict; and yet, when we know that period a little more nearly, what noble figures it reveals. What grander company of Christian men and women, and these occupying the thrones of the earth, would any where greet us than greet us here:—Otto the Great, and Brun, Archbishop of Cologne, his brother, these two, the layman and the priest, working so zealously together for the spread of Christian missions among the wild heathen races that raged and stormed around the fortress of German Christianity; while, completing this royal group, there is Matilda, the mother of these; and Otto's queen, well worthy to share his toils and his throne, our English Edith, grand-daughter and undegenerate scion of Alfred the Great?

Or take that cruel and wicked fifteenth century—an unlovely time, if such there was ever. The interval which parts two eras, it displays all the evils which usually wait upon times of transition; being as they are times when the old, although all or nearly all its virtue has gone out of it, is not yet dead and buried, but still haunts and cumbers the earth ; while the new and the better is only uncertainly feeling its way, and little by little learning to use the power and fulfil the duties which have lapsed to it. Look at that age, with all its cruelties and crimes ; and at the same time remember that it was the century of Thomas à Kempis, of Gerson, of Hus, of the author of the *German Theology*, of Joan of Arc, of the Brethren of the Common Life, of Savonarola. It was a century in which one, seeking to estimate the state of religion round him, could say, " It is a laudable custom with many of both sexes, and these not of the humbler classes only, but magnates and nobles, to set apart at least one hour at some set time of every day for the recalling and meditating on that highest benefit bestowed on the human race, the passion of Christ." It were to be desired that so laudable a custom of the fifteenth century had not become nearly extinct in the nineteenth. We do ourselves, we do the Church of Christ much wrong when we fail to recognize and to dwell with thankful praise on the grand and beautiful souls which in every age have been trained by Him for his heavenly kingdom. What mightier attestation of the divine character of Christ's religion than the fact that all which men have so perversely mingled of superfluous or mischievous with it, has not robbed it of its power to heal and to bless, and to fashion elect souls as polished corners for the temple !

The Church of the Middle Ages, as indeed has been the case with the Church in other ages as well, was on several occasions arrested in the downward

path of spiritual declension and decay, quickened to a
new life, by what we should now call a Revival. The
Revivals of those times may not have been, and were
not, revivals exactly after the pattern which we, with
our clearer lights, but perhaps not stronger affections,
might wish them to have been; but seeing that unhappily we cannot reform our ancestors, we must take
such times of refreshing as they were, giving credit to
them for all which they had of healthy and good; and
heartily regretting that what cannot be qualified as
such had any part in them, leaving them, as no doubt
it did, less fruitful of abiding good than they otherwise
would have been.

Thus, to enumerate a few of the beneficent waves
of high spiritual emotion which in the ages wherewith
we have to do, swept over Western Christendom,
there was the revival of the better elements of monastic life, the recovery of discipline, the rekindling of
zeal, whereof the religious foundation of Clugny was
the centre and the hearth (910). There was again,
when this revival had spent itself a little, the Cistercian reform, in which St. Bernard (b. 1091, d. 1153)
led the way. Of both of these I have spoken already.
Again, there were the Crusades, which we as much
misconceive when we leave out of sight the nobler
and purer impulses which were at work in them, as
when we see in them nothing else but these. There
were the early days of the Mendicant Orders, with so
much of promise about them that men wise and good
hailed in them the dawn of a more glorious day than,
as it proved, they should ever usher in. There was
Scholastic Philosophy for those who sought to know
that they might love, and the Mystic Theology for

those who sought to love that they might know ;—nor do these at all exhaust the list.

I alluded just now to blemishes which cleaved to the Medieval Revivals, and, without destroying, more or less impaired their worth. Certainly the most serious of these blemishes was the immense increase of the worship of the Blessed Virgin which signalized so many among them. The growth of this cult, the causes which led to it, the shapes which it assumed, all this I should find it impossible historically to treat of; but it is a phenomenon of these ages altogether too significant to allow me to pass it over with merely a transient notice. It would be long to tell of the cycle of greater feasts instituted in her honour, which was not counted complete till it had reached the mystic number seven; it would be endless to recount the innumerable lesser feasts and local devotions. Titles of honour were invented for her, as Queen of Heaven, Star of the Sea, Mother of Pity, Refuge of Sinners, which not merely had no sanction in Scripture, but had no analogy in anything there; ransacked though Scripture was, that so it might yield prophetic or mystic anticipations of the glories which should be hers. What was not ascribed to her now? She was the new and the better Eve; and in the *Ave* of the Angelic Salutation there was traced a significant reading backward of the name of another, from whom and from whose disobedience all death had proceeded, in favour of a better Eva, from whom and from whose obedience all life had flowed. She was the Wisdom which builded her house with the seven pillars (Prov. ix. 1); and the Bride of the Canticles, this Song of songs being an Epithalamium of which she is the object; and the woman clothed with the sun and having the moon beneath her feet (Rev. xii. 1) ; and she, the Ever Virgin, the East gate of Ezekiel's Temple, by which the Prince of the people entered once, but which henceforward was shut for evermore (Ezek. xliv. 2). Jacob's ladder, linking earth to heaven (Gen. xxviii. 12), was a mystic symbol of her; and the Bush that burned and was not consumed (Exod. iii. 2); and Aaron's rod that budded (Num. xvii. 8); and Gideon's fleece (Judg. vi. 37) ; with much more in like kind.

But Scripture was submitted to worse usage than this. It was directly falsified so to do her the more honour. A profane travestie of the Psalter, sometimes ascribed to Bonaventura, but not the work of the "Seraphic Doctor," was a favourite book of devotion in these ages. In this, to take one sample, the opening words of the 110th Psalm, "The Lord said unto my Lord," reappear as "The Lord said unto my Lady;" with the rest to match. After such handling of the word of God, it will sound as a small matter that the Church's grandest hymn should be dealt with in the same fashion; that side by side with a *Te Deum* there should be a *Te Virginem laudamus.* She was addressed as the Mother who could command her Son —language which, as we learn from an interesting communication of Dr. Newman's, has recently been authoritatively condemned and forbidden at Rome. All power on earth and in heaven was declared to have been committed to her; as without the Son nothing was made, so without her, the Mother, nothing was remade. He was the Mediator, she was the Mediatress. If a distinction was still maintained between the worship addressed to her and to the several

Persons of the ever-blessed Trinity, there was also a distinction drawn in the opposite direction between the service addressed to her and that offered to any other of the Saints. Falling below the one and rising above the other it occupied a middle place between the two.

This cult of the Blessed Virgin,—in the pushing of which to well-nigh insane excesses Peter Damiani obtained a bad pre-eminence,—fell in with the spirit of chivalry which was everywhere abroad, encouraged this, and was itself encouraged by it. In such names as Our Lady, Notre Dame, Madonna, we hear the language of gallantry and devotion blended into one; and it is not easy to measure the extent to which these evoked and mutually sustained one another. The fact that this cult inspired a poetry and a painting of beauty the most transcendent,—creations of loveliness that without these springs of inspiration would never have come to the birth,—all this may be freely accepted; but accepted without any acceptance of a conclusion which is often deduced herefrom, namely that what is so beautiful must also be true. This does not by any means follow. Greek Art, in many ways unsurpassed and unsurpassable, roots itself in the Greek mythology. There were the gods of the Greek Pantheon, a Zeus or a Pallas Athêne, gods which were no gods, that inspired a Phidias; but that Greek mythology receives no seal or attestation of its truth hereby. There is a world far higher than the world of Art; and when our youthful poet, "the young Marcellus of our tongue," exclaimed, "Beauty is truth, truth beauty," he was transferring into the present imperfect condition of things that absolute identity of truth and beauty which shall only come to pass in that glorious future which is still waiting to be revealed.

The immense development of the sensuous and the symbolic, of which I have spoken elsewhere,—the mistaken confidence that men might be effectually taught by means of these without the living and interpreting voice,—did much to throw into the background that divine ordinance, the preaching of the Word. Do not suppose when I say this, that there were not illustrious preachers in the Middle Ages. Of many such we know, and these many are few as compared to those we do not know. Not a few famous in other lines were also famous in this ;—as St. Bernard, as Thomas Aquinas, as Innocent III., as Bonaventura. Others there are whose reputation with the after world mainly rests on their excellence as preachers. Let me name, among the Dominicans John of Vicenza (cir. 1230), author of a wonderful revival in Italy,—a revival indeed marred, like that of Savonarola, by the mixing of a political element with it ; and Vincent Ferrer of the same Order (1357–1419), indefatigable in this work, by one means or another making himself understood in so many lands that men ascribed to him the gift of tongues. More famous still is Bertholdt of Ratisbon (d. 1272), popular as the best Franciscans knew how to be ; and of whom we are better able to judge than of many, a large number of his sermons having reached us. It must be allowed that the new style of popular preaching, mainly introduced by the Mendicants, if it had its merits, had also its defects and dangers. Bertholdt's own sermons, with much worthy of admiration, sufficiently attest this. These preachers from the people, addressing themselves to the people, and more *ad plebem* than *ad populum*, sought by methods sometimes questionable,—by legend, by jest, by buffoonery,—to obtain a hearing for themselves and for their message. In the Capuchin of the *Prologue* to Schiller's *Wallenstein* we have a sketch of this popular preacher at a somewhat later date, yet no doubt very much the same man as he was two centuries before, and seeking to make his effects by the same arts. But the history of Medieval preaching still waits to be written.

I have spoken to you already on the system of Indulgences, which assumed so fatal a prominence in the later Middle Ages. When we have at all realized to ourselves what a system like this in actual working must have been, we are tempted to wonder how any high Christian life could have maintained itself at all, in the face of a machinery so disastrously adapted for the lowering of the tone of that life, for robbing God's judgments of their terrors, and man's repentance of its earnestness. We can only account for the survival of this life by the fact that there are very few who in actual practice push the principles which they profess, and the truths which they believe, to their ultimate consequences. The good which men embrace does not make them so good as they might and would be if they followed it to all its legitimate results; nor yet the bad so bad. "Pardons are from hell"—this might be quite true, which once a Franciscan friar in his righteous indignation exclaimed; but despite of these "pardons," and of men's trust in them, and even then when these were most in vogue, there were numbers who strove to enter by the strait gate, and whom God had taught in his own school that the means for making this entrance sure were not remissions of sin bought with money, but faith and penitence and prayer.

We have dwelt on some aspects of Church life in those ages which are, or ought to be, a grief and sorrow to us ; but that life had much fairer sides as well. In all ages, wherever the Gospel comes with power to the hearts of men, it shows itself full of mercy and good fruits, It would be a serious injustice to the Church of the Middle Ages to suppose it barren of institutions for the relief of human wretchedness and woe. So far from this, the multitude and almost endless variety of these are among the most attractive features which those Ages present. When we bear in mind the imperfect social organization of those times, how little the State undertook to look after its children—indeed, it can hardly be said to have undertaken to look after them at all,—it is easy to imagine to what frightful heights this misery might have risen except for the alleviations of it which were thus afforded. If, after all was done, the open sores of society were not healed then, we must in fairness to those times remember that they are as little healed at the present. The wretchedness that was in the world outstripped then, as it outstrips now, the most earnest efforts to overtake it. But the efforts were not wanting ; and they had their measure of success. Whether in proportion to means and opportunities these efforts were as great or greater in those ages than they are now, He only can tell who notes in the book of his remembrance all that is done, and all that is not done, for the least of his brethren. Let me here speak a little of the heavenly plants which then as now, spring-ing up under the shadow of the Cross, and twining round its stem, were by it sustained, being watered and kept green by the precious dews which evermore drop and distil from that sacred Tree.

In ages when pilgrimages were so rife, and in these I include that armed pilgrimage the Crusade, there naturally did not lack houses of rest and refreshment for the reception of those who were on their way to Holy Land, or to some sacred shrine:—these houses by the very necessities of the case being hospitals for the sick and worn and way-weary as well. The Hos-pitalers or Knights of St. John were at the outset no more than male hospital nurses, who waited, for the love of God, upon the sick, first under the walls of Acre (1191), and afterwards elsewhere in Palestine. These, after they had added to the duties first under-taken by them the warring against the infidel, did still, by the aid of lay-brothers who were associated with the Order, remain faithful in a measure to the objects of their first institution.

The Monastery, whatever might be the disorders, whatever the relaxation of discipline within its walls, rarely forfeited its character for an hospitality extended to rich and poor alike. Nor is it possible to read with-out admiration the gracious courtesies which, accord-ing to the Rule of St. Benedict, should evermore ac-company the reception within cloister walls of the wayfarer and the wanderer; the whole purpose and aim of these being to make all who shared this hospi-tality to feel that they rather conferred a favour than received one. When some made a charge against these institutions, that, by an almost indiscriminate distribution of alms, they fed and fostered the poverty which they professed and seemed to relieve, this no doubt is true; but what is it after all but saying that they shared in the economical errors which were universal in their time; while if herein they offended more than the rest of the world, this was only because their bounty was on a larger scale?

I need hardly mention that the Penitentiary for the rising to a new life of holiness women who had fallen deeply into sin is no modern invention. The Order of Fontevraud, founded by Robert of Arbrissil (1094), made these unhappy ones its peculiar care. And as little is the Foundling Hospital a modern experiment. Whether this in actual working does not generate more evil than it prevents may well be a question; but with the widespread prevalence of infanticide, not in the heathen world only, but in the nominally Christian, it was inevitable that earnest men should make proof whether some help was not here to be found. Lay Guilds too there were—they still survive in Florence and in other cities of Italy to the present day—which occupied themselves with the decent and reverent carrying of the Christian dead to their last home. There was a Leper-house, Muratori tells us, in almost every city of Italy—rendered necessary as these were by the prevalence of leprosy, and its malignity as it then existed, a malignity which the disease now retains only in the East, if, indeed, in the worst forms it retains it even there. For the ministry of these houses there were organized companies of men and women, not seldom drawn from the noblest families of the land, who did not shrink from the most revolting offices which this service entailed.

It is very interesting to note the thoughtful care which devised charities such as would have scarcely or not at all suggested themselves, where there was not a very lively sense and a 'tender consideration of the wants of others. There were Bridge-builders, associated for the building or keeping in repair of bridges for the use of way-farers,—of pilgrims above all. There were guilds for the waiting on and ministering to criminals condemned to death, a far more numerous class under the rough and ready administration of justice which prevailed in those days than they are at present. Then too there were associations, monastic or semi-monastic, as that of the Trinitarians, which took as their distinct mission the redemption from slavery of such as by evil hap had fallen into the hands of the infidel. There were found heroic souls among these, who, when other ransom was not forthcoming, and when for one reason or another the case would admit of no delay,—as for instance, when there was danger of a perversion to Islâm,—bought the liberty of a captive at the price of their own. Indeed, an engagement not to shrink from this last act of self-sacrifice, if need so required, constituted a fourth vow which was taken by those who entered these Orders for the redemption of captives, in addition to the usual three.

There were other benefits, and they were not small, of which the Medieval Church was the source and spring in times wherein men, owning, as it was, very few and slight restraints on their passions and appetites, would, except for those by the Church imposed, have owned none at all. To the Church was due the attempt, not wholly unsuccessful, to set some sort of limit to the prosecution of private feuds, by the institution, in the eleventh century, and first in Aquitaine, of what was called "The Truce of God." By this it was forbidden to wage these hateful private wars on certain days of the week;—not on Thursday, being the day of our Lord's Ascension; nor on Friday, as that of his Passion; nor on Saturday, as that when He rested in the grave; nor on Sunday, as the day of his Resurrection,—not, that is, from Wednesday night until Monday morning; the Truce was also to find place during certain sacred seasons of the year. At the same time the Church took under her protection clerics, monks, lay brethren, pilgrims, labourers going to or returning from their work, women and children, —all of whom were to remain unmolested and free to move backward or forward in the midst of the men at arms engaged in these quarrels. It need hardly be remarked that all these ordinances of mercy were very imperfectly observed, were continually violated; but they were very far from being wholly inoperative or without their value, as some might suppose.

Then, too, it was from the Christian Church that any effectual impulses proceeded for the amelioration of the condition of the slave and serf, and for the final extinction of slavery and serfdom. Travelling in the lines marked out by the Apostles themselves, and chiefly by St. Paul, the Medieval Church did not, any more than the Apostolical, denounce slavery as a wholly unlawful institution; nor seek with revolutionary violence to overturn the whole existing framework of society with its several orders and conditions of men. But while she bore with this, she at the same time always taught that he did an act well pleasing to God, who, either in his lifetime, or by testamentary disposition and, as it was then called, "for the remedy of his soul," gave freedom to the servile members of his household.

Much too the Church effected for the bettering of their condition for whom the hour of their emancipation had not as yet struck. It was impossible that the equality of all men in the world to come,—and before God already in this world, as in a present kingdom of heaven,—could be proclaimed, as in every act of the Church it was proclaimed, without seriously modifying the relations between master and slave. There might still be room only too large for the exercise of cruelty and caprice ; but something, nay, much was in this way accomplished. Nor did the Church in this matter teach by precept only, but also by example ; pointing as she was able to do to the hinds and labourers on lands held directly by ecclesiastical bodies, and to the comparatively thoughtful kindness and humanity with which they were treated, as a pattern that secular proprietors might do well to imitate. Some in late years have sought to deprive the Medieval Church of the honour which is her due, as the prime mover in the emancipation of the serf and the slave ; or, where her influence reached not so far, as rendering less intolerable the hard condition of these. In such attempts there is manifest injustice. Many causes must have wrought together for the gradual diminution, and in the end the extinction, of slavery in Western Europe ; but here was very far the most effectual cause of all. It is no more than justice to acknowledge this.

LECTURE XXIX.

THE EVE OF THE REFORMATION.

LET us plant ourselves, so far as this is possible, in the times which immediately preceded the Reformation. To one who took but a superficial view of things, at no time would the Church have seemed to have a better right to say, " I sit as a Queen, and shall see no sorrow." She had come forth to all appearance not seriously damaged from the profound humiliations of the Avignonese Popedom, and the great Schism. The decrees of the Three Councils, by which it had been sought to place some limits on the absolutism of the Popes, had been, some secretly evaded, others openly set at naught or solemnly reversed. At the same time the Councils had done for the Papacy what probably no other, friend or foe, could have done for it. By their aid the enormous scandal of Pope and anti-pope anathematizing one another had ceased, and has never since revived.

In many other ways too the position seemed improved. The sects which had been so threatening once,—which, in a mistaken confidence of their own strength, had challenged the Roman Church to do battle for her very existence,—which had honeycombed the very ground on which she trod,—these, so far as they still existed, were but the thin ghosts and shadows of what once they had been. The conflagration kindled in Bohemia by a spark from Hus' funeral pyre, had fairly burned itself out. The sword of the crusader and the scaffold of the inquisitor had proved more than a match for the Manichæan sects, the whole elaborate network of whose organization had perished. A like fate had befallen the Libertines,—Brethren of the Free Spirit and others,—by whatever name they are known. There were scattered Manichæans and Libertines still, but these only too glad to escape notice. The Waldenses alone as a visible body survived, even as they alone deserved to survive; but these also thrust back into their Alpine retreats, and neither in numbers, nor organization, nor aggressive energy calculated to inspire any serious uneasiness.

More really formidable had been the single Reformers before the Reformation, who, during the later Middle Ages, had in different quarters lifted up their voices against the corruptions in doctrine and in practice of their time, often with the foremost Universities to back the protest which they raised. But here too the contrast was remarkable between the violent revolt of the first half of the fifteenth century and the submissive acquiescence of the second. These also had passed away, leaving, as might seem, no successors behind them. Of Wiclif I have already spoken at large, and of Hus. John Wessel, of Gröningen,— *Lux Mundi* his admirers called him, but his enemies, matching one exaggeration with another, *Magister Contradictionum,*—protected by powerful friends, had died in a peaceful old age (1489). John Von Wesel, often confounded with one who is so nearly his namesake, uttered some brave words against Indulgences, but had closed his days in confinement (1482) ; having

only by a timely retractation escaped the fiery doom
to which his writings were delivered.   Savonarola (b.
1452, d. 1498), the fervent Dominican of Florence,
would fain have reformed the State no less than the
Church; but his grand work, through this error and
through the mingling of his own apocalyptic fancies
with the word of God,—as if those were of equal authority with this,—had early made shipwreck ; and he
had fallen only too easy a victim to the hatred of the
wickedness among the Popes, namely Alexander VI.
(1498).   Many more might be mentioned whose dead
bodies lay unburied "in the street of the great city
which spiritually is called Sodom and Egypt :" and to
whom the voice from heaven, " Come up hither," had
not yet been spoken.

The only Theology in which there dwelt any origi-
nality and power, that of the Mystics, if it did not take
upon it the defence of the Papacy and its pretensions,
as the Scholastic had done, yet evinced no hostility,
was quite content that these should stand.

But, however fair might be the outward show and
semblance of things, there lurked danger behind, and
this danger was everywhere.   The embitterment of
men's spirits against the Church and her whole manner of acting was widely spread and intense.   Western
Europe had outgrown its minority, and felt that it had
outgrown it.   That long course of discipline by precept and prohibition, to which untutored races newly
brought within the pale of the Church, German and
Slavonic and others, had been submitted, may have
been necessary, might very ill have been spared ; but
it was not the less felt as a vexatious and meddling

tyranny now that these races were conscious of having arrived at full age, and entered into the liberties which belonged to this. The rudimentary Christianity, the "elements of this world," to which they had been subject so long, had served in their time as a "schoolmaster to bring them to Christ;" and the education through which they had passed, though rather of divine sufferance than of divine appointment, and though mixed with much that was of the earth, bore a certain resemblance to that which the earlier people of God had gone through, while they too were under tutors and governors. But such a condition of things, to justify its existence, must be merely transitional. Rome, however, was determined that the bondage should be eternal; that the children, not any longer in their nonage, should be treated as children to the end. Religion may be, as our old poet has so grandly put it, "Mother of form and fear;" yet, if true Religion, she proves in due time mother of far fairer things than these. To her belongs not form only, but also spirit; not fear only, but also love. This was the truth which they whom it most concerned that they should see it, were resolved not to see nor understand.

Much else too there was which the rulers of the Church either could not see, or would not. Grey hairs were upon her, and she knew it not. In manifold ways strength had departed from her, and gone over to the side of her adversaries; while weakness, wearing indeed still the treacherous semblance of strength, was all which remained to her. Thus, what apparently could have been more triumphant than the issue of the struggle with the Councils? These, which had been the objects once of so much hope and so much fear, had utterly failed in securing any liberties for the Church, or in compelling a gradual and peaceable amendment of things therein which were amiss; but they had not the less left a profound impression on the heart and conscience of Christendom. Of this, however, I have spoken already.

The Monastic Houses had been at one time so many fortresses in every land, with the monks a garrison on whose fidelity the Church of Rome could safely rely. It is difficult to estimate at too high a rate their value to her. They brought her reputation; they furnished her with men trained for any work to which she might send them. The Papacy indeed without the Monks would have been impossible. The Orders still existed, but fallen how far! the oldest fallen the farthest, but all of them fallen; and, if one thing they hated, hating to be reformed and resolved that they would not be reformed; prepared to oppose the fiercest resistance to every attempt to bring them back to any strict, or indeed to any decent, manner of living. He was a bold man who attempted, though armed with the Papal authority, the visitation of one of their Houses; he might have to carry it through at the peril of his life. Of course there were honourable exceptions: religious Houses in which a godly discipline was maintained; but such, by the confession of all, were exceptions.

It is the misfortune of institutions which are merely human inventions, that after a while they overlive themselves. Having contributed all which they were capable of contributing to the Church's good or the world's, they thenceforward cumber a ground which they may have profited once. The reason of their

existence having ceased, there is now one supreme
favour which they could confer, that is, not to seek to
exist any more. It is seldom, however, that those who
are bound up with institutions which have thus over-
past their time, see things in this light; while yet the
falseness of their position, and the consciousness of
this falseness, which they cannot wholly escape, in
many ways tell injuriously upon them. The elevating
sense of a true vocation is gone. The sphere in which
a healthy activity is possible has grown much narrower, or has quite disappeared; and under these
conditions it is almost inevitable that a rapid deterioration, moral and spiritual, should follow. This
was eminently the case with the older monastic bodies.
The decay of discipline, the dissolution of manners, the
dying out of all sense of corporate life, were everywhere making themselves visible to the eyes of all.

And if it fared thus with them, it fared only a little
better with the Mendicants ; to whom good men and
great men had so fondly looked at their first appearance, hailing this appearance as little short of a new
apocalypse. These too had betrayed the hopes thus
built upon them. They might not have fallen so far
as the earlier Orders had fallen ; but their fine gold
had become dim; and the most hopeful, if any were
hopeful still, were compelled to own that the regene-
ration of the Church, its joyous return to the days of
its youth, its renewal of itself as an eagle, was not to
come to pass through them.

The Scholastic Philosophy, which was to have reared
new bulwarks for the faith, which had so long borne
the word for the Papal system and defended it before
the intellect of mankind, could not pretend to do this

with effect any more. Its alliance and moral support invaluable once, was now rather an embarrassment than a help. As a theology properly so called it had almost ceased to exist, and now only survived as a logic and a metaphysic. Spinning all its threads out of its own consciousness, and persuaded that there was nothing which it could not spin from thence, it had absolutely refused to learn anything from experience and history; and thus, wilfully closing one of the two main inlets by which knowledge comes to man, it had never been better than a Cyclops with a single eye: but even from that one eye vision was now going or had gone. Drier, harsher, thornier every day, it was the object of ridicule to some, of a deep indignation to others, who saw these husks set before the people instead of the wholesome food of God's word. When too Schoolmen could be found to affirm that what was false in philosophy might yet be true in theology, the reason of their existence had manifestly passed away; for, indeed, what did they exist for unless to witness against such a God-denying lie as this, and to assert the ultimate identity of all truth?

And worse than all the rest, or rather summing up all other failures in one, the central institution of those ages, the Papacy itself, had broken down. This at least might have been demanded of an institution to which every other had been sacrificed, namely that it should secure the unity of the Church. But what had been the fact? Again and again between rival claimants to the highest throne upon earth, a power external to both had been compelled to decide which was a lying impostor, and which the divinely appointed judge and dogmatist of mankind. Then too, in place of setting herself at the head of the movement for a reformation in head and members, with a frank confession of past sins and shortcomings, now for a century and a half Rome had made it her main business to baffle and defeat every attempt at reformation : when weak, to put off those who demanded this with illusory promises ; when strong, to punish, so far as her strength reached, all who dared to suggest that any serious amendment was required. What fatal success attended her in both these undertakings we have seen.

And then, while abuses were never rifer, while the lives of the Clergy were never fuller of scandal, while the Papal Court was never more venal, nor could less endure the beating upon it of that fierce light which leaves nothing hid,—the Invention of Printing (1440) multiplied a thousandfold every voice which was raised to proclaim an abuse or to denounce a corruption. A Censorship and an Expurgatory Index might do something in the way of counteraction ; but much escaped or defied the most vigilant control. And marching hand in hand with this wondrous Invention there was the Revival of Learning. This, among its other consequences, bringing men into nearer acquaintance with the early ages of the Church, made them aware how little the primitive times had known of a Pope or a Papacy in the later sense of these words ; how slowly and by what gradual encroachments on the rights of others, in the face of what remonstrances and of what resistance, the system had grown up. It was easy now to detect and expose the falsehood and forgery of some of the most important documents on which the Roman Canonists relied. The False Decretals are but one example of these.

It takes much to stir men to any earnest indignation against evil, unless that evil in some way touches and hurts themselves. But the enormous wickedness of so many among those who, during the latter part of the fifteenth century and the beginning of the sixteenth century, filled the Papal throne, the immense contradiction between them and the office they held, patent as this was to all, could not fail to rouse many thoughts. This contradiction indeed was immense. Those in the high places of the Church were as men who, having escaped a huge danger, were prompted by the sense of impunity to audacities of evil which they would not have dreamed of before. Shame itself had perished. What had been veiled, concealed, withdrawn out of sight, was now openly transacted, avowed, and defended. There had been bad Popes before ; but then, alternating with these, there had been also good,— men of personal godliness, who would fain have set straight, if only they had possessed the insight and the power, some part at least of all which they saw so crooked around them. But regard the Popes from Paul II. to Leo X. (1464–1521), including both ; what less lovely spectacle has the Church or the world ever presented? " The very precursors of Antichrist" one living at the time, and a faithful son of the Church, does not fear to call some of these. I shall not enter into particulars. There is much which I do not care to tell, not a little which I could not tell.

And yet one signal difference between these and such as went before them, and that for the worse, I cannot forbear to note. Boniface VIII., Pius II., with others whom I might name, were not model Popes, nor models in any way. For all this they had some

thought of Christendom as a whole, took some sort of
oversight of it as a kingdom ; and if they abused their
grand position, yet did not miss or ignore it altogether.
But the men who sat on the Papal throne immediately
before the Reformation—their horizon was limited to
the pettiest and paltriest politics of Italy. The chief
value which their office possessed lay now in the opportunity which it offered to snatch some worldly advantage for the family which they were founding, or at
best to enlarge the so-called Patrimony of St. Peter.
Who that knows anything of Italian history during the
century before the Reformation will deny that for objects such as these they schemed, intrigued, struck alliances and broke them, made war and made peace,
conspired, betrayed, confounded in worst disorder
things temporal and things spiritual to the infinite dishonour and degradation of both, invoked the most
awful thunders of heaven to do the most unworthy
work upon earth ?

Such were some of the moral aspects of Western
Christendom on the Eve of the Reformation. A few
more words before we conclude. I have endeavoured
in these Lectures to trace the manner in which all the
great events and tendencies of the medieval times
were leading up to the Reformation as to their goal;
destined as that was to prove an unspeakable gain to
the whole Church, and not to one section of it only.
For indeed, while its full blessings belong to us who
made it fully our own, even those nations of Christendom which, after a brief hesitation, put it back from
them, could not escape the gains of it altogether.
Hard words are often spoken of it by those who then

refused it—some of these, it may be, just, not a few unjust. Unjustest of all are these words, where the things we are reproached with having lost or let go, it was Rome herself who, by her long abuse of them, tempted the Reformers in a not unnatural indignation to cast away. Certainly I do not consent with those who set out with this maxim, " The farther from Rome the nearer to the truth ;"—but I can understand them: and whatever fault may cling to this violent and exaggerated reaction, lies not wholly at their doors, but in part assuredly at hers who had done so much to provoke it. Thus, to take an example, the whole subject of the Intermediate State, beginning with our Lord's Descent into Hades, is one which the theology of the Reformation has almost shrunk from touching ; and this because of the terrible mischiefs which had attached themselves to the Romish doctrine of Purgatory. What have been the losses hence ensuing may be guessed, but not fully measured, by the loud and angry denials that there has been any loss at all, which will instantly follow any assertion like that which I just have made.

But let there be in these reproaches which are thus cast upon us what amount of truth there may, such as utter them owe an incalculable debt to that which they reproach. Where would the Roman Catholic Church be now, except for the great searchings of heart, the diligent setting of her house in order, the strengthening of the things that remained, which all by this visible judgment-act were forced upon her? Matters had come to such a pass, ills had become so inveterate, that it was no more possible for her, of a free spontaneous impulse, to have reformed herself, than for a man to perform a painful surgical operation on his own body. This which may be done for him, he cannot do for himself. Where would now be her St. Teresa, her Philip Neri, her Charles Borromeo, her Francis Xavier, her Francis of Sales, at this day her just blazon and boast? They were not the fruit which the Church of Alexander VI., of Julius II., of Leo X., was in the way to bear, or would have ever borne. Whatever Rome can boast,—and this is much,—of the grander forms of piety and devotion during the last three hundred years, she owes to the mighty reaction and revival of spiritual life in the sixteenth century, forced upon her, as I would again repeat, by the Reformation; by the aid of which reaction and revival she encountered and put some bounds to the advancing wave that at one time threatened to submerge her altogether—nay more than this, recovered much that for a while appeared to be lost to her for ever.

But these reproaches do not reach us from that quarter only. We too ourselves are sometimes tempted to say, and more often to think, that on those labour-pangs of so many centuries there might have followed a more glorious birth than any that we actually behold; for who among us, looking round on the Reformed Christendom which now is, will affirm that it has fulfilled the expectations that might have been cherished once? What remains but to acknowledge and to accept the fact with which in my first Lecture I started, and with which in this last I conclude; namely that everything here, in this world of imperfections, is more or less a disappointment and a failure; that this law of shortcoming, being universal, does not exclude the highest and the best; and that so it will continue until HE comes who shall make all things new, the Restorer and the Reformer of all. Much at that period to which I have brought you, and where I pause, through the sin and impatience of men was ill-done, undone or overdone. Let us own it freely; but not the less freely declare that in what the Reformation rid us of, in what it obtained for us, in all that would have been impossible without it, there is matter for everlasting thanksgiving. "Thou sentest a gracious rain upon thine inheritance, and refreshedst it when it was weary."

INDEX.

———•———

441

299 1127

N

DATE DUE

DATE DUE

JUL. 27 1979		
OV 1 3 1984		
APR. 19. 1990		
GAYLORD		PRINTED IN U.S.A.